HARPER TORCHBOOKS / The Cloister Library

(continued on next page)

HARPER TORCHBOOKS / The Science Library

(continued on next page)

P. M. Sheppard	NATURAL SELECTION AND HEREDITY. Illus. TB/528
O. G. Sutton	MATHEMATICS IN ACTION. Foreword by James R. Newman. Illus. TB/518
Stephen Toulmin	THE PHILOSOPHY OF SCIENCE: *An Introduction* TB/513
A. G. Van Melsen	FROM ATOMOS TO ATOM: *The History of the Concept* Atom TB/517
Friedrich Waismann	INTRODUCTION TO MATHEMATICAL THINKING. Foreword by Karl Menger TB/511
W. H. Watson	ON UNDERSTANDING PHYSICS: *An Analysis of the Philosophy of Physics*. Intro. by Ernest Nagel TB/507
G. J. Whitrow	THE STRUCTURE AND EVOLUTION OF THE UNIVERSE: *An Introduction to Cosmology*. Illus. TB/504
Edmund Whittaker	HISTORY OF THE THEORIES OF AETHER AND ELECTRICITY: *Vol. I, The Classical Theories,* TB/531; *Vol. II, The Modern Theories,* TB/532
A. Wolf	A HISTORY OF SCIENCE, TECHNOLOGY AND PHILOSOPHY IN THE 16TH AND 17TH CENTURIES. Illus. *Vol. I,* TB/508; *Vol. II,* TB/509

HARPER TORCHBOOKS / The Academy Library

ROBERT PAYNE

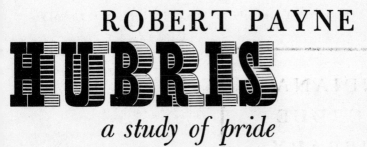

HUBRIS

a study of pride

FOREWORD BY
SIR HERBERT READ

HARPER TORCHBOOKS   The Academy Library
HARPER & BROTHERS   NEW YORK

TO THE HAPPY MEMORY OF CHARLES WILLIAMS

HARPER TORCHBOOKS / THE ACADEMY LIBRARY
ADVISORY EDITOR IN THE HUMANITIES
AND SOCIAL SCIENCES: BENJAMIN NELSON

HUBRIS: A STUDY OF PRIDE

PRINTED IN THE UNITED STATES OF AMERICA

THIS IS A REVISED EDITION OF A BOOK FIRST PUBLISHED
IN 1951 BY WILLIAM HEINEMANN, LTD., LONDON,
UNDER THE TITLE, THE WANTON NYMPH: A STUDY OF
PRIDE

FIRST HARPER TORCHBOOK EDITION PUBLISHED 1960

Contents

The illustrations follow page 314.

FOREWORD TO THE TORCHBOOK EDITION

ROBERT PAYNE is one of the most remarkable writers of our time. I know that "remarkable" is a question-begging word, but it conveys the sense of his stature, without involving one in a value-judgement, for which this is not the occasion. He is one of the most prolific writers of any age, so prolific that he has to resort to various pseudonyms and several publishers. It was under ambiguous circumstances that I first became acquainted with him, about twenty-five years ago. I was at that time acting as a reader for the English publisher, William Heinemann. One day I received a manuscript purporting to be a translation of an epic story by the Russian writer Valentine Tikhonov. It impressed me very much, especially by its vivid presentation of Russian character and landscape. I consulted a Russian friend about the author—and yes, he knew him and admired his work. I then arranged to meet the translator and in the subsequent conversation about copyright and royalties, the young man before me had to confess that the book was not a translation at all, but all his own work.

From that moment we became friends, and I have followed the career of this writer with increasing admiration and ever-renewed amazement. His range is immense—from passionate romance to the theology of the early Christian Fathers; from lyric poetry to contemporary history—his *Chungking Diary* (1945) is one of the most illuminating documents of our time. His restless spirit takes him to China or Persia, India or California—I never know where he is and I see him but rarely. But his books appear as regularly as the daffodils and the swallows, and are always as welcome.

The present book is characteristic. Mr. Payne relates in his introduction how it was first suggested to him and it is not surprising to me that it came about as a result of conversation with a writer so inspiring as Charles Williams in a coffee-house well known to me. But what is characteristic is that Robert Payne should immediately seize on a subject that would involve him in a survey of world literature from Ancient Greece to modern France, and that he should reveal his familiarity with such neglected authors as Ennius and Statius, Cassian and Alanus de Insulis, Capaneus and the York Mystery plays. All this learning is worn lightly and dispensed to the general reader with grace and appositeness. It is not learning for learning's sake, but rather a converse with great minds on a subject of immediate importance. Pride, whether worldly or spiritual, is the most significant of all human sentiments, the "wanton nymph" that throughout all history has lured men to their destruction; but its significance lies, not so much in its own fateful consequences, as in the contrast it offers to the virtue of humility. This book is perhaps not so much about pride as about humility: when the author has reviewed the noisy triumph of pride, we hear the still small voice of humility, and that is the enduring impression. And yet it is not a simple contrast, of black and white, of good and evil. In the dialectic of history, as in the vital tension of the human spirit, pride is as necessary as humility is desirable. Mr. Payne does not simplify the problem—he knows that human nature is eccentric and human destiny inscrutable. However much we may be impressed by the immensity of his knowledge, it is finally the sensibility of the poet that makes this a book exceptional for its insight and wisdom.

HERBERT READ

Frate, la nostra volontà quieta virtù di carità, che fa volerne sol quel ch'avemo, e d'altro non si asseta.

Brother, the quality of love stilleth our will, and maketh us long only for what we have, and giveth us no other thirst.

Paradiso, iii, 70

A phrase, then, of impatience, thud of Blake's wings of excess. I hear the ruin of all space, shattered glass and toppling masonry, and time one livid final flame.

JAMES JOYCE, *Ulysses.*

Introduction

THIS book came about as the result of conversations with Charles Williams in a coffee-house in Ludgate Hill. He had spoken, I remember, of Wordsworth's "unknown modes of being", and from there he had gone on to wonder whether it was possible to write a history of the naked human soul divorced from accidental history, for it seemed fairly clear that the human soul had nothing to do with changing dynasties, Acts of Parliament or indeed anything recorded in our history books. "Surely," he said, "the human soul has a history, for it grows, it changes, it is never the same. The poor thing, which is after all the most important thing, has been forgotten. It ought to be written, but I suppose no one will." He paused, sipped his sherry and went on: "I don't know, but I have a feeling one could do it from the poetry." He mulled this over, but it occurred to him that poetry was lacking in definition, and though in poetry you hear the soul babbling to itself, you are never sure whether it is telling the truth. In his book *The English Poetic Mind* he made sorties against the invisible fortresses of the soul, but retired from the combat with the feeling that the poetic mind was not an unimpeachable witness of the truth; I think he said as much in discussing Shakespeare's *Troilus and Cressida*.

It was some weeks later, after a re-reading of Hooker's furious diatribes against pride, that it occurred to him that the history of pride might offer a solution to the problem, for was not pride the soul confronting itself in a mirror, overjoyed at the recognition? But not only pride—there were other things, and most important were those concentrated moments of consciousness when the spirit

1

goes wheeling on its own: the epileptic visions of Dostoievsky, the rages of King Lear—it would be necessary to find the connection between these extraordinary moments and the normal ambiances of the soul in search of mirrors. Clearly they were related. The difficulty was to find out where the relationship lay. "We could write it in a volume as large as all the Cambridge Histories put together, or in 300 pages, and let the scholars add the footnotes and the impedimenta. Heaven knows, we must save the thing from extinction."

It was heady wine. For a year of Saturday afternoons I burrowed in the British Museum. There were occasional discoveries which seemed of importance, and these would be reported to him. The mulling went on, and then the war came, Charles Williams disappeared to Oxford and I to the remote valleys of China; and there seemed no purpose in reviving even in myself a discussion which must be fruitless, for if the human soul talked nonsense in poetry, how much more nonsense he talked when he became the sin of pride gesticulating in front of mirrors. One morning, after the war, there arrived from the Oxford University Press a heavy parcel with Charles Williams' signature. It had survived the bombing of Amen Corner and his own death. I carried the parcel on my travels. One day, in San Francisco, alarmed by its accusing state, I began to put my notes in order.

I wish Charles Williams had written the book. He would have shed over it the light of his humour and grace: he would have dealt with pride more humanly and possessed more pity for it, and joined the parts together more ably. Also, he might have solved one of the problems which a history of pride presents. It seems to me now that a history of the naked human soul in its pride and self-consciousness—there are, of course, distinctions to be made between pride and self-consciousness—can no longer be written. It is too late, or too early, in our history. To write it well, it would be necessary to introduce a history of time and a history of space, the two continually changing co-ordinates of our existence—the Egyptians, for example, lived under a different dispensation of time and saw a wider space—and it would be necessary to introduce the apocalyptic time of the Middle Ages, which reduces the historian to tears. What is certain is that no history is really possible unless we have the measure of these two things, and perhaps nothing is more ludicrous than the efforts of historians to write the history of man (who is the envelope of the naked human soul) by the calendar and without reference to the changing space around him. In China history becomes a series of anecdotes—it seems the more honest and the more human way.

For what is oddly disturbing to the historian of the human soul is precisely its humanity, the anecdotes it tells against itself. In spite of the antics of Hubris and Nemesis, the heaven-leaping pride and the descending punishment, in spite of the perpetually distorting mirrors, in spite of Lear's eye-gauging and Dostoievsky's hysteria and Leonardo's "obstinate rigour", the human soul in its perambulations around itself has a strangely human eccentricity. I have read somewhere of how a friend came upon Tolstoy when he was alone, and listened to him saying as he gazed in a mirror: "Well, my dear, hurry up, hurry up—what a handsome boy you are," and then leering at himself. Those who conclude that Tolstoy was insane are almost certainly wrong: they have said as much to themselves in their shaving mirrors, and will continue to do so as long as the mirror represents man's nearest approach to himself. The inevitable distortion remains: we cannot escape from it: the mirror hides as much as it reveals: and pride, as we watch it through the centuries, is as much a tribute to man's credulity as to his vision. Not all the things that the self-regarding soul is reported to have said to itself, not all its admiring glances or sudden rages, are authentically recorded. We must take the words of the soul on trust: and since a kind of development (but to what end?) is visible, much of the evidence finds its own corroboration.

But not all the evidence is available. There are places where we walk with extreme danger, hardly knowing or recognising the pathological landscape of the soul. There are places where there are mists and storms, and other places where there are mirages, and who shall say whether a mirage is a real, tangible thing? Under its many disguises, Pride, the sharp cutting-edge of the self-confronting soul, resembles the witches in the Indian fairy-tale who split themselves in two, and one points towards the other, saying: "There is me," but by the time the hunter has tracked her down, she has disappeared or changed into something else, and we cannot ask comfort from the original speaker, for she has vanished entirely. And any discussion of pride must inevitably partake of a stirring of a witch's brew: the serpents, the chameleons and the hippogriffs abound. In such a landscape reality sometimes eludes us. It is this which is worrying, for we shall not touch the human soul until we touch reality, and Plato has told us already that in the world of Ideas all things are intangible save one, and it is splitting hairs to discover its name. This one tangible thing is certainly not the naked human soul wandering along its greasy pole between one abyss and another. Even to define the nature of its nakedness is impossible. It would appear that the difficulties are endless and may never be solved.

What then can be done? We can tell the story of pride as it emerges, catching it on the wing: these eagles, flying high, turning their blind eyes to the sun, are our legitimate prey. We can at least record the genus and the habits of these high-flyers, examine them through telescopes, survey their nests, sometimes it may even be possible to see them caged. It is true that when they are caged, the sheen has gone from their feathers. We shall not see them living unless we follow them to their high altitudes or lonely crags. We must do the best we can. Perhaps all that can be done is to discuss those anecdotes in its history for which there is reasonable authenticity, and sometimes—in case the thing becomes too tenuous —to discuss persons. So Pascal has his place, and the nymph Hubris is treated as a real personage, as indeed she may well have been. I have begun with this wanton nymph, the mother of Pan, and ended with Paul Valéry's nymph gazing in the same waters, if only because one must end somewhere.

This then is a short history of the European soul as it shows itself in its pride. It would have been better if the soul could have been divorced from its admirable reflections, and if the writer had not been so obsessed with the thought that the soul in regarding itself saw itself, as we do when we see ourselves in a mirror, reversed; or more poignantly, like the light-rays on the nerve-cells behind the eyes, upside-down. There are complexities which even the theologians never thought of, and it is no purpose of this study to increase them beyond the fantastic dimensions they have already acquired.

The Nymph Hubris

THIS nymph with the honey-sounding name is the most mysterious of all, for she was to leave upon the people of Greece indelible traces, but of her origin nothing is known. She was to become as great as the gods and more powerful than the most powerful men, yet we know neither where she was born nor what sacrifices were offered her, what costume she wore or what streams she bathed in, nor where she first struck down the men who opposed her determined will. We imagine her with a spear, naked and shining among the snowy cliffs of the Arcadian hills, a goddess of solitariness and curious waywardness, descending at intervals to the lowlands to strike panic from the earth; she may have been goat-footed; perhaps a horn grew out of her head; all that is certain is that she has about her a terrifying evil purpose, for men who were touched by her immediately went mad. She was not pride only, but the terror of pride, with power to massacre as she willed.

We may never discover where the nymph Hubris first came into existence; there are few legends about her; her history is as dark as her birth. When we meet her in the Greek dramas, she is already fully-armed. If it is true, as Apollodorus informs us, that she was the mother of Pan by Zeus, then we may expect to find her hidden away in the place where Zeus and Pan are known to have been in partnership together, on Mount Lukaion, in Arcadia; there, on the sacred enclosure of the topmost peak, no object was said to cast a shadow. Here, too, mysterious human sacrifices were offered to Pan on every ninth year and the man who performed the sacrifice must hide for the following nine years wearing a wolf-skin. Somewhere, lost in Arcadia, there must have been legends concerning her, and though we construct one at our peril, the sacred enclosure on the peak, the shadowless grove and the hunted sacrificer disguised as a wolf all seem to belong to her ritual. As we see her coming dimly through the enchanted woodlands, we do not know whether she was originally the spirit of exultant freedom or someone with a more evil purpose. Pan, the hoary goat-god, was once a spirit of the pastureland; so too was Nemesis, goddess of the greenwood tree, though she was to become later the most terrifying of portents. We shall meet them all again later, but it is the nymph Hubris who tantalises us, and whose influence seems to spread out among them all, like the ripples of a pool when a stone is flung, bequeathing insolence to men whenever they are touched by her wand.

But if we know nothing, or nearly nothing, about the nymph Hubris and can only guess at the reasons which led her to bear the goat-god, we know considerably more about the goddess Nemesis, who later became the implacable deity of those who allowed themselves to be touched by Hubris. Yet when we first come upon her statue, there is no hint of her strange powers. There is a marble relief, found in the Piræus and now in the Louvre, which shows her resembling any young goddess of the woods. She is winged, carries a wheel and holds a bearded serpent in her hand. When we look closer, we see she is standing on a naked man, and Artemidorus has written on the pedestal the astonishing inscription:

> I am the Nemesis of men,
> Lovely-winged, immortal, dwelling in the sky:
> I flit through the world exulting,
> And have all mortal tribes within my power.
> Artemidorus, proud and wise man,
> Wrought me in stone as an offering.

Why the bearded serpent? Why is she winged? Why the wheel? Why should Artemidorus beg the question by describing himself as proud? The mystery grows greater when we discover Pausanias going out of his way to record that no statue of Nemesis was ever winged, "not even the holiest wooden images of the Smyrnaeans," while Ammianus Marcellinus refutes him, observing that she is always winged, and the wings were given to her by the fabulous past in order that she might come running towards men with swiftest speed; he says she carries a steering oar in her hand and a wheel beneath her feet, so that none may fail to know that she travels through all elements and rules the universe. From Ammianus Marcellinus, also, we learn that she was the daughter of Justice, and for unknown centuries she has regarded the creatures of the earth from her high place. She is the goddess of fortune—this we might have suspected—but she is also given the title of Arbiter of Events, Queen of All Causes. He adds that she "binds the swelling pride of mortals with indissoluble bonds of fate, bending and weakening the necks of the proud."

These two accounts of the goddess do not necessarily conflict. The legends of the gods come from so many sources, are so inchoate, fuse so readily that we are not astonished by surface changes. In some remote age she seems to have been a real goddess of vast powers with a seat in Olympus, among the highest gods; gradually she lost favour, and only the Smyrnaeans continued to hold her in the highest favour. She must have been worshipped at a temple in Athens, for Phidias made a statue of her in Parian marble at the time of the Persian wars—it was said that the marble itself was brought by the Persians to Marathon. She was curiously panoplied. She wore a crown of stags, there were apple-branches in her hands and, most strangely of all, she held a cup adorned with Ethiopians! Pausanias explained the presence of the Ethiopians by saying that they dwelt near the river Oceanus. He says that Oceanus was her father, and then hesitates: perhaps there were oceans—it is possible, he says, that she derives from that other ocean bordering on Britain. It is all mystery, for him as for us. We remember the strange presence of Oceanus in the Homeric myths, the god of the Flood, mysteriously hinted at, never explained. Pausanias goes on to say that Nemesis was the real mother of Helen; Leda only suckled her. The bearded snake suggests a goddess of the dark underworld, but it is hardly from the dark underworld that Helen came. When Paris desires to make love to Helen after emerging with doubtful honour from a battle with Menelaus, she answers: "I will not go—Νεμεσσητὸν δέ κεν εἴη; it would be a thing to feel Nemesis at," and we feel that a curtain has half lifted and dropped before we have been able to glimpse more of the mystery beneath. Hesiod says that Night was the mother of Nemesis; then, at last, we find ourselves on safe ground, for so mysterious a personage could come from nowhere else.

The known history of the goddess, as a figure to be worshipped, is not quite over. There has been found an altar erected in 199 A.D. sacred to Nemesis the Queen and Diana; there, too, are the apple branches and the stags, suggesting that the legend described by Pausanias was still in vogue. But in Upper Pannonia, in the year A.D. 259, there was erected a statue of her which follows the totally different description of Ammianus Marcellinus. She wears a short *chiton* which leaves the right breast bare, there is a crescent moon on her head, on her feet are high hunting boots; there is a winged griffin on one side of her and a wheel on the other. Her right hand holds a rudder and a whip; her left hand a sheathed knife. Dio Chrysostom relates that at Smyrna there were two goddesses with the name of Nemesis. Perhaps there were two all over the empire. All that we know for certain is that she becomes more complicated and more debased as time goes on, and is no longer the terrible avenging angel of the Attic tragedies when we see her last. We walk away, disturbed because she could have explained so much and haunted by the suggestion that she was once among the Smyrnaeans wingless, but greater than the other gods.

The tantalising mystery of the nymph and the goddess remains. Nemesis is at least tangible—there are statues, discussions on her parentage, her habits, the favours she offers to mortals; Hubris hides among the Arcadian woods. Apollodorus alone offers a hint at her credentials. When Pindar says that Hubris was the mother of Koros, or Satiety, we are not impressed; we know no more than we knew at the beginning. We cannot trust Apollodorus when he says she was the mother of Pan; this, too, may be only a mythological shorthand, meaning that she was of the same kind as Pan, a thing of witchcraft and sudden terrifying rages. There are even moments when she disappears entirely, to become, as she became for Sophocles, a bloodless category of the mind. She has a honey-sounding name and seems half-sister to the Hyblaean bees, but there is a hissing note in the name which suggests that she derived more likely from the wind in the trees. It is possible, but not certain, that she derived *from the wind in the highest trees*, that strange and unaccountable rustle in the forests which filled the Greeks with alarm, for they feared all that could not be explained, and how could you explain the trembling in the forest when there is no wind?

It is possible, but not certain, that the explanation lies here. Seneca, discussing the holy dread of men when confronted with the wild forces of nature, places first in the category of dreadful things a grove of ancient trees higher than the rest:

> When you enter a grove peopled with ancient trees higher than the ordinary, and whose boughs are so closely inter-woven that the sky cannot be seen, the stately shadows of the wood, the secrecy of the place, and the awful gloom cannot but strike you, as with the presence of the deity; or when we see some cave at the foot of a mountain penetrating the rocks, not made by human hands, but hollowed out to great depths by nature; it fills the mind with a religious fear. We venerate the fountain-heads of great rivers; the sudden eruption of a vast body of water from the secret places of the earth obtains an altar: we adore likewise the springs of warm baths, and either their oqaque quality or their immense depths hath made some lakes sacred. (EP. AD LUCILIUM, XLI)

These are territories where argument fails: if we do not feel these things, it is doubtful whether we shall ever understand what it was that moved our ancestors in their prayers. As for Hubris, she is half-nymph, half sigh from the beginning, and never seems quite to emerge into the daylight. Among these shadowy trees we must leave her.

If it is difficult to trace the origins of Hubris and Nemesis, it is still more difficult to trace the origins of the Titans, those who were the first of gods to commit the crime of insolence. Was Prometheus, who stole the fire from heaven, originally a volcano? a meteorite? the first man who rubbed sticks together? This, too, we may never know, and when we come to disentangle the story of the Titans we find ourselves in confusion at once. There are twelve Titans, six sons and daughters of Uranus and Gaea. They may have been, and probably were, the accepted gods of the Greek tribes before Zeus and Olympus became the centre-poles of Greek theology. It is when we come to the names and powers of the Titans that the confusion becomes alarming, for they are not sons and daughters in any ordinary sense. There is Iapetus, the father of Atlas and Prometheus; Themis, the mother of the Hours and the Fates; Mnemosyne, the mother of the Muses; Cronus, the god of harvest; Hyperion, the god of the sun; Oceanus, the crab-clawed god of the sea, and six others. There was never such a rag-bag of gods. Gaea incites the children to rebellion. Cronus mutilates and overthrows the father, then seduces his sister Rhea, and becomes by her the father of Zeus, Demeter, Hades, Poseidon, Hera and Hestia, the goddess of the hearth. Later Cronus swallows all his children with the exception of Zeus, who was mysteriously hidden in his birth-place on Mount Ida in Crete. From this moment on, Zeus begins to assume the power of lordship over the father. With the assistance of the sea-nymph Thetis he makes his father disgorge the other children, and afterwards hurls his father and the other Titans into Tartarus. The new dispensation begins. One epic ends, and a new epic opens. There occurs, as a footnote to this epic, the story of Prometheus, who was chosen to present a sacrifice to Zeus, but instead of offering a whole sacrifice he heaped the bones together and covered them with fat, keeping the lean and tender meat for himself. It was in his rage against the presumption of this sacrifice that Zeus refused to give men fire. Prometheus thereupon rebelled, stole the fire, hid it within a fennel-stalk and came to the Caucasus. To torment him, Zeus shaped a woman for him "of shameless mind and most subtle manner"; together with the woman went a dowry in the form of a jar containing all the evils. Prometheus opened the jar, the evils flew out, casting a spell about him; he was then easy to capture. By orders of Zeus he was bound in adamantine chains to a pillar on the Caucasus; every day there came an eagle to consume his liver, which grew again each night. Finally, Hercules killed the eagle and set Prometheus free.

Such, in brief, is the story of the Titans, mostly as it was related by Hesiod, who tells the story with amazing detail and conviction. He knows all the complications, reveals all the alliances, mentions names of gods who have no existence beyond his pages. Everything is in confusion. We are made conscious that three or four cosmologies have been fused together, and it should be, but is not, possible to separate them. There is not one rebellion, but three main rebellions and a host of minor ones. Hesiod even hints at a state of *continual rebellion*. Prometheus, who challenges Zeus, is not the first to have challenged him; that honour belongs to Menaetius, "the insolent one", who for some unexplained reason was hurled into Erebus after being struck by Zeus's thunderbolts. Then the first proud man disappears forever, to be mentioned twice by Apollodorus, who adds nothing at all to the little we know of him.

There is no easy path through the history of the Titans. Hesiod accomplishes miracles of compression. There is about the whole work a curiously compulsive air, as though he were describing things which *must* be described, otherwise guilt would fall on him. What is it all about? We do not know. He hints at some primitive blood-guilt. Incest, sodomy, supernatural crimes, endless tortures, eternal rebellions—this is their terrible history, he seems to be saying, before Zeus arose on the calm and white heights of Olympus. It is all delightfully clear when Zeus emerges at last through the battle-smoke. There are at least two separate descriptions of the creation of man. There are pieces that do not fit, and perhaps were never intended to fit. We see rebellion under different skies, at different times, on different levels. The revolt against Cronus and the revolt against Zeus belong to entirely different worlds and different mythologies, but he employs scissors and paste, and admirably joins them together, so admirably indeed that we can almost hear the loud laughter at his own success. But something is deliberately concealed: that at least we know for certain. And what it is he has concealed we can only guess at.

It is a nightmare world, written down at a time when ghosts were almost palpable on long winter nights. Some of these figures, we suspect dimly, are ghosts. They fight so desperately; they win their battles in a way which has nothing in common with the battles of Homer; they swallow their enemies; blood drips everywhere; incest is more common than wedlock. Gaea revolts against Uranus, who was produced from her own womb by Chaos. She gives birth to giants, and from the blood of her mutilated husband there spring the Erinyes, the snake-haired fates with the blood-shot eyes. Horror is piled upon horror. This is not the quiet world of *Genesis* before the Fall; nothing so gentle as a temptation ever manifests itself. All is tumult, lightning, vague shapes coming out of the storm-mist, and somewhere above the clouds the gods are rejoicing. There is a primal terror again, but it is not the terror men suffer when they enter the grove of ancient trees and listen in holy dread to the gathering silence. That was impersonal; this could not be more personal. It is a world which is menacingly close to us, because it corresponds so closely to sexual dreams.

Who, then are the Titans, who are most responsible for this terror? The clue, perhaps, lies in the name, which can only come from τίτανος, meaning "white earth". Now, Harpocration explains that when the Titans tore Dionysus to pieces they were covered with a coat of white clay, while Nonnus says "they were whitened with mystic gypsum." We know that in the heroic age in Greece bodies were cremated and the ashes were carefully gathered and placed in urns. We know of white gypsum that it is a fertiliser and like asbestos it is unaffected by fire. We know too, or we can guess, that there survived into the heroic age the belief which was common among the ancient Mediterranean tribes that the dead remained in some unexplained way sexually alive, shedding the *mana* of their lost fertility on the living; that the dead did not entirely die and they were as much the bringers of victory and harvest as the living. The white clay or gypsum, which did not burn, helped harvests and possessed the colour of human seed and of human ashes, was related to the dead, and in order to uncover the future or penetrate the secrets of the dead, the sorcerer had only to smear himself in white clay and enter a trance. The Hippocratic Corpus says that "if anyone sees the dead in a dream dressed in white, it is a good omen, for from the dead come food and increase and seed." It is possible that the Titans are the white clay men, the ghosts who have been burned to ashes and battle to return to life. If this is true, the revolt of the Titans is the revolt of the dead.

There are gaps somewhere. There is further evidence to buttress the theory, but it is with the greatest difficulty that we attempt to understand the sentiments of the ancients towards the dead. We need to know far more than we know about the Roman attitude towards death, and under what aspect they beheld the Titan gods. We are nearer to a solution in Plutarch, who, in his *Roman Questions*, asks, "Why did not the Romans marry in the month of May?" and answers his own question: "Is not the reason that in this month they perform the greatest of purification ceremonies?" and he goes on to explain that "this greatest of purification ceremonies" consisted of throwing puppets called *argeioi* ("white men") into the river as offerings to Saturn. But Saturn is Cronus in his Roman dress, and these puppets, made of rushes in the shape of men bound hand and foot, possessed great and mysterious importance, for it was the *pontifices* who carried them to the Tiber and the Vestal Virgins who threw them in the river. Who they really represented the Romans never said, but they seem to represent the white clay men, who come from beneath the earth, the Titans who have been overthrown and who must continually be overthrown, if the State is to survive.

Hubris represents one form of pride; the Titans represent another. Hubris comes from above, the Titan pride comes from below. One pride sleeps and the other wakes. These forms of pride obey different laws and follow different patterns. In psychological terms, one represents the overweening demands of the unconscious, the other represents the overweening demands which men make when they are most conscious of themselves. The pride of Hubris, therefore, is clean-cut and towering, while the Titan pride turns steeply inward towards the vast dream-world, where power manifests itself in terms of sexual dissensions: incest, sodomy, the desire to emasculate the father and sleep with the mother; a dream-world where titanic rages abound. In this world sexual frustrations are compensated for by imagined triumphs, everything is vastly magnified, all actions are compulsive and the landscape is heavily coloured and haunted by the legendary beings men have inherited from the unknown past. One pride leaps high, the other descends into the underworld: one is pure light, the other is darkness shot through with feverish colours.

It is necessary to distinguish these two forms of pride, otherwise we shall be faced with confusion. Occasionally, it is true we shall hear the authentic notes of Hubris proclaimed from the underworld. The Titan Prometheus belongs to both worlds, and almost he seems to hang between both worlds, a mediator between them. But the gods punish the mediators, and when at last Prometheus is freed from his chains, he still wears the marks of his servitude—an iron ring on his finger and a crown of willows. With these, like the wandering Jew, he is marked through all eternity.

What is strange and delightful is that even Zeus may be guilty of Hubris. That Zeus can speak like Prometheus we know from a fragment embedded in the Homeric epic. He exults in his triumph:

Hearken unto me, all ye gods and goddesses,
I shall say unto thee what my heart biddeth me.
Let no god or goddess come between me and my desire,
Or attempt the thing I shall do.
Come, make trial, O ye gods, that ye may know.
Bind to the heavens a chain of purest gold,
Lay hold of it, O gods and goddesses,
Though with all your might ye hold it, none shall overthrow me,
Even though he useth all his force, from highest heaven.
But should I desire to draw ye up by my chain,
Then should I draw up with thee the whole earth and sea,
And tie the chain like a ribbon round Olympus,
Leaving thee hanging in space.
So I am greater far than any gods or men.

(ILIAD, VIII, 5)

The golden chain of pure power is the emblem of Zeus's pride. "It is not possible to deceive or over-reach the mind of Zeus," says Hesiod, remembering his Homer, "and even Prometheus could not escape from his hard wrath; a great chain binds." But the holder of the golden chain is free of all chains.

This portrait of Zeus in his pride introduces a new note, and a new landscape, into the mythology of the Greeks. Nothing comparable to this young, dauntless and exuberant Zeus is to be found in Hesiod's catalogues. This is man detaching himself from surrounding space, as the archaic statues of Apollo gradually detach themselves from the rock. It is pride-in-action. When, at a period in human development comparable to the emergence of Zeus, the pure sun-god of Ikhnaton is made to say:

> I am the God Aton, I who alone was,
> I am the God Re at his first splendour.
> I am the great God, self-created, God of Gods,
> To whom no other God compares.

we are not made aware of any action, only of passive self-contemplation: this god is wholly remote from men and indifferent to their fate. Zeus is man himself acquiring new powers, exulting in his own prowess, and he is not wholly dissimilar to the heroes who crowd the pages of the *Iliad*. He is like Hector, who says to Polydamus: "We scorn augury," or like Achilles when accused by Phoinix of an overwhelming desire to succeed:

> O Achilles, master thy proud spirit.
> It is not for thee to have a pitiless heart:
> The gods may bend, and they have virtues,
> They exalt their gifts of honour and great worth.
> So it is their hearts shall turn from wrath
> When offerings of incense rise before them:
> Vows and spilt wine and smell of sacrifices
> Are needed by them when proud men turn to sin.
>
> (ILIAD, IX, 496)

Achilles is one of those proud and indomitable heroes who thread their unwary way through European story. He defies the gods. Therefore Nemesis comes, and it comes in the shape of the ancestral Flood. Achilles pits himself against Oceanus as it sweeps across the plain:

Achilles, the hero, leans against the stream,
Seeing all the immortals in heaven in fury against him,
While the heaven-fed river hangs upon his shoulders.
Furious he springs to the high ground, knees trembling
With the weight of the river below, the earth shifting beneath.
Over all the plain lies the flood of water,
Fine armour, youths slain in battle, all these are floating.
The high ground escapes him, and the Flood rushes on.

(ILIAD, IX, 265)

This is what might have happened to Zeus exulting on Olympus. Uranus, the old Titan god whose powers were stolen from him, asserts himself and returns to take vengeance, for he is the Ocean and the Flood; and it is not man, but lame Hephaestus who at last brings the flood to an end by boiling it away with the heat of thunderbolts. In that singular flood we have been made a witness of the heavenly powers, and though Achilles survives by the miracle of the thunderbolts, he has suffered irremediably, and some of the *mana* has gone out of him.

When we come to the *Odyssey* the atmosphere of pride changes; the weather is sultry, the menace is brooding and does not come from the high gods, but from Ulysses himself, the heavy-jawed and beetle-browed hero, eternally malignant in spite of the pleasant miracles which Athene continually prepares for him. Demodocus had an eye on his audience when he sang for Ulysses at the court of Alcinous: "The slow catch the swift, the lame Hermes can conquer Ares and Aphrodite in their bridal beds." It is one of the terrible moments of the drama, this prophecy of what is about to come. But if Ulysses resembles the lame Hermes, he also resembles the wandering Prayers who are "halt, wrinkled and cross-eyed". He has the determined malignancy of Ivan Karamazov, and the same violent belief in his own powers. "Still in my strength unbroken," he cries; and though his pride is as great as the pride of the wooers, he wins only by the grace of the gods.

Where the *Iliad* is full of the pride of morning, the *Odyssey* is full of the pride of late afternoon. Darkness will soon be descending. In this world Ares, the war-god, rages confusedly— ἐπιμὶξ δέ τε μαίνεται "Αρης. Nemesis comes swiftly. Once Ajax was heard saying he has passed through the tempest in spite of the gods. "Then Poseidon heard him boasting and seized a trident in his huge hands and smote the rock of Gyrae apart, where Ajax was sitting, his heart blinded; and bore him down into the tumultuous ocean, where he perished, having drunk of the salt sea." It was one of Ajax's many deaths, all of them incurred by the sign of Hubris. But worse is to come for the wooers, "overweening in their insolence". Their crime is clearly stated: it was not that they had seduced Penelope from her daily tasks; it was not even that they had taken over the wealth of Odysseus; it was that they "honoured no one among men upon the earth, whether evil or good, whoever came among them; therefore it was through their own wanton folly that they suffered evil." The end came with the famous slaughter. When the wooers were butchered, Ulysses and Telemachus prepared calmly to scrape the blood off the wooden floor, and the handmaidens who had offered themselves to the wooers were casually hanged in a row on a single beam.

Yet it is an unfair conquest. Once again we are conscious of evasions, some important element left unexplained, and there is duplicity in Ulysses' relationship with Athene, who was at once the goddess of war and the goddess of peace, the hurler of thunderbolts and the protector of the growing olive-trees. In some way unexplained the story of the *Odyssey* seems to be the sequel to a *gigantomachia*. Holy vengeance is invoked; there is also unholy treachery. The pride of Achilles in his youthful strength and defiance is exchanged for a new kind of pride, more contemplative, and heavier. There is a fall from grace, an exile like the exile of the Titans: Ulysses is the wanderer on whom there reposes a curse. Permanence has gone, and the hero's life is a wanderer's unhappy journey from coast to coast. And there must be some significance in the fact that when the exile returns home at last, the bloodshed only begins.

Like Shakespeare's *Tempest* and Corneille's *L'Illusion*, the *Odyssey* is a drama where the magic is intimately connected with power, with what the French call *prouesse*. But the power which is revealed has an oddly baroque quality; it is intermittent; too many spells are spoken for us to believe in their total efficacy. One thing is certain: the weather of the soul is full of storms, and the unexpected is always happening. We feel that the incidents on Calypso's isle, the bewildering war with the Cyclops and the wonderful interlude at the court of Alcinous are all perfectly in keeping, but they lack the precise inevitability of the wars of the *Iliad*. Once there was war among the shining heroes; now there is war against dominations and powers, against demons and goblins. And the mind of Ulysses, dealing with darkness, recoils in horror upon itself. Some clue to the origins of these states of mind is given by the names themselves: Odysseus means *hater*, Achilles seems to mean *the man fated to die*, the name arising from a root-word connected with ἀχλύς, the veil or mist that comes over the eyes of the dying.

Death, a dark death, not the bright deaths of the *Iliad*, hangs over the *Odyssey*. The clouds lift only with the figure of Telemachus, who makes his own boast: "No, it is no bad thing to be a King, for soon one grows rich and oneself is held in honour." This is not the boast of Ulysses, who desires a greater glory—to be god-like.

The pride of Telemachus, his delight in earthly honour, is something entirely new to Greek poetry, though it is foreshadowed by the calm glory which hangs over the court of Alcinous. So Alcinous himself might have spoken, rejoicing in his wealth. It is pride removed from the threats of the gods: the gods are invoked only because it is delightful to invoke the gods. Following Telemachus, Pindar announces a human glory and warns against the desire to be god-like. He is continually repeating the warning. He describes the athletes, praises their grace and beauty as they have never been praised before, and sometimes, and most especially when he is carried away by some peculiarly heroic action, we realise that only a razor's edge separates them from the gods—so beautiful and heroic they are. At such times it is impossible to take his warnings seriously. These oiled and handsome athletes have received the total grace; and seeing them, all questions of divine envy and human pride become irrelevant, not because men have reached the stature of gods, but because they lived according to a divine law within themselves. Sometimes, when Pindar introduces some flashing history of the gods, we hardly know whether he is describing the gods or these youths. Against the weight of known mythology Pindar could say: "Everlasting Zeus set free the Titans." It was not true, but he believed it to be true: freedom was in the air, all sins were to be forgiven, the world would begin anew, and how better could it begin than with cities formed of the young heroes of the races? "When anyone is born of prowess," he wrote in an ode on a young boxer, "so he may, with the help of the gods, whet his keen spirit and reach a greater glory." The "greater glory", he seems to be saying, is in every man's reach. But what is glory? He never completely defines it. It is "the joy which is the light of life in recompense for all labours." It is also fame, the fair name, the statue of the hero erected in the market-place. Death itself holds no terrors for those who have achieved glory. "Death is fair when the hero has left to his dearest offspring the grace of a good name, the greatest of treasures." But he is not talking of Hubris or the Titans. A new element has entered the scene. The beloved champions, the poets and the actors, all those who partake in the games are endowed with possible fame. The human animal, conscious of his own beauty and intelligence, but not too conscious, proud but not tormented by pride, steps on to the stage.

By some miracle, with the light of the gods shining on him, Pindar resolved the two forms of pride, and he does this by placing men almost within the company of the gods while they are still living. He admonishes men continually—"the uncourageous hand" of pride is always striving to draw men back from their glory—but he is on the side of the angels, and refuses to believe that the terrible hand is as powerful as we had imagined. He sees the world filled with shining men and gods, and the market-place and the stadium are hardly less holy than Olympus. "All is holy," he says; and across the centuries we hear the answering voice of Blake, saying: "Holy, holy, holy!" in the gardens of Felpham.

At such times the voice of the nymph Hubris in the grove and the groans of the Titans in the depths of Tartarus are stilled; and it is all one to us whether there are gods or demons, the world is filled with a shining glory and the athlete on the steps of the Temple of Zeus as he lifts his hands to the crown of wild parsley is neither the greatest of men nor the worst, but man seen, as he should always be seen, through the gates of song.

The Rage of the Lions

THERE is no end to the theme of Greek pride. The Greeks understood the pride of Hubris and the pride of the Titans, but they also examined at great length and with infinite cunning all the permutations and combinations of pride. The problem absorbed them, and they hunted after a final answer, a final settlement, with the enemy, who was pride.

Pindar saw the world in a calm light; the golden heroes moved among the green and scented fields. Æschylus, his contemporary, swept the veils away and saw the world under darkening clouds. Again and again Æschylus draws the portrait of the proud man, and nothing is more terrifying than the manner in which he commends them to their punishments. In Æschylus, the nymph Hubris does not sing from the high branches; she screams or croaks her baleful warnings. Here all is mist, destruction, the foretaste of terror, the evil in the air and the bloodstains upon the path. "Dark and shadowy are the pathways of Zeus," he says. "From their high-towering hopes Zeus hurleth down to destruction the race of men. Sitting on his holiest throne, in ways unknown to us he bringeth his will to pass." This Zeus resembles the vindictive, implacable Jehovah of Job: terror destroys the proud hopes of men, ruin swift and ignominious—αἴσχιστα καὶ τάχιστα—accompanies their destinies. In this world, demonstrably not the world of Pindar, the heroes are slain.

In the world of Æschylus the boasts are louder, the punishments more ferocious. "Alone, and of my own will and choice I did it." The poet delights in the craggy landscapes, the haunted landscapes of the lost souls, "the farthest verge of the world, where the Scythians wander in unearthly desolation." In these places there exist the temptations of the desert; and like the anchorites of the Nile, the heroes are tempted to feats of pride. Here, too, the mind is given no rest, men speak under the stress of unconscious compulsions, crime follows on crime, men are trapped by their own fatality—a great hunger moves them. It is a dream-like world, comparable with Hesiod's, but starker. No sunlight shines, dark shadows wheel among the rocks, and for the first time in our literature there is heard the cry of those who, having given no mercy, are content to receive none; they walk alone through the *wildes einote*, the wild loneliness of the spirit, ambassadors of their own self-seeking pride.

Pindar had seen the world in clean-cut lines; the lines of Æschylus are jagged. Pindar's Zeus is benevolent; the Zeus of Æschylus has never set free the Titans. It is not only that there is guilt, but guilt hovers over the whole landscape. The gods of Æschylus stand aloof; they are the keepers only of deeply religious men (οἰκοφύλαξ ὁσίων ἀνδρῶν); and whoever dares to disobey the law of heaven is remorselessly hunted down, his honour and his name destroyed, annihilated into a black shade; then it comes about that the hero still lives among the damned (ἐν ἀΐστοις), and there is remembered by men, but only as a terrible warning. Heracleitus said once: "You should put out insolence even more than a fire." Æschylus assumes the task of one of the chief firemen.

In this world of leaping flame and pillars of flame, there is no trace of Pindar's simple vision, no belief in the blessedness of high deeds. It is impossible to conceive Æschylus saying: "In time the deeds of the ambitious youths are bathed in light and lifted aloft into the air of heaven." The delightful mysticism by which a deed becomes a ray of sunlight leaving the earth and penetrating heaven is not only foreign to him, but there are moments when he comes to believe that high deeds will produce rays of darkness. "Want," wrote Aristotle later, "is not the sole incentive to crime. The greatest crimes are caused by excess, not by necessity." Æschylus sets out to explore the landscape of excess, and he is disposed to find it in the least likely places, as when Agamemnon fears to tread on the purple carpets when entering his palace lest some evil eye should harm him. The rage of Æschylus to see the proud destroyed is unwavering; never has a poet written with so many thunderbolts employed as pens.

Previously, the nymph Hubris had been a dim goddess in some unapproachable fastness of the woods. Now, though she is invisible and no words are ever put directly into her mouth, she becomes the chief character of the plays. She is no longer a bloodless abstraction; she glows with supernatural light: she is the goddess of the fatal triumph. "In the hour of triumph, when fortune presents herself unexpectedly at a man's side, then the conqueror is in deadly peril." The words were spoken by unhappy Diodotus in Thucydides, but they describe the belief of Æschylus: like Shakespeare he believes that the tempest drowns the most outrageous sins:

> He who transgresses through overweening pride
> Or brings upon himself treasures unjustly acquired,
> For him there comes a time of retribution.
> He, when he sets sail upon the evil ocean
> Is like a ship with the yard-arm split asunder,
> Though he cry out his voice will not be heard.
> He shall struggle in the wild waves.
> And the gods shall laugh, seeing him.
> Having boasted of enduring fortune,
> All is taken from him.
> Riding the wave-crest he is tossed like a weak thing,
> To perish unwept and unseen.
>
> (EUMENIDES, 553)

It is a world of dark seas and impatient shipwrecks; the lightning plays on the rocks; the drowned sailors litter the shore.

In *Prometheus Bound* the pride of Zeus and the pride of Prometheus wage pitiless war. Prometheus claims that he has not acted through pride:

> It was not pride that drove me to this fate,
> Nor wilfulness that makes me silent now.
> Agonised thoughts devour my vitals.
> The rebel gods derived their powers from me.

I shall not speak of these things now; other thoughts
Burn within me. Besides, these things are known to you.
I shall speak of the miseries that beset mankind:
Once they were witless, and I gave them sense.
I gave them reason and the power of thought.
I say this now for no unruly purpose.
Simply: I gave them gifts.

(PROMETHEUS BOUND, 436)

But this portrait of Prometheus does not describe a Titan; it describes the emergence of political power.

When Atossa speaks of her dream, of the great figures of two women, one in Persian robes and the other in a loose-flowing Doric gown, the sculptural effect is magnificent, and for the first time we see Hubris and Nemesis as they must have been imagined by the Greeks:

Then saw I these two women gloriously arrayed,
One wearing Persian clothes, the other Dorian.
They stood before my eyes. O, they moved
In mortal majesty beyond all knowing,
Like sisters of a perfect beauty, glowing
With supernatural fire; and they did dwell
In lands apart, one on the barbaric coasts,
The other in Hellas. Then it seemed
Dissension rose among them, and my son
Striving to restrain them, yoked them both
And reined their harnessed necks to his twin chariot.
Exulting in her rich array, the Persian gave
Obedience to the reins and she smiled proudly.
The other with indignant fury spurned
The car, and rent the harness with her hands,
And tore the yoke to pieces. . . .

(THE PERSIANS, 181)

The classic situation has been stated: we know now that the Persian Kings in their nightmare must follow the course to the end. It is not only that nothing is left for the imagination, but the actors are like marionettes held on strings; they have the frightening *dependence* of those medieval marionettes which are still shown in Spain, as tall as human beings, but completely expressionless; only the shadows of the candle-light give vicarious expression to their faces, so that they look horrified when they are supposed to look tranquil, and murderous when they are being murdered.

Æschylus was conscious that he was dealing with shadow-plays, or at least he was not averse to dealing with vast abstractions which can only be imagined in terms of menacing shadows. The great chorus in the *Agamemnon*, the *locus classicus* of Æschylean *hubris* seems to be played out like a drama of vast shadows in Plato's cave. The red fires burn outside, and within the cave the authoritarian shadows play:

> There has come down from of old
> A saying made by men:
> Prosperity as it grows
> Comes to its waxing time,
> And from good fortune flows
> Evil upon men's seed,
> When they have grown too bold—
> Evil's fiercest crime.
> I hold my mind apart:
> Evil breeds evil, I say,
> Like to its own breed,
> But in a righteous hearth
> Children are blessed indeed.
>
> Old Hubris is a maid
> Who brings on the evil day,
> At the fatal hour of birth
> A young and arrogant heart—
> And none can ever say
> What tattered violence comes
> On to these cursed homes.
> Eternal insolence flows
> Among black shadows.
> So on golden houses falls

The shadow of these funerals,
And hope departing with averted eyes
Fulfils their insolent destinies.

(AGAMEMNON, 750)

For Æschylus the laws of destiny are violated by the insolent heart, and all his work is no more than a footnote to the power of old Hubris (παλαιά ὕβρις), who incessantly gives birth to children, who are the heroes in the toils of fate. When the gods for their own purposes desire to destroy a hero, they sent down not *hubris* but *âte,* a mental delusion or infatuation which prevents men from foreseeing the consequences of their sins. It is *âte* which makes men reckless, to become the immediate servants of pride. Then they are hardened (βροτοὺς κρατύνειν), and have no fear of the future, but blindly encompass their own tragic ends, and every step they take is only one more step to an anguished death, and the annihilation of their tribe, for the curse is not on one man, but on all. The dark shadows are always there, Æschylus seems to be saying; they cannot be wished away; only those who travel along the narrow path of symmetry, self-restraint and moderation (συμμετρία, σωφροσύνη, μετριότης) need have no fear of God's vengeance.

In this arid philosophy all Æschylus' sympathies appear to be on the side of the tragic hero. We watch him with bated breath. When, unknown to himself, the hero passes beyond the appointed law of heaven (θέσμιον), the chorus exercises its right to utter its eternal complaint against man's folly; yet the chorus is colourless compared with the regal hero on his way to his death. There is a proper time and season for all things, but how incomparably dull and empty would be our lives if we obeyed the ordinances of the gods at all times! Yet the plays have their tragic purpose, to re-mind us that the ordinances are there, immutably engraved on the rocks of heaven, and we ignore them at our own peril. Against the dark shadows only pure righteousness, piety towards parents, love for the stranger at the gates are of any avail; and all extremes of conduct lead to a tortured death.

It is the great merit of Æschylus that he could dramatise so barren a philosophy until the conflict between the heroes in their royal robes and the encompassing shadows becomes real to us, and we hear the rustling of the heavy robes, and the fluttering of arrogant wings. His purpose is the clear purpose of warning. He will deliberately so arrange the fate of his heroes that their greatest triumphs occur at their greatest moment of defeat. We see them pressing forward to the triumph, unconscious of the pit. Clytemnestra welcomes the victorious Agememnon. "What day," she cries, "so bright, so blessed, as when the wife greets the returning husband! Throw wide the gates of welcome; go and meet him and tell him that his wife is waiting for him, unchanged and unchangeable! No pleasure have I known but the thought of him, and have watched like a faithful guardian over his treasures and his honours!" Then Agamemnon enters, seeing the purple carpet laid out before him. The carpet is like the pit of Hell, for if he walks upon it, he is taking to himself the prerogatives of the gods:

> O treat me not like a soft and delicate woman,
> Or gazing open-mouthed, give me acclaim,
> As though I were barbarian. These tapestries here
> Will draw the envy of wide heaven should I touch them.
> So are the gods worshipped.
> No mortal ever walks on rich embroideries.
> So treat me as a man, with a man's honouring,
> Not as a God. The voice of rumour takes
> These gifts and spreads them wide.
> To be of humble mind is God's best gift.

(AGAMEMNON, 918)

There occurs then the intervention of a god who is unnamed, but whom we have later come to call Irony, for Agamemnon is persuaded to tread the purple, *though he insists on removing his sandals as a sign of his humility*. When the procession enters the palace, it has already assumed the shape of a sacrificial progress. "So it has always been," Æschylus seems to be saying, for there is no regret in his voice, though there is a sorrowing pity for the abstract laws of Fate, which have been wounded by the crime. The triumph of Clytemnestra will be followed by her inevitable defeat, and the defeat of all her children to the last descendant of her house. Iron irony rules; and it is as though, on a scale embracing a whole family, we were in the presence of the medieval torture which insisted that as the flesh wasted away, the iron chains should be brought closer to the flesh. In the lost fragment of the lost *Niobe*, Æschylus announces clearly the inexorable fate: "God planteth in mortal man the cause of sin whensoever He wills utterly to destroy a house."

In Æschylus the scale of vengeance is complete, pitiless, violent, continuing and absurd. Reduced to its logical conclusions it allows no hint of mercy to the world; predestination enters on a scale which was not envisaged by Calvin. Yet it is important to observe that a kind of pity remains: a profound pity for the dead. Æschylus sees the world through the frame of death, and all the honour that survives after death. This at least remains, for the fallen hero as for the simple peasant who has worked dutifully in his fields. "If disaster must come," says Eteocles, "let it be disaster without shame. A man's honour is the only thing that remains to him after death." For Æschylus the dead are everywhere, their *manes* must be exalted, and justice will execute the wrath of the dead— τοῦ θανόντος ἡ Δίκη πράσσει κότον. Here at last compassion enters, for he sees a Justice which immutably concerns itself with the affairs of men, but towards the dead there is only the justice of men's regard for them: they are beyond the consolations and the fear of the gods. For him the workings of fate are an affair of Time, and every man approaches to his own ripeness. It is no good expecting the fullness of things before their proper time, but for the dead there is no time, no fullness, only a continual pleading to be in every man's favour; and in a sense the calamities which occur to those who go beyond the bounds of σωφροσύνη are the vengeance of the dead.

To understand the profundities of the Æschylean mind and temper we must travel more than two thousand years forward to Dostoievsky. When Father Zossima on his death-bed cries: "There are those who remain proud and fierce even in Hell—they cry out that the God of Life should be annihilated, that God should destroy himself and his own creation, and they will burn in the fire of their own wrath forever, and yearn for death and annihilation. But they will not attain to death," he is speaking in the tones of a Dostoievskian chorus which is also an Æschylean chorus. For

Æschylus the act of stepping over the boundaries of σωφροσύνη implies that "God should destroy himself and his own creation," and the whole world will descend into the primeval chaos which existed before Zeus became supreme among the gods. *The Brothers Karamazov* postulates a world where the crimes are the same as those which preoccupied Æschylus. When Ivan Karamazov cries out at his trial, in complete lucidity of mind: "My father has been murdered, and they pretend they are horrified. They keep up the sham with one another. Liars! They all desire the death of their fathers!" he is speaking as an Æschylean hero might have spoken secretly to himself, knowing that the ceremony of patricide had causes which lie deep in the human soul. All Æschylus is there. It is as though he wrote in horror of the myth, but saw life through its ritual, and dared not step an inch from the path which the myth laid down for him, and in doing this he is no more than the servant of his time, suffering with the heroes he had created in his darkest nightmares.

With Sophocles the sun shines. The myth, seen at the bottom of the pool, rises to the light. The same compulsions occur, the punishments are just as terrible, the ferocious Fates are forever lying in wait, but man is more assured of his freedom than ever before. The archaic Apollo has stepped out of the Caucasian rock, and man is at last master of his destiny, of some part of his destiny. The Rhamnusian Nemesis still holds her scales adverse to the hopes of man, and on her pedestal there are still written the words: "Be thou not lifted up!" but now for the first time in drama man may be upheld as the master of the territory he surveys:

> Many wonders there are, but none so wondrous as man,
> Who by his power channels the white seas
> With ships driven by storm-winds
> From the south, and the breaking waves
> Beneath his paths are perilous.
> Yet man wears upon himself the earth,
> Eldest of the gods, immortal, never-sleeping,
> Turning his furrows by his horse-teams:
> So does the plowshare travel year by year.

> (ANTIGONE, 332)

But this is not the end of man's mastery: he traps the birds, tames the wild beasts, yokes the horses, teaches speech and "windswift thoughts", and is a councillor of his government; he has resources against all things except Death. He has found release even from sickness, the most cunning ideas abound in his brain, and when he swears by the gods and keeps his city holy, he possesses an enviable perfection—so Sophocles in a singing chorus announces the triumphs of man, as Pindar had announced his glory.

It is an astonishing portrait, and is wholly inconceivable in any gallery of portraits painted by Æschylus, who saw dim shapes more powerful than death. When Sophocles speaks of the splendour of man he is not in the least ironical, for it was Sophocles who brought the third actor on the stage, as though wearying of the interminable dialogue of the self with the self, determined that there should be others to insist upon the reality of the self; and it was Sophocles who first dressed his tragic actors in the most vivid colours, giving them jewelled chaplets, embroidered girdles and robes of saffron and purple falling in long graceful folds. In the *Antigone*, it is not the laws of the Thunder-bearer which are made to rule, but the laws of human custom and what Keats called "the holiness of the Heart's affections and the truth of Imagination." The chorus in praise of man comes at the very moment before *Antigone* appears in manacles, arrested by order of Cleon because she has flouted his order that Polyneices should remain unburied.

Not man only, but man's love is celebrated by Sophocles, and almost in the same terms with which he had celebrated man, for if man travels by sea, so does love, and if man is unconquered, so is love:

O Love, unconquered in fight, who makest the havoc of wealth,
Who keepest vigil beside the maiden's tender face,
Thou who wanderest the seas and huts of the wilds,
No immortal can escape thee, nor any man
Who lives for the day: thou makest him mad.

For even the wisest are turned to folly by thee.
So do they come to their ruin; thou stirrest the feuds of the kinsmen;
Victory shines in the love-kindling light of the eyes

Of the decorative bride; thy power is enthroned
Beside the eternal laws: all bow to invincible Love.

(ANTIGONE, 786)

At this moment, for the first time, Love comes upon the stage,
demanding her own sacred rights, and Nemesis Adrasteia, "she
whom none may escape" is exchanged for Love "whom no immortal can escape". Between Nemesis and Love there could be no
fiercer war, and in a sense the war between Love and Fate was
only resolved with the coming of Christ.

The choruses of *Antigone* may therefore be said to announce the
full emergence of man. In the words of Protagoras: "Man is the
measure of all things." Man becomes, too, the measure of the gods,
who are depicted exactly as though they were the champions of
the race, Hercules clearly modelled on a living wrestler, Hermes
on a runner and Athene on a village maiden. Only Zeus, half lion,
hugely bearded, looks like a god any more. Man's cunning is now
celebrated; the worst that can happen to him is not that he should
be struck by the gods, but that he should be deprived of his
citizenship:

> Cunning beyond the wildest dreams man has,
> Such is his fertile brain which leads him to evil and good;
> When he honours the laws of the land and has justice
> Upheld by a solemn oath sworn before the gods,
> Then proudly his city shall stand; but cityless is he
> Who departs from the just ways by reason of his pride.
> Never may such a man sit by my hearth or share
> My thoughts, who sins unreasonably.

(ANTIGONE, 367)

So, in the most beautiful of Sophocles' plays, Œdipus comes at last
in old age to the place of his death, a wanderer from a curse. As
his death approaches, he curses his sons, but even this curse is not
held against him by the divine fates; Apollo whispers that in spite
of his crimes he will find rest at the seat of the Awful Goddesses.
Æschylus describes the Furies as "Gorgons, not women, and yet I
will not liken them to the Gorgon mould: they are wingless, black,
utterly horrible." Heracleitus spoke of them as "the allies of justice,

finding out the sun, if he passes his limits." Sophocles is the first to call them merciful. Œdipus dies; his children ask Theseus where his grave can be found, and Theseus replies:

> Weep no more, maidens; the mercy of
> The dark-winged powers is now stored among us.
> There is no room for mourning: Nemesis would follow.
>
> (OEDIPUS IN COLONUS, 1751)

In these lines the weight of Nemesis is lifted, and the dark-winged powers are seen to be providing by their mercy a store of graces for the community; Œdipus' death is a liberation and a promise of peace for the people; Nemesis will follow grief, but not the acts of men, for men are, in the Christian phrase, saved by the divine sufferings of Œdipus, and on the place where Œdipus died, there is erected an altar which shall protect Attica from invaders.

When Maximus of Tyre wrote that the Greek custom was to represent the gods by the most beautiful things of earth, because "the idea of those who make divine images in human shape is that the spirit of man is of all things nearest to God and most godlike," he was expressing the theme of Sophocles, who could say of men that there were many wonders, but none so wondrous as man. It was an age when men were very close to being their own mediators between themselves and the gods, and the gentleness of the Eleusinian mysteries had come to temper the nightmare of Nemesis which haunted the Greeks of an earlier age.

But Nemesis and Hubris remained. Occasionally Plato was to find himself conscious of their presence. "Love sends men mad," says Plato's Socrates, but so too does the love of wisdom and so too does pride. In the *Laws* Plato touches pride with velvet gloves:

> Of all the faults of the soul the gravest is the one inborn in most men, and they all excuse it in themselves and make no effort to avoid it, and this fault is conveyed in the maxim that "everyone is naturally his own friend", and that it is only right and proper that it should be so. Yet in truth this same violent attachment to self is the constant source of all manner of misdeeds. . . .
>
> (LAWS, V, 731 D)

There is a failure of nerve somewhere; Plato never entirely got to grips with pride. When Callicles in the *Gorgias* denounces the slave morality of law, and proclaims "the will to power," Socrates is made to laugh it off as an absurdity. Plato defends power mightily. The Platonic definition of existence in the *Sophist* is based on power, "for everything that possesses any sort of power to affect another or to be affected by another, however trifling the cause and however slight and momentary the effect, has real existence; and I hold that the definition of being is simply power." It was not only the Sophists who argued in this way. Power is still seen to be the ruler; in the *Laws*, its rule is absolute, and in the name of naked power the most tyrannical dictatorship is elevated to the role of the desirable empire.

For Aristotle power is still supreme, but the proud man is surveyed at greater leisure and with a greater insistence, not on his failures, but on his triumphs. A new co-ordinate is introduced—the co-ordinate of the *megalopsychos*, the great-souled and magnanimous devotee to culture, the man who dares to live alone in the secret worship of his own soul. "The man who lives alone," wrote Plato, "would partake of the character of the god or the beast." Aristotle attempts to show that he partakes of neither, and that his desires, instead of being easily satisfied or productive of never-ending despairs, are indeed insatiable. Æschylus remarked sadly in *The Persians:* "If you have lived alone, you find out how bare is that furniture." Aristotle's *megalopsychos* answers gravely that in the interior of the soul there is very little need for furniture. It is a voice of extreme gentleness and cultivated *ennui*, and the portrait is delicately painted, so delicately indeed that we begin to suspect that Aristotle is engaged on a self-portrait, though Hegel unaccountably suspected that Aristotle was describing Alexander the Great. It is a description that could come only at the end of the era. So Marcus Aurelius might have described himself, and so might M. Charlus, and it is unthinkable that Plato or Socrates would have derived pleasure from this portrait or excitement in the painting of it. In Aristotle the excitement, of a most cultivated kind, brims over:

The *megalopsychos* (the man of great soul) is especially concerned with honour and dishonour. Great honours, afforded to persons of worth, afford him a moderate pleasure, for he will believe he is receiving what is due to him, or even less, for no honour can be adequate to the merits of perfect virtue. Nevertheless, he will deign to accept such honours, because they have no greater tribute to offer him. Honour rendered by common people, or on trivial grounds, he will utterly despise, in the belief that he does not merit them. He will also despise dishonour, for no dishonour can justly attach to the man of great soul. He is a man, as I have said, who is especially concerned with honour, a man who will not rejoice overmuch in prosperity, nor grieve overmuch at adversity: *for he does not care much even about honour*. Because he regards honour of little price, so all other things are regarded by him as of little price, and it is for this reason that he is thought to be proud.

(NICHOMACHEAN ETHICS, 1124 A)

The terrible "split in the soul" is announced almost at the beginning of the portrait. He is especially concerned with honour, and he cares nothing at all for honour, or at least he cares more for the gift of it at the proper time and place than for the glory of possessing it. His glory, Aristotle suggests, lies in the accolade rather than in the perpetual wearing of the order of knighthood. It is a grim portrait, implying the highest degree of detachment, but Socrates had previously issued the appropriate warning in the *Phædrus*, saying in words that have a Buddhist ring: "But detachment, Phædrus, and preoccupation with form lead to intoxication and desire, they may even lead the noblest among us to frightful emotional excess," and the "stern cult of the beautiful" would make him the first to condemn these excesses. The *megalopsychos* is immune to "the stern cult of the beautiful", even though he values beauty above most things. Aristotle has by no means finished. There are four folio pages of discussion on *megalopsychos*, who is treated as though he was some rare specimen of animal whose appearance must be celebrated in a manner worthy of him. He values few things highly. The consequences are manifold. "He will not run into danger for trifling reasons, and indeed he is not a lover of danger, for there are few things he loves, but he will face danger in a great cause, and when doing so he will be ready to sacrifice his

own life, since he holds that life is not worth having at any price."
The portrait of Aristotle himself imperceptibly merges into the
portrait of the Athenian man described in the funeral speech of
Pericles, and something of the Athenian pride confronted with
Spartan barbarism continues as the portrait unfolds:

> It is characteristic of the *megalopsychos* never to ask help
> from others, or only with reluctance, but to render it willingly;
> and to be haughty towards men of position and fortune, but
> courteous towards those of moderate station, *because it is dif-
> ficult and distinguished to be superior to the great, but easy to
> outdo the lowly*—it is like putting forth one's strength against
> the weak.
>
> He will not compete for the common objects of ambition,
> or go where other people take the first place, and he will be
> idle and slow to act except when pursuing some high honour
> or achievement; and he will not engage in many undertakings,
> but only in such as are important and distinguished. He will
> be open both in love and in hate, since concealment shows
> timidity; and he will care more for the truth than for what
> people think, and he will speak and act openly, for despising
> other men, he is always himself outspoken and frank. He will
> be incapable of living at the will of another, unless a friend,
> and he is not prone to admiration, since nothing is great to
> him. He does not bear a grudge; he is no gossip; he will not
> talk either about himself or another. He likes to own his own
> useless and beautiful things rather than useful things that bring
> a return, since the former shows his independence more. He
> has a slow gait, a deep voice and a deliberate utterance.
>
> (NICHOMACHEAN ETHICS, 1124-1125A)

There is much more of it; there are the most delicate and involved discourses on the measurement of honour, on charity, on
the degrees of elevation above one's fellows.

The description of the *megalopsychos* is not always convincing.
There are too many repetitions of the phrase: "for he values
nothing highly." One begins to imagine that he values many things
highly, including himself, and is whistling to keep his courage up.
In the great Greek phrase, it was the duty of creators to see fair—

τὰ ἴσα νέμειν—in the handling of their creations. Aristotle does not see fair. The dice are loaded in favour of magnanimous virtue, but the implications of magnanimous evil are also there. Aristotle is trying to define the most enviable, the most cultivated, the most honourable man, but students subjected to the professor's exaltation of the *megalopsychos* might be excused if they found in vice an agreeable consolation for so formidable a virtue. Surveying this strange incubus, we realise that even the nymph Hubris is more colourful, and the vengeance of the gods more desirable; for what Aristotle has succeeded in doing is to present the hero without any heroism. So in our own day we present Christianity without miracles or Hell-fire.

The god-like man who does not suffer, the hero who performs no task except the cultivation of himself, eternally immersed in his own splendour and his own honour, remained to colour the Aristotelian tradition, and to give an impulse to those descendants of the Greek philosopher who gloried in themselves, admired themselves and walked in the places of honour unaccompanied by anything except themselves. When Philo of Alexandria taught that God was unqualified Being, had no need of the world, and even after the Creation remained "without suffering, without fear, having no hand in evil, not to be influenced, without care, unwearied, full of unclouded blessedness," he was subtly reflecting Aristotle's portrait of the magnanimous man raised to the heights of the magnanimous God.

Philo was a neo-platonist who attempted to form a bridge between Judaic scholasticism and the scholasticism of the Academy. Half-Greek, half-Jew, a contemporary of Christ, he was compelled to face the problem of pride, for there were curious similarities between the Hebrew and Greek mythologies. Was not Adam a kind of Prometheus hurled from heaven? Azazel, too, in the *Book of Enoch*, shows some of the features of Prometheus. The theme of pride runs through the Old Testament; it is the central theme of Christ's temptation. Lucifer crying: "I will exalt my throne above the throne of God," or Satan crying ironically: "I yield to thee who are the greater wrestler," are the exemplars of pride, but not the only ones; medieval scholars delighted in demonstrating the pride of Aman at the Court of Ahasuerus, the boasts of Deborah and Barak, the overweening claims of Saul and Joab; and Jeremiah was astonishingly fertile in his imprecations on pride. So, too, was Philo of Alexandria:

> Let us build ourselves a city, they say: and this means, let us fortify our resources and fence them in with strength, that we may not fall easy victims to the onset of the foe. . . . Let the tower be built as a symbol, as a citadel, as a royal and impregnable castle for the despotic vice. Let its feet walk upon the earth and its head reach to heaven, carried by our vaulting ambition to that vast height.
>
> For they say, "let us make our name." What monstrous and extravagant shamelessness! What is this you say? You ought to be hiding your misdeeds in night and profound darkness, and to have taken, if not true shame, at least the simulation of it to veil them.
>
> What sort of name, then, do you desire? Is it the name that best befits your deeds? Is it one name, only? One general name, perhaps, but a thousand specific ones, which you will hear from the lips of others even if your own are silent? Reckless-ness with shamelessness, insolence with violence, violence with murder, seductions with adulteries, unbridled lust with un-measured pleasures, desperation with foolhardiness, injustice with knavery, thefts with robbery, perjuries with falsehoods, impieties and lawbreaking, these and the like are the name for deeds such as yours. It is indeed a fine course for pride and boasting, when you pursue so eagerly the repute which these names give you, names at which you should in all reason hide your heads for shame.   (CONFUSION OF TONGUES, III)

So, across the centuries, Philo rebukes the *megalopsychos;* and Cicero, inveighing against Catiline, could not have thundered louder. The knives of patristic invective are being sharpened; in some such way Jerome will inveigh later against the habits of Roman virgins. There is something almost vicious in the relentless determination to crush the enemy underfoot, and then to turn sharply on the heels, but Philo is conscious of the self-regarding gaze and long before the fathers went out into the desert, he saw its dangers:

Many have exalted their senses, as though they were a tower, so that they have touched the boundaries of heaven, that is symbolically our mind, wherein range and dwell those divine forms of being which excel all others. They who do not shrink from this give the preference to sense rather than to understanding. They will use perceptible things to subdue and capture the world of things intelligible, thus forcing the two to change places, the one to pass from mastery to slavery, the other from its natural servitude to dominance.

(CONFUSION OF TONGUES, 133)

Even in translation the power of the horror comes through; it is taut, keeps close to the object and chooses the method of the countermine to disenthrone the enemy. Here there is no bright ring of words; no Aristotle perpetuating, on a full stomach, the hungers of the spirit. It is measured despair, coming out of wounded certainty and throwing the words hard on the page. The admirable performance has none of the weaknesses of complaisance which infect the Platonic dialogues. When Socrates in the *Republic* warns against excess, there is mellowness in the acceptance of the fact and no energy in the rebuke:

Answer me, do you see greater pleasures—I do not mean the greater number, but those that are greater in violence and intensity—occur in a life of overweening pride (ἐν ὕβρει) or in a life of moderation? Think well before you speak.

I see what you mean, and the difference I perceive is great, for moderate men are ever kept in check by the well-known proverb "nothing too much", which restrains them, whereas ignorant and profligate men are possessed by pleasure to the point of madness and wild shouts.

Well said. And if that is true, it is obvious that the greatest pleasures and the greatest pains are to be found in a bad state of mind, and not in excellence of virtue.

How delightful the absence of rebuke, the quiet contemplation of excess, as though excess in the nature of things was no more disturbing than a line drawn with a crooked stick on the sands beside the Ilyssus! Excess is indeed to be abhorred, but let us abhor it politely, and consider how virtue may be best cultivated. Philo is a barbarian compared to the Platonic *megalopsychoi*. He thunders, his voice trembles, he invokes divine vengeance and he is careful that his periods should end in organ-notes:

> Those who assert their ownership of soul, sense and speech receive the heritage their miserable state deserves: a soul malevolent, a chaos of unreasoning passions, held down by a multitude of voices: sometimes mauled by greed and lust, like a strumpet in the stews, sometimes fast-bound as in a poison by a multitude of ill-deeds, with habits which an unanimous judge have held worthy of arrest; speech brow-beating, keen-edged against truth, working to the harm of its victims and the shame of its employers; sense insatiable, ever imbibing the objects of sense, yet through its uncontrolled avidity incapable of reaching satisfaction, regardless of its monitors, blind, deaf and derisive of all they preach for its benefit.

(WHO IS THE HEIR?, 109)

Philo, by his exhilarating invective, does not solve the problem of man's pride. Swept forward in the flood of his own rhetoric he is a new Jeremiah employing the resources of the Academy to defeat his private opponents.

When we reach Plotinus the air is thinner, and we live on heights where rhetoric becomes meaningless, for the quiet urgencies of the soul cannot be described in purple prose. He delights in the legend of Narcissus. He says calmly that "if any man would know God, he must become God-like," a phrase that would have appealed to Angelus Silesius. Elsewhere, he says that "God is present in all things, though we are ignorant that he is so, for we fly from him, or rather from ourselves." In the pure landscape of spun glass Plotinus has his home, but though he speaks gently of the mystery of man's consciousness regarding itself, and would seem to agree with Plato in the *Theages* that "everyone in the world would like if possible to be master of all men and above all of God," we are no nearer a solution to the problem; his own pride chills his prose; we walk among his mirrors, and they are not our own.

The debate on pride, the constant annotations, the feverish determination to penetrate the heart of the matter, all these are Greek;

they were perhaps the first to feel the pangs of self-consciousness, the first to realise the terror that lay behind the mirror. Pride was death-dealing, as Narcissus knew, and Narcissus was the least of the tragic heroes: Œdipus and Antigone died in greater agony of soul for a similar crime. Inevitably the legends continued, changing as time went on. We have to wait until the fifth century A.D. before the strands are drawn together. Then the half-pagan, half-Christian poet Nonnus, living in Egypt, decided to sift the legends of the Titans and make a consistent story of their progress. Writing nearly a thousand years after Hubris has first appeared on the scene, he describes how Zagreus-Dionysus (the name Zagreus means "one who is torn to pieces") stormed heaven and for a while secured the throne of Zeus:

But he did not hold the throne for long. In their fierce envy of implacable Hera, the Titans cunningly smeared their round faces with mystic gypsum, and while Zagreus contemplated his changing countenance in a mirror, they destroyed him with their infernal weapons. Where the limbs of Zagreus were cut piecemeal by the Titan knives, the end of his life was the beginning of a new life, as Dionysus. He appeared in another shape, and assumed many forms, now young like crafty Cronides shaking his ægis cape, now as ancient Cronus, heavy-kneed, pouring rain. Sometimes he resembled a curiously formed baby, sometimes he was a mad youth whose first flower of down darkened his rounded chin, or again he was a lion who roared in snarling rage as he lifted his neck shadowed with a thick mane; then he became an unbroken horse raising his neck and shaking out the imperious bit, until again he was seen to be a curled and horned serpent covered with scales. Watch him: he becomes a young tiger striped with grey markings. Watch him again: he is a roaring bull. So he fought for his life, until Hera in her envy uttered a curse and then the fierce bull collapsed, and immediately the murderers set upon him, each eager for his turn with the knife, chopping the bull-shaped Dionysus to pieces. So the first Dionysus was slaughtered, but afterwards he learned the trick of the mirror with the reflected image.   (DIONYSIACA, VI, 169)

It is the classic text: here all the impedimenta of pride are brought together in a single story. Here are the knives, the white gypsum, the identification of Cronus and Ocean, the enchanted gaze within the mirror, the images of huge power, the war to the death and the continual bringing to life. Finally, never elucidated but as inevitable as sunrise, there is "the trick of the mirror with the reflected image."

The Roman Triumph

WHEN the Roman conqueror returned to Rome to receive a triumph, he rode on a chariot adorned with ivory and drawn by four white garlanded horses. His face was smeared with red paint. Splendid in his isolation and glory, he wore a tunic of Tyrian purple embroidered with golden palm-shoots, and a toga decorated with gold stars; there was a crown of laurels on his head, and he held an ivory sceptre surmounted by a golden eagle. A slave held the crown of Jupiter Capitolinus above his head, the crown sparkling with rubies and emeralds. He was the pride of the Roman race, but he did not himself lead the triumphal procession. The Roman senators led the procession; they were followed by the trumpeters, and these in turn were followed by the spoils of wars. Then came the white sacrificial bulls with gilded horns led by bare-foot boys in white, and behind the bulls came the manacled prisoners, men, women and children, their wounds showing, the look of death on their faces, for they would have their throats slit before the procession reached the steps of the Temple of Jupiter. The conqueror was still far behind. Lictors, musicians and a long train of choristers swinging censers separated him from the prisoners. At the end of the procession, behind the choristers, almost obscured in the blue smoke of the censers, came the conqueror.

It is worth while to watch the conqueror closely, because it is possible that never in human history has there been such pomp of naked power as when the triumphant Roman general rode from the Campus Martius to the Via Sacra on his way to the Capitol. He is the god of war incarnate. To him is granted all the splendour and honour the Roman state could conceive, but as he rides through the garlanded streets, among the falling petals and to the triumphal cries of the people, deafened by the noise and seeing everything discoloured by flowers, he is also the object of the fiercest taunts and the coarsest jests. Running beside his chariot, making obscene gestures, were painted clowns and satyrs dressed like wantons, and though the conqueror wore a crown of laurel, they wear crowns of gold. Among them there is a single satyr dressed in female clothes who taunts the victor louder than the rest. She has a place apart. She is treated with great ceremony by the clowns. Her croaking voice gave out more than abuse; it curses the general to the last generation of his sons, invents a rude genealogy for him; sometimes she will run straight up to the low chariot and scream in his face.

Who is she? Why is she alone among the clowns dressed in female dress? Why is she given a special position among the clowns? No one knows, but it is at least possible that she comes from the same origins as Hubris and Nemesis.

The procession goes slowly forward. Whips crack over the bound and bleeding prisoners. The conqueror is tense and nervous; if we observe him carefully, we see he is holding in one hand a rat's foot or a dried-up cockerel's comb, an amulet against the evil eye. A slave stands behind him, a slave who himself wears a golden crown and who holds the crown of Jupiter Capitolinus above the victor's head. All the time he whispers urgently: "O Conqueror, look behind you, and remember you are mortal." So the procession winds towards the Capitoline Hill, the oxen are sacrificed, the prisoners are murdered (because there is no place for them in the sacrifice,) and within the Capitol itself the victor offers a magnificent entertainment for his friends. It was dark when he was led home to the sound of music in the glare of torches.

The extraordinary triumph of a Roman conqueror was so carefully elaborated, and so slavishly copied over the generations that we are justified in attaching to it a quite extraordinary importance. It was in this form that Roman power, the *mana* of the Roman state, was celebrated. It is a strange and disconcerting spectacle, and oddly *neutral,* for with every effort to exalt the conqueror there is a corresponding effort to debase him. He is all that every Roman desired to be, and at the same time he is made to pass through an ordeal that no one would assume willingly. Why the red paint smeared on his face? Why the obscene jests? Why is he placed at the end of the procession? We can only guess at the springs of the Roman character, but it would seem that the red paint was the sign of his divinity, the obscene jests were deliberately cultivated to remind him of his humanity, and his place in the triumph arose by the accident which had fused together three separate triumphal processions deriving from different cultures, Etruscan, Roman and Greek. What is so extraordinary at first sight in the Roman triumph is the deliberate employment of sexual symbols to avert *hubris*, so that a conqueror would sometimes carry in his chariot, as a reminder of his common sexuality and also as a *fascinum* to avert the evil eye, a red-painted *phallus*, which he would show triumphantly to the people. The Greek triumphs were not like this. The Greek equivalent to the Roman triumph is the naked athlete crowned with parsley who stands alone on the steps of the Temple of Zeus, while the priestesses sing hymns.

That the Roman conqueror should hold the obscene amulet is surprising enough; what is still more surprising is that a public slave, and not a priest, is deputed to whisper warnings into his ear. The general who gives the order for slaughter is warned of his own slaughter by a slave, the proudest is placed next to the humblest, and like the warning death's head in the medieval *memento mori*, the slave reminds the conqueror of the limping Fates who come up from behind and cut the thread of life.

In the Roman world, even at the moment of the greatest triumphs, we are made aware of the presence of inchoate fears, which tug remorselessly at the Roman soul. Auspices are continually being taken. A host of "critical" and "black" days mark the calendar; all the days following the calends, nones and ides are to be regarded with fear because severe defeats were received on those days. There is so great a reliance upon auguries that *imperium* and *auspicium* become almost interchangeable terms. A harsh fear inhabits the people who have taken over from Greece gods who were entirely foreign to them. When the Romans worshipped they were veiled —the single exception occurred on the 15th March when they threw the bundles of white reeds into the Tiber; when the Greeks worshipped they were bare-headed, and faced the sun. There is something inhuman in Roman religion, and it does not surprise us that they forbade the making of statues in the first two hundred years of the existence of the Roman state; instead they worshipped Jupiter in a flint-stone, Mars was represented by a spear and the Vestals by fire. Even the conqueror relied on auguries, and as he climbed the steps of the Temple of Jupiter, he would glance hurriedly at the behaviour of the wild bulls being led to the sacrifice, for if they bowed their heads all would be well, but if they raised their heads grave harm would follow. The Romans were hag-ridden with a sense of guilt, and the old Roman curse, *Ultimus suorum moriatur*, seems to have been there from the beginning.

Anyone who wanders through the scattered remnants of the poetry of Ennius cannot fail to observe the obsession with blood. "Bronze resounds, spears splinter, earth sweats blood," he says in one fragment. In another, Thyestes, the descendant of Tantalus, speaks in the pure Titan tradition:

> Come not near me, stranger. Draw back from me.
> My contagion is—my shadow harms thee.
> So great an evil clings upon me.
>
> (REMAINS OF OLD LATIN, I, 352)

When we see Thyestes again, he is clinging to the stern rocks, and all his intestines are drooping down the mountain-side, "a mess of black blood." It is the Roman Nemesis. It does not terrify as Œdipus terrifies, when he plucks out his eyes and we hear the thunder of Zeus. The Roman obsession with viscera was so enduring that Augustine was to comment upon it in *De Civitate Dei*; they were men who had seen the bodies cut up on the battlefield, and could not get out of their minds the terrible yellow flowering of the entrails. But once or twice in Ennius there are passages which hint at the causes of shame. When Cicero quotes Ennius: "It is the beginning of disgrace to bare the body among fellow-citizens," we are immediately aware of the difference between Greece and Rome. And once, quite suddenly, we are brought face to face with a legend concerning Pan which suggests once again, but most tantalisingly, the mountain in Arcadia where the nymph Hubris may have been born. "Once Pan led Zeus up to the mountain which is called the High Pillar (*Coeli Stela*)," he says. "When he had climbed it, he then contemplated the world far and wide, and on this mountain he built an altar to the Sky; on that altar Jupiter first sacrificed and burnt the whole victim." But who the victim was, and what was the final purpose of this journey we may never know. Was Hubris present? Was the High Pillar on Olympus? Is this the beginning of the legend of Olympus? All that we know for certain is that Pan, whom we had thought to be a wood-god, belonged to the eminences, or at least led Zeus to them. The credentials of Hubris, posing as Pan's daughter, become more certain.

There are still other fragments of Ennius which suggest how the Roman theme breaks down the Greek gods into abstractions, thereby making them more dangerous and more compulsive, for a popular religion worshipping abstractions can end only in a kind of despair, a desperate belief in abstractions for their own sake, until they lose all validity and are exchanged for more tangible gods. All that the Stoic *apatheia* meant is already contained in those lines of Ennius where, speaking with pathetic emotion, he insists on the vision of duty:

> *Caelicolae, mea membra, dei quos nostra potestas*
> *Officiis divisa facit.*

> Dwellers of heaven, my own members, gods made
> By the division of my power into duties.
>
> (REMAINS OF OLD LATIN, I, 450)

So ample an enunciation of *pietas*, which is more than reverence and nearly as much as plain duty, comes surprisingly from the earliest of Latin epic-writers. We are oppressed once more by the suspicion of some *arrière-pensée*, a deliberate journey against the stream. No one would invent so arid a philosophy unless he had departed from a sense of duty to the living. The *veneratio vitae* is absent, and we remember that the Roman word *religio* means awe, scruple, fear, nervousness, and that it never meant what it means to us today. We remember all the various attempts to change the site of the capital, as though a curse had been laid upon it, and the mass of credulous superstitions which it was the purpose of Lucretius in *De rerum natura* to discount. The blessedness of the gods was foreign to the Romans; for them the valid and terrible appearance of the gods lay in the brilliant and blinding lightning-stroke.

"To desire the impossible is a disease of the soul," said the ancient Greek proverb. The Romans, however, were always desiring the impossible. The demonstrable and physical sign of this desire lay in the great aqueducts they built across the mountain valleys, so huge and forbidding that two thousand years later Rousseau could say that nothing was easier than to lose oneself in the immensity of the aqueduct at Nîmes; seen against this giant aqueduct one becomes an insect. The Roman roads belonged to the same order of things. These roads left the gates of the Eternal City, and marched straight onward, over mountains, across rivers, through frozen fens in one perpetual straight line, until they reached the sea. *Primum in mondo fecit deus timorem*, wrote Tibullus. "God brought the fear first into the world." The immense roads, the huge aqueducts, the great columns, the vast empire—all these give the appearance of being a form of escape from a primal fear.

Why the fear? Perhaps St. Augustine was right when he suggested that Rome fell because there had been a tradition of bloodshed and crime and pride from the beginning. Romulus, the founder of Rome, murdered his brother and his two foster-fathers, continually exalted himself, dressed in purple, saw people when reclining on his couch, and was at last mysteriously murdered near a place called the Goat's March, on a day when, according to Plutarch, "sudden strange alterations took place in the air, and the face of the sun was darkened, and the day turned into night, and it was not a peaceable night, but one shot through with terrible thunderings and winds from all quarters." The first walls were stained with a brother's blood, and the murder had been one of revolting cruelty. The echoes of the murder can be heard throughout Latin literature. Troy had fallen through pride—*cecidit superbum Ilium*—but Rome was built on the foundations of pride; the working out of the evil was long and dangerous. The Roman triumph was the Roman sorrow; the more lands they conquered the more impossible became the hope of holding the empire. Through Roman history tyranny rides rough-shod over the people, until the last of the Cæsars becomes an insane giant of monstrous talents, as murderous as Romulus, as disposed to glory as the father of the nation, and as unscrupulous.

Lucretius reduces the myths of the Titans to facts of the human soul; Nero plays out within himself the dreadful conquests of the Titanic powers. Nearly all the emperors were afflicted with the disease of an insane pride. Hadrian, whom Tertullian describes as *curiositatum omnium exploratorem*, the first man to ascend Mount Etna and Mons Casius, slew handsome youths in order to inspect their entrails, deified his lover Antinous, and ordered cities to be built in his lover's honour. Caligula instituted a temple of priests in honour of his own divinity, sacrificed peacocks and flamingoes to his own statue, dressed in women's clothes or paraded with a gold beard fixed under his chin like an Egyptian pharaoh, and sometimes wore the costume of Venus. Suetonius relates that he would take his gold statue of himself to bed with him, and embrace it, whispering: "Raise me to become a god, or else——" When some kings visited his court, he shouted after them: "Let there be one king, one prince." The Romans, shocked by his insane madness, were still more shocked when he adorned himself with the breastplate of Alexander the Great, which Augustus Cæsar had removed from the open tomb. Still more irreverently, he ordered all the most famous images of the gods to be brought from Greece, then lopped off their heads and substituted his own. The madness of the Roman Emperors was prodigious, but none equalled Nero either in cruelty or in pride. He made a colossal statue of himself 120 feet high. He wore the dress of a woman, married his slave Pythagoras to his eunuch Sporus, acted the part of Achilles on the stage and delighted in throwing handfuls of diamonds and pearls at the people; he murdered his mother, with whom he had had incestuous relations, and behaved with a calculated wantonness which is still frightening, not only because he was insane, but because he was capable of the most exquisite good sense when it was profitable to him. Even the most commendable Emperors allowed themselves to be worshipped as gods. Julius Cæsar after Pharsalia allowed his statue to be set up side by side with that of Jupiter in the temple of Quirinus. Octavian, hailed as *divi filius* after Actium, allowed divine honours to be paid to him in the provinces, and in the year B.C. 9 permitted

himself to be called Saviour of the present and the future. To com-
memorate his birthday an inscription was set up in Asia Minor:

> This day has given the earth an entirely new aspect. The
> world would have gone to destruction had there not streamed
> forth from him who is born a common blessing. . . . The
> providence which rules over all has filled this man with such
> gifts for the salvation of the world as designate him the
> Saviour of us and of future generations. . . . By his appear-
> ing the hopes of our forefathers are fulfilled. . . . The birth-
> day of God has brought to the earth good tidings that are
> bound up in him.

We are not asked to believe this nonsense, for by the time of
Augustus there were few who seriously believed in the gods. The
Roman augurs were observed to wink at each other during the
obsolete religious ceremonies they solemnly celebrated. "From his
birthday," continues the inscription, "a new era begins." Even
Virgil did not completely believe that a new era had begun, though
he accepted it as an article of faith, and wrote the *Æneid* in an
effort to prove the unprovable. But there were other and more
pressing reasons for writing the *Æneid*. There was guilt somewhere: it was necessary to reveal the sources of guilt, open the
seals. Virgil digs deep into the unconscious memory of the race,
while Dante erects over the human condition a tent of belief, or
rather he wraps layer upon layer of nacre around the obscure irrita-
tion, and proceeds to form that immense pearl whose colours still
dominate our lives: his movement is outward and upward, until the
pearl will embrace the whole earth, the whole of hell, purgatory
and the heavens. Dante was to end his epic with the vision of the
quiet light radiating from the godhead; Virgil ends his epic in
nightmare and flame. And where Dante in his pride sees himself as
a kind of Christ harrowing Hell, Virgil sees himself as Æneas, the
father of the race. He looks back to see the walls burning in the
senseless wars, but nothing is explained, and least of all does he
explain the sufferings of men.

In the end they were never explained; there were only hints,
tremendous gleams in the darkness, revolving wheels of light which
lit up the strange taut figures in the cave, blood-red and menacing,

caught in the attitudes of violence, not yet dead. Turnus, fighting his last desperate fight in a world gone mad, having no trust in the gods and little enough in men, has his belief in destiny, and little else. For him too there must be the final act of violence and audacity: *tu ne cede malis sed contra audentior ito.* "Do not give way to tribulation, but go relentlessly, audaciously forward." It was a motto well worthy of a Roman, but what if the voyage was not worthy of the effort, and what if the sign-posts were turned in the wrong direction? Perhaps indeed there was no explanation, or the real explanation lay in the fact of man's existence. This was not the point where Virgil started; he was after bigger game than man. Somewhere above the brooding melancholy of the small wars there is the vast shadow-play of greater wars; behind the scenes of conquest we seem to see the greater conquests of the Titans. "The Æneid is so inchoate", he wrote in a letter to the Emperor Augustus, "that I think myself mad to have embarked on it." But it was only by embarking upon it that he could see the depths of madness that haunted the Roman soul.

Perhaps, too, we are too fond of seeing the heroic gestures and hardly ask ourselves what the causes were. The Romans, like ourselves, worshipped labour: the mere act of labour was an act almost of divine creation. Virgil had written once in the *Eclogues: omnia vincit amor.* "Love conquers all." But in the *Æneid* it is not love that conquers, but relentless and treacherous labour: *labor omnia vincit improbus.* And this "treacherous labour" was the working of pride, from which there was no escape once it had begun. The name of Rome must be graven deep across the earth, the name of Æneas likewise. This was not the desire of Achilles. To come straight from Homer to Virgil is to come from the sunlight to the oppressive dusk. There is no sun in the *Æneid*. All is tempest, flashes of lightning, wounded soldiers in moonlight, funeral pyres— the Gothic horrors are piled up in a monstrous evocation of the discords in the Roman soul. Terrors are everywhere. The Cretan minotaur haunts the conquered lands, as once before he had haunted Crete. Behind the heavy notes of grief we hear the softer songs of lament: we hear them again in the strange hymn of Horace to the departing snows, a lament which goes back to the Egyptian *Song of the Harper* and forward to the *Dies Irae*. And on the proud the day of wrath, which is constantly in Virgil's imagination, falls most heavily.

What remains in Virgil, as he wanders round the dusky battle-fields in autumn, is the deep sincerity which makes his poetry tangible, his *"high solayn solemne port"*. Sir Thomas More's *Dialogue of Comfort against Tribulation* echoes the same kind of journey which Virgil undertook, and it is there that this delightful phrase is to be found, with much else concerning pride. But for Virgil pride was not the only, or the major, enemy; like Pascal he has his abyss and waits trembling for the end, but always so humanly and with such quiet determination to exalt the Romans that they still live for us. For him the vengeance of the gods was real and had to be worked out among men. He could not, like the Emperor Tiberius, when a man was put on trial for insulting the memory of the dead Emperor Augustus, stop the proceedings by saying "the gods could avenge their own wrongs": *deorum iniurias deis curae,* for the gods did not avenge their own wrongs. The fatality of mortals was to thirst for peace, though the gods denied it to them. Like Phèdre he recognises the ever-wakeful gods whose intransigence is so great that men must humble themselves before them:

> . . . *ces dieux qui dans mon flanc*
> *Ont allumé le feu fatal à tout mon sang,*
> *Ces dieux qui se sont fait une gloire cruelle*
> *De reduire le coeur d'une faiblesse mortelle.*

There is hardly a line of French which moves with so tremulous a Virgilian horror as these lines of Racine; the cruel glory remains —it is all that can ever remain in the contest when it is fought to the end.

There was one other Latin poet who threw himself into the heart of darkness and returned with the spoils. He was not a great poet, though there are moments when he speaks greatly. When Virgil describes a funeral pyre, we are conscious of the desperate sadness of the thing. With Statius the pyre shines with a fascinating glory: "Never was so sumptuous a blaze: precious stones crack, huge streams of molten silver run, and gold oozes from out the embroidered raiment, the boughs are fatted with

Assyrian juices, pale saffron drops hissing on the burning honey."
Yet when Statius described Capaneus threatening heaven he is
excellent:

> O arms and trumpets, swords and wounds I sing, and now
> Is Capaneus raised to battle with the starry vault.
> No more shall I sing the customary songs of poets.
> I summon a greater madness from the Aonian grove.
> Dare with me, goddess, all! Whether this madness was
> Sent out of darkest night, whether the sisters of Styx
> Dogged Capaneus' banner and forced him to assault
> Jove's majesty—was this the headlong virtue of the proud?
> Or love of glory? or final destined ruin?
> Or pride of mortals going to its doom?
> For now in the hero's eyes all earthly battles were
> Small things, and he was tired of endless slaughter.
> His weapons spent, his right arm weary, he
> Gazed fondly at the sky. His frowning gaze
> Measured the lofty ramparts; so he brought
> A heavenly ladder made of endless steps
> Fastened to tree-trunks, and terribly from afar
> He brandished flaming torches of oak faggots,
> His armour glowing red, his shield all fire.
> He cried: "Now my high-stepping valour bids me to Thebes,
> Where the great tower is slippery with Menoeceus' blood.
> Now I shall see what sacrifices avail, and whether
> Apollo plays me false." He spoke and climbed exultant,
> Jumping the steps. . . .
>
> (THEBAID, X, 827)

The prodigious portrait of heaven-vaulting pride glowing with
red flames seems to have been written in the white heat of the
imagination. No one else had ever cried: *Mecum omnes audete
deae!* To emphasise that Capaneus was taking on the whole hosts
of men and gods there follows a passage where Capaneus is seen
hurtling through the air, while javelins and Balearic slings and
stones are thrown at him from the earth, but what hope is there,
Statius says, in javelins and the vague flight of arrows? The huge

rocks which were thrown upon the Titans are now thrown up against Capaneus by powerful engines. Still he is undaunted:

> So hovering in empty air he drew himself onward,
> As though he walked on earth; striving forward,
> Forever drawing nearer to destruction.
> So does a river gnaw at a bridge's roots
> With never-resting waters, and beams are loosened,
> Stones gape and crumble: ebb and flow of tide,
> Summoning violence saps at the foundations,
> Till the swift current bursts through all the fastenings,
> And then the violent river draws its breath,
> And flows unfettered along the open reaches.

(THEBAID, X, 861)

Once again we see the Flood which nearly drowned Achilles in the *Iliad*. It is part of the quality of the imagination of Statius at his best that he can make these things palpable and visible. Capaneus continues to climb. He stands above Thebes "in towering height" and gazes down at the trembling city. The Thebans are terrified by his huge shadow. He taunts them with the cry: "What glory is there in overthrowing a fortress built by a feeble lyre?" Then in a rage of destruction he destroys the city; the bridges fall away, the stone curbs melt in the air, huge rocks are thrown at the temples. There is panic in Heaven, only Zeus remaining undisturbed. Then the voice of Capaneus is heard rumbling from below. "Are there no gods among you?" he taunts them, "who stand for panic-stricken Thebes? Semele's ashes and her tomb are in my power. Come, thou, and strive with all thy flames against me, Zeus! Why, all you ever do is to frighten maidens with your thunder." Status breaks up his lines. The authentic excitement is conveyed, and when he shouts: *Nunc age, nunc totis in me conitere flammis, Iuppiter*, these words, coming at the end of a long catalogue of crimes against Jove's majesty, possess an almost quiet force, as though Capaneus has come to the end of his patience and is about to take Heaven by violence. Jove laughs and shakes his thick locks. *Tunc etiam feriendus?* He speaks almost casually. He is still hesitating when the gods come running to him, crying out for avenging weapons. Then Statius draws a picture of

the revenge as it accumulates: the clouds approach the throne of
Zeus, though no wind blows:

> The heavenly palace thundered, but still no sign
> Was given, only the thundering clouds
> Came racing forward though no wind had risen.
> Midway the hero stood in the dizzy air,
> Summoning the gods to furious battle with him.
> The gods turned pale and marvelled at the stranger,
> And doubted whether thunderbolts would fall.
> Then from the summit of the Ogygian tower
> Strange thunderclaps were heard; the sky lay dark
> Around them; in the darkness he who held
> The ramparts saw no more, but sometimes flames
> Came from the lightning, and through the clouds they raced
> Tearing them through and through.
> Then Capaneus: "Here are fires to use against my Thebes.
> I take my torch from here. The smouldering oaks
> Shall now renew their flames." But as he spoke,
> With all his power Jove hurled the thunderbolt.
> The crest of Capaneus vanished in the clouds,
> His blackened shield-boss fell, his limbs were shining.
> And down below him all the armies fled,
> Afraid that he would fall, whole armies crushed
> By the descending flame of the hurtled hero.
> The hissing of the flames Capaneus heard;
> His hair and helmet blazed, he pushed away
> The galling cuirass with a burning hand
> Which touched the breastplate smoking there.
> So he stood, his gaze upon the heavens,
> Leaning his smoking breast on the hated battlements.
> But now the earthly frame flees from the hero,
> His spirit dies, and had he waited longer
> A second thunderbolt, hurled from the hand of Zeus,
> Had consumed him utterly.

(THEBAID, X, 913)

It is not, of course, great poetry, but the astonishing quality of
the imagination reminds us that no one else had ever attempted

such a portrait of the "engagement with Heaven". Dante delighted in it, and there are echoes of Capaneus everywhere in Dante's discussion of pride—even the red glare on the face of the hero appears in the red glare on the face of Satan in the *Inferno*. Statius has solved too late one of the problems which face the epic-writers; he has employed *montage* and cuts, like a modern cinematograph film, and the pace is so quick that we are not always sure whether we are reading about the inhabitants of Thebes or the inhabitants of Heaven. Like a scenario-writer, he has no time to explain all the details. We do not know why the sky-ladder is fastened to two trees. Surely the inhabitants of Thebes could cut the ladder at its roots? Or are the trees the supports of the interminable stairway? Nothing is explained; and there is no need to explain, for the furious pace is maintained. It is not quite the end. When we see Capaneus again, he has something of Ahab's fury. The great-souled hero, *magnanimus Capaneus*, falls, leaving on the walls of Heaven the track of the avenging flame. Victorious Jove with his right hand composed the shaken vault, and when the gods welcome him, he has about him the air of someone who has fought in mortal combat, as though he were breathless and weary. Down below, on the ruins of Thebes, Capaneus lies, "grasping the fragment of a shattered tower, with a scowl on his face, leaving deeds for all the world to tell of, which even the Thunderer might praise." Not until Gregory the Great writes his *Commentary on Job* shall we find again a phrase which so superbly defines the magnanimous soul.

Now at last it is all over except for the shouting. Capaneus lies prostrate on the earth, where the heavenly sulphur rises to remind men of his fall. He is the new Titan *in excelsis*, and appropriately he becomes a sulphur field. Thebes draws breath again, the suppliants rise in the temples and women dare to place their children on the ground. But before leaving Capaneus for ever, Statius introduces an image of unholy grandeur to describe the broken giant. "Vast as in Avernus lies outstretched the defiler of Apollo's mother, whom even the birds beheld aghast as they emerge from his cavernous breast and view his huge extended limbs, while the wretched fibres grow again to feed them, so burdens he the earth, flung prostrate."

Who was Capaneus? We know little about him. No epics in his name have survived. He appears for a brief moment in *The Seven Against Thebes* of Æschylus. He is the type of *hubris*. A scout reports that Capaneus cared nothing for Jove's thunderbolts and lightning flashes, and likened them to the rays of heat at noonday. His shield was marked with the portrait of an armourless fire-bearer holding a torch; in letters of gold on the shield there is inscribed the message: "I will fire the town". If he has something of Prometheus about him, a Prometheus who vaunts in the destructive power of his captured flame, he is also the terrible portrait of the first warrior who made war using flame as his weapon, the ancestor of all those who have scorched the earth. The scout in *The Seven Against Thebes* says: "Against such a warrior do thou send—who will meet him in the foray? Who will abide his onset, his heart not turned to terror at his boasting?" He was all that the Greeks meant when they spoke about their helpless fear of fire, and as though to emphasise his ancestry the chorus introduces a curse which sounds like a curse against those who burn the city:

> May he perish who boasts against the city!
> May the thunderbolt slay him
> Before he enters the house,
> And may the spear of flame
> Not burn my maiden home!
>
> (THE SEVEN AGAINST THEBES, 452)

Perhaps, too, his ancestry is even older. As the Greeks crouched in winter beside their hearts, seeing the blazing sparks hurtling towards the smoke-hole (κάπνη), the legend of the hero Capaneus may have had its birth in the showers of sparks. So pride is seen as the rush of flame from every man's hearth, Lucifer rising in fire to vanish in mysterious darkness in the heavens. Then at last we understand why, of all the things he could have stolen from heaven, Prometheus chose flame.

Statius was the last of the great line of Roman poets. The wheel turned full circle, and Roman epic poetry ended as it began —in a note of grief and horror, without any complacency, in terrible uncertainty, and with no hope in the future. In the end only colourless Stoic resolve was of any avail. Helplessly the great kings like Marcus Aurelius watched the world rushing past. "To a stone," he wrote, "it is all one whether it is thrown upward or downward; it is no harm for it to descend, nor is there any good in its climbing." The philosophy implicit in the phrase is one of blind despair. He sees the world from the high eminences, where the people seem small. For him there is no engagement with the gods, no physical struggle, no Jacob wrestling with the angel. Capaneus says once: "Never shalt thou escape my stroke, whether thou be the savage inmate of the trembling grove, or a delight granted to the gods—never even if thou broughtest a giant to battle upon these towers." Perhaps the savage inmate of the trembling grove—*pavidi ferus incola luci*—is the nymph Hubris herself; it is certain that Marcus Aurelius never saw her approaching through the grove, or ever trembled before her.

Perhaps, after all, it was Seneca's Jason who told the Roman truth when he shouted after Medea as she rode in the upper air on the necks of two serpents: "Go through the lofty spaces of high heaven and bear witness, where thou ridest, that there are no gods." The lofty spaces of high heaven—*alta spatia sublimi aethere*—may have possessed no gods or nymphs at all.

The Medieval Monument

FROM the anchorites in the desert Christianity derived an immense strength. These athletes of God, *athletæ Dei*, led by the desire to confront God naked and to wrestle with Him, were the real fathers of the Church; it was from them that the Church derived its second impetus. But the desert was a hard master, it made many claims on the lonely anchorites, and if it strengthened, there were also times when it weakened. In the desert there were mirages, unaccountable excitements, the strangest of sexual desires. Also, in the extreme loneliness of the desert, the will multiplied. The abbot Arsenius was asked why he fled into the desert, and answered: "I go to the desert, for God knows that I love you, but I cannot be with God and man. The infinite number of the angelic powers has a single will, but men have many." Arsenius feared the multitudinous wills of men, but he feared also the many wills of one man, the various levels at which the will operates, its gamut of desires.

St. Anthony, the first of the desert fathers, seems to have fought on all levels of consciousness. The Devil came to him in the form of a woman, and in the form of a prince who offered him all power and majesty: in a hundred shapes the Devil tempted him; but he refused to be tempted and lived quietly in the desert, alone to the alone (*solus ad solum*), slowly and with great determination killing his body, but when he appeared to the people he showed no signs of ill-health. He gives the impression of having been a quiet, princely and most gentle recluse, deprecating the fame that came to him, and considerate towards all things, even towards the Devil. Many stories concerning the Devil's temptations of pride were told of him. It was said that he saw the earth covered with snares, and it seemed scarcely possible to lay a foot down without falling into them. St. Anthony cried out: "Who, O Lord, can escape them all?" Then he heard a familiar voice of warning in the clouds saying: "Humility, O Anthony." That was all; but in that single engagement St. Anthony had perhaps fought his greatest battle against pride.

The stories told by the monks of the Egyptian desert have sometimes the fragile perfection of the quite similar stories told by the Zen Buddhists. A gentle illumination flows from them. It is recorded that when the Devil appeared to a hermit as an angel of light, he was greeted with the cry: "I know thou art the Devil: no angel of light would ever come to me." There is the same delicacy in the response of Alonius when he was asked what contempt was. He replied: "To be below the creatures that have no reason, and to know they are not condemned." But the battles fought in the desert were not always of such gentle kind. There was an *ascesis* in the minds of the monks which demanded resolute and desperate solutions. The war against lust was relentless; there were always the dangers of the high, thin, rare, continual worship of the self-absorbed.

Rome fell fifty years after the death of St. Anthony. There followed the age of Ambrose, Augustine and Jerome, the great fathers who set about consolidating the foundations of the Church. The days of the desert were over, but the will survived.

Augustine has related that it was the example of St. Anthony which led to his conversion. St. Anthony had destroyed the will. Augustine, who had once belonged to the strange sect of the Manichees, which worshipped a founder who had been crucified and possessed the sacrament of the bread and the fruit, found himself continually at the mercy of the will, and the most tortured pages of the *Confessions* describe how he wrestles with the two wills, the good and the evil, and how these wills multiplied in the struggle. He who had wanted in his youth, as he said, nothing better than "a shining kind of body," threw himself heroically into the contest of wills, and did not emerge unscathed.

It is a strange portrait—the proud young Berber attempting

to divest himself of his pride. He portrays himself accurately;
we are conscious of the African fevers in his blood. He is always
impulsive, he loves to ride on the wave-crest, he delights in his
own brilliance even when he is discussing humility. He says he
was deafened "by the clanking of the chains of pride in his youth,"
but their grave music was to be heard years later.

He sees pride everywhere. Pride is a continual, fiery contest.
He struggles nakedly with pride like Jacob struggling with the
angel. He takes walks with pride in broad daylight, arguing with
it, and then when the argument seems to have concluded, pride
itself shows its secret weapons, and the argument continues more
abundantly than before. At night he will lay traps for pride, and
bait them; then when pride comes, he pounces on it even before
the trap has sprung, buries his knife in it, dissects it, holds it up
to the faint light, waits patiently for the morning, and lo! it is
still there, still living, still answering him with its unfathomable
unscrupulous arguments. "Where, and in what country can pride
be resisted?"

We are conscious sometimes of the desperate resistance of words,
as if he were hacking them out of solid rock, or chipping them
out of his own breast-bone. Eagerness and a feverish desire to know
the truth, obstinacy, all these spring from his dramatic southern
mind, but with them goes a remorseless impulse to pursue the
quarry even to the extremes of weariness, when it can no longer
defend itself, when at last, run to earth, it waits for the final, the
most damaging blow. For Augustine the pursuit was more difficult
than for others. He was not naturally ascetic, his mind was highly
coloured and the furniture of his soul glowed like the jewelled
windows of his native Hippo. He will say: "Even the Devil will
only conjure up seven sins," and think to outwit Satan's majesty
by an appeal to mathematics, but the next moment the Devil displays
the values of his wares, and no mathematics can compute them;
and even in *De Civitate Dei* he remains faintly envious of "this
superb and envious angel, this prince of devils who turns away
from his creator towards himself and makes himself into a tyrant."
Something of that proud obstinacy which he imputes to the Devil
can be heard again when, like Father Allois, he interrogates himself
in the famous question of the Soliloquy: "*Deum et animam scire*

cupio." "*Nihilne plus?*" "*Nihil omnino.*" The self could be a tyrant, and it is never certain whether he entirely disapproved of glory, even though he inveighs against it, and once he quoted with approval the lines of Virgil:

Pars mihi pacis erit dextram tetigisse tyranni.

Some peace, I hope, by touching the tyrant's hand. But by this time he had confused the tyrant with God himself, deliberately and without malice, because the Virgilian context demanded a wider audience.

What is strange in Augustine is his continual desire to be fair to the enemy. "Man born of carnal desires," he wrote in his epistles, "needs to live and cannot live without setting himself as an object of his desires." But in his commentary on *Corinthians* he attempts to frighten men into humility by the statement of God's powers: "God has constituted all things by the word of his majesty, and by that same word he can destroy them all." Yet in his commentary on *John* he develops the theory of God's humility: "Why dost thou make thyself proud, O man? A god has made himself humble for thee. You blush perhaps to imitate a humble man; then imitate a humble God." There are moments such as these when we are never quite sure whether he is speaking out of the simplicity of his heart, or with a ferocious casuistry. Occasionally, with one of those blue lightning streaks which illuminate his whole work, he will say quietly, in words that might have been spoken by one of the apostles: "God humbled himself in order to be exalted." Then at last we are not conscious of an *arrière-pensée* or any struggle between the wills, only of the acceptance of a tradition and of his own incomparable statement of it.

But there are many levels on which pride must be fought. "The desperate and impious obstination in sin, with a proud refusal to humble oneself before God" admits many interpretations. He wrote once: "Other sins find their vent in the accomplishment of evil deeds, but pride lies in wait for the good deeds to destroy them." It was on such psychological levels that progress in interpretation could be made, but there was also the historical level: all the first part of *De Civitate Dei* is an effort to prove that Rome fell by the sin of the angels. Had not Romulus, the founding father, been torn to pieces by his own senate for his pride? It was a rumour, believed only by a few Roman historians, but Augustine seized upon it eagerly. He had read in the lost *Hortensius* that on the death of Romulus there was an eclipse of the sun—it was one more proof. The rape of the Sabine women was another. "The Romans slaughtered their own step-fathers in the field, whose daughters they had already enjoyed in their beds." The impious course of Rome followed the development of a Greek drama, the sin of sexuality going hand in hand with the sin of pride: the endless massacres and evils, the sense of guilt from the beginning were only God's curse on the Roman world. But if God was endowed with foresight, then the fall of man and the fall of the Roman Empire were both preordained; and at this point confusion enters, for if God has the only will, then man is incapable of free-will, and Augustine must strive against the current to prove that free-will remains, for how otherwise can man offer himself freely to God? But in fact man does not offer himself to God. He must will firmly, with the uttermost of his will—"for going thither and coming there is nothing else than the will to go thither, and to will with full power (*velle fortiter et integre*), not to waver and be tossed to and fro with a divided will, which now rises up and now sinks down in the struggle." No one had ever spoken of the will in these terms before; no one had ever shown such artistry in depicting the perverseness of the will:

> The spirit orders the body, and it obeys instantly; the spirit orders itself, and it refuses. The spirit orders the hand to move, and it does it so quickly that one can scarcely distinguish between the act and the command; the spirit commands the spirit to will, and although the same it will not do it. Whence this monstrosity? It is a disease of the spirit that prevents it from rising up; the will is split and divided; thus there are two wills in conflict with each other, one good and one evil, and I myself it was who willed and who did not will.

The same deliberate confusions return to haunt the fathers of a later age; the problem of the will is never resolved—the one against the many, the many against the one. Peter Lombard will throw himself headlong against the knives of the will; Duns Scotus will dissect the anatomy of the mind with his trembling and incisive hand, only to discover that the will seems to be everywhere. In the end Augustine follows Paul and resolves the problem to his own satisfaction by invoking a paradox: *Deo servire vera libertas est.* To serve God is true liberty. Then at last all the conflicting impulses of all wills are ambiguously united.

But pride remains, even in the service of God, and more and more desperately he attempts to ring pride and starve it out by blockade. In his work *Concerning the Morals of the Manichees,* he explains that evil is not an essence, but a deprivation and a disorder. "Everything that has an internal principle of disorder tends to dissolution, but the goodness of God forbids things to arrive at this place; and even in those of His creatures who miss their end, He gives such order that they are placed in their most congruous place, so that by regular effort they will again ascend to the rank whence they have fallen." The words have a hard, unnatural ring; the beautiful ladders cannot carry such things as heavy as sins; and as far as pride is concerned, he denies the whole thesis in his commentary on Psalm LVII: *Primum peccatum superbia est, ultima poena ist ignis æternum.* The ultimate punishment is eternal flame.

There is something almost pathological in his hatred of pride, his consciousness of his own strong will. The pride of the Manichees overwhelms him, and he is still speaking of the Manichees when, in one of his most tragic passages, he begs for the supreme punishment of him "who aspired to advance his throne in the north, that, all darkened and frozen, they might serve him, as he imitates thee in his wry and crooked ways." There is a harshness in the original which comes from the heart, a cold horror wholly lost in the translation. The Devil is a host of echoing sibilants—*qui statuit sedem suam ponere in aquilone, ut te perversa et distorta via imitanti tenebrori frigidique servirent.* In the end perhaps even the blessed paradox is insufficient to wrest men's minds away from the *perversa et distorta via:* free servitude works less miracles than the consciousness of God's mercy. So he writes in his long essay *On Grace and Free Will:* "Lest human pride should tempt us, all the merits which may be secured by monastic discipline were but the gift of God." Then, and only then, does it seem that for St. Augustine the battle is won.

The desperate romanticism of Augustine is wholly lacking in his contemporary, Jerome, whom Luther hated with such a passionate hatred that he said: "He deserves hell more than heaven, and writes only of fasting, virginity and such things." No estimate could have been more inaccurate. It is true that Jerome wrote delicately and far too often for his own peace of mind concerning the most intimate habits of virgins, but he could be violent like Augustine, only with a cold classical violence. When Augustine hates, he hates like a thunder-storm; Jerome simply makes a catalogue of evils to be avoided or describes his enemies with delicate precision, as when he describes a certain type of Egyptian priest: "Everything with them is done for effect: loose sleeves, big boots, clumsy dress, constant sighing, visiting virgins, disparaging the clergy, and when a feast day comes they eat so much that they make themselves sick." He is so eminently sane that he is prepared to examine the question of pride in cold blood, and he insists that pride is permissible if it is pride in God. He wrote to a young married woman a gentle letter of warning, reminding her of her duties to God, then he urged her not to associate with those who are distinguished with earthly riches:

> I would not have you consort overmuch with married women or frequent the houses of the great. I would not have you look too often on what you spurned when you were a virgin, and desired to remain one. You must know that women of the world plume themselves if their husbands are judges or hold high positions. If an eager crowd of visitors flocks to greet an Emperor's wife, why should you insult your husband? In this regard you must learn a holy pride; know that you are better than they. (EP. XXII, 16)

It all looks innocent enough; but the trap is sprung in the last sentence: *Disce superbiam sanctam, scito te illis esse meliorem.* The mind rebels at all the possibilities the casual phrase implies. More than a thousand years later St. Alphonso Liguori was to repeat the phrase to his novices. It was the first time that *hubris* had been officially encouraged, but Jerome makes it clear that he meant only a pride acceptable to God. Commenting on the text in Isaiah: "Ye shall eat the riches of the Gentiles, and in their glory shall ye boast yourselves," Jerome says: "We are proud in the glory of the martyrs, not with that vicious pride which God resists by giving grace to the humble, but that which becomes his power and his glory." A gloss on Jerome's commentary adds more simply that there is a good and an evil pride, one which God resists and another which denotes the glory he bestows. Jerome was the first to make the distinction.

He seems to have been conscious of the dangers of the phrase, and returns to the attack in the *Commentariorum in Sophoniam:*

> He who glories in dignities shall perish; he who is puffed up with pride (*inflatur*) will perish; he who glories in the strength of the body perishes. But he who shall arise and be proud with a sacred pride (*superbire sancta superbia*), he shall be with the apostles, and he who shall be worthy to suffer disgrace for Jesus Christ's sake shall be glorified with the apostles, who exult in tribulations, knowing that tribulations give birth to patience, patience gives birth to hope, and hope confounds the enemies of God.   (PATROLOGIA LATINA, XXV, 1350)

The distinction is clear, but one begins to suspect that the saint who invented the *fama de sanctitate* knew more concerning pride than he cared to admit. He continues to inveigh against false pride, that deceptive sweetness and tickling devil (*fallax suavitas, blandus dæmon*), but he insists too much, and for the first time we are made aware of the infinite delicacies of pride. "Pride masquerades," says Jerome, "in so many ways that they are past counting." Almost, he seems to suggest, the task of eradicating them is too much. It is everywhere: it hides under the grossest humility, it blandishes in extreme servility, or in any kind of servility. Give a woman clothes and jewels: she is proud. Take the clothes and jewels away: she is proud in her nakedness. Then let her body become rough and miserable, let her cringe before her confessor, and she will be proud in her humility. Only children seem to be exempt from the catalogues of pride. There are moments when the cultivated scholar's voice is almost heard thundering. He has gazed for interminable hours into the human heart and discovered all its weaknesses:

Beware lest your contempt for the world's boastfulness breed in you a boastfulness of another kind. Harbour not the secret thought that as you have ceased to please in cloth of gold, you may now try to please in homespun. When you come into a gathering of brethren and sisters, do not sit in too lonely a place, nor pretend that you are unworthy of a footstool. Do not deliberately lower your voice, as though you were worn out by fasting, nor lean upon a friend's shoulder imitating the gait of one who is completely exhausted. Some women actually disfigure themselves, so as to make it obvious that they have been fasting. As soon as they catch sight of anyone, they drop their eyes and begin sobbing, hiding the face, all but the glimpse of one eye, and this they keep open to see the effect they have made. They wear black dresses and girdles of sack-cloth; their feet and hands are unwashed; their stomachs alone —because the stomachs cannot be seen—are busy churning food. Of such people the Psalm is sung every day: "The Lord will scatter the bones of them that please themselves". Other women change their garb and wear men's clothes; they cut their hair short and lift up their chins in shameless fashion; they blush to be what they were born to be—women, and they prefer to look like eunuchs.

(EP. XXII, 27)

It is one of the classic texts of pride, as relevant to its time as Aristotle's great portrait of *megalopsychos*, but he has failed to give the corresponding portrait of male pride. Suddenly, for no reason whatsoever, Jerome's horrible infatuation for viscera enters the scene. "Your bellies! think of what is happening in your bellies!" he shouts. "Don't be proud! The most terrible things are happening in them!" The scholar's deliberate calm, his irony, his gentle impatience, all vanish at the thought of the viscera which reduce all people to the same humble level; or would, if only we were conscious of their grinding tribulations and utter ugliness. Immediately afterwards he is once more contemplating these girls with their strangely modern air who resemble eunuchs, put up their chins and wear short hair.

The tradition of the desert had survived: men who had been for long years in solitary contemplation in the desert were susceptible to wantonness. The story of Heron, the monk of Nitria, was well-known. He carried the mortification of his senses to such an extent that he could run for thirty miles in the desert under the scorching sun, without food or drink, endlessly repeating passages from the Bible, and he could live for three months on nothing but the bread of the Eucharist and wild herbs. He became so proud that he acknowledged no earthly superior, received advice from no one and considered it beneath his dignity to take part in the communion. Then the restless fevers which come to all monks in time sent him helplessly to Alexandria in search of women. He frequented the theatre and the circus, and abandoned himself to every kind of excess, until a severe illness brought him to his senses; then he returned to the desert, where, says the historian, he died in peace.

Jerome was conscious of the dangers of contemplation, just as he was conscious of the ever-present danger of women. The Devil's mania for laying snares, the unwearying battle to be fought against temptations, sometimes gives a hoarse edge to his voice. Almost, it seemed to him, it was better to castrate oneself and tear out one's eyes; and he quotes with approval the text of Jeremiah: *By our windows death came in.* Sometimes, too, in his anguish he will talk of a woman's navel when he means something else entirely, and the cultivated disgust is more unpleasant than anything in Augustine, who speaks at length of his mistresses and how he delighted in them. And like Augustine he was captivated by the poetry of violence. Augustine has related that when he was going through the crisis of conversion, he was fascinated with the famous phrase in St. Matthew relating how "the kingdom of Heaven suffereth violence and the violent take it by storm". He was so overcome with his own emotions that he flung himself down in astonishment, his voice changed, his face, eyes and colour expressing his meaning more clearly than his words. It was a moment of almost ecstatic desire to lay siege to heaven immediately, that very moment. When Jerome remembers the same phrase in a letter to the virgin Eustochium, there is almost the same romanticism: "Unless you use violence, you will never seize the kingdom of Heaven. Unless you knock importunately, you will never receive the sacramental bread. Does it not seem to you to be truly violence when the flesh desires to be as God and to ascend to the place whence angels fell that it may judge angels?" * In our modern age we may feel that the scales are too heavily weighted against the devils and that there is no particular pleasure to be derived from judging the fallen angels in their toils; yet at that time and place there were few joys more exceedingly sweet than the joy of paradisiacal revenge. Christianity had not yet won its laurels. The enemies were all around, and the motive of revenge, even if vicarious, is always useful in welding the flock together. But in his commentary on violence Jerome had also defined the extent of *sancta superbia:* it was the violent desire of the flesh to be as God and partake in the judgment of the damned.

At intervals in the history of pride the *sancta superbia* returns. Alyosha Karamazov is perhaps the greatest expression of it, but Hippolyte, in *The Idiot*, runs him close, for he openly despises pride and most of all does he despise sacred pride. It returns at odd and unexpected moments in Bossuet, and it shines through the aphorisms of St. John of the Cross, though he has no desire to partake in the judgment of the fallen angels, and has hardly any real conception of their existence. For a brief moment the ever-changing face of pride has become a holiness, but it is rarely referred to officially afterwards, the holiness is almost forgotten, and when we see pride again he has something of the measured stride of the *megalopsychos.*

Cassian of Marseilles was born ten years after the birth of Jerome, whom he knew and reverenced. He had known the desert, he had stayed with Jerome at Bethlehem, he had wandered into the famous communion at Scete, and he spent the greater part of his life in the monastery in the south of France. He was never sanctified, yet Gregory the Great regarded him as a saint and Urban V engraved on the silver casket that contained his head the words "Saint Cassian". His famous *Institutes* were the moral text-books of his time, but concerning the vice of pride he had nothing to say that had not been said already, until he came to talk of the proud men; then, with that peculiar transparent glance, he writes like an angel. "Pride," he thunders in his catalogue of vices, "is the most savage

* Nisi vim feceris, cœlorum regna non capies. Nisi pulsaveris importune, panem non accipies sacramenti. An non tibi videtur esse violenti, cum caro cupit esse, quod Deus est, et illuc, unde angeli corruerunt, angelos indicatura conscendere.

of all evil beasts, and the most dreadful, because it lies in wait for those who are perfect." "Pride, with its dreadful bite devours those who have almost obtained the consummation of virtue." We have heard it all before. Then, quite casually, he introduces us to the portrait of the monk he must have known:

> A man who has such dislike of spiritual talk in his heart that, if such a conversation should happen to arise, he cannot keep his eyes fixed on one spot, but his gaze wanders emptily here and there, and his eyes shift hither and thither. Instead of wholesome coughs he spits from a dry throat: he coughs on purpose without any need: he drums with his fingers and twiddles them, and scribbles like a man writing: all his limbs are continually fidgeting, so that, while the spiritual conversation proceeds, you would think he was sitting on the very sharpest of thorns.   (DE INSTITUTI COENOBIORUM, XII, XXVII)

The portrait of "the man who knows all the answers", lost in his dreams of befuddled superiority, is the counterpart to Jerome's anathematised virgins with short hair and uplifted chins. For the first time we come face to face with the ancestor of Faust. He is altogether smaller than Heron, less ambiguously certain of himself, no longer contained within the desert nightmare; but after the centuries he will rise and throw his ink-pots at God, as Luther threw his ink-pot at the devil. We see him now awakening from the trance of *acedia*, that mournful disease to which all scholars are subject. But the dreams end, and sometimes like Faust and like Hitler there arise from the depths the monstrous children of emergency, desperate to put an end to their own fidgeting sense of superiority, and it may happen that they come to possess the force to sway millions. Cassian of Marseilles is the midwife of this succubus.

Jerome wrote from Bethlehem; Augustine from northern Africa; Cassian from the south of France—as pride drives westward it gains a greater subtlety. Prudentius was superbly equipped to describe the battle between the virtues and the vices. A Spaniard steeped in Latin poetry, a Christian and a magistrate under Theodosius, he writes as Virgil might have written if Virgil had been a Christian; yet there is something vaguely disappointing in his *Psychomachia*, his Battle of the Soul. It is in the hymns of the *Cathemerinon* that he rises to full stature, eloquent with grief and praise. In the *Psychomachia*, the virtues are set in combat with the vices one after another, but the conclusion is foregone: no poetic *catharsis* occurs: the landscape of inevitable victory is only too well known. But here for the first time we meet Pride wearing the battle-dress of the Amazons, helmeted and gleaming, riding on horseback against the miserable virtues and almost trampling them down. Almost against his will, Prudentius must give her a glory:

> *Forte per effusas inflata Superbia turmas*
> *Effreni volitabat equo, quem pelle leonis*
> *Texerat, et validos villis ornaverat armos*
> *Quo se fulta jubis jactantius illa ferinis*
> *Inferret, tumido despectans agmina fastu,*
> *Turritum tortis caput accumularat in altum*
> *Crinibus. . . .*

(PSYCHOMACHIA, 178)

In this astonishing picture of Queen Pride rushing to the attack in a fluttering mantle, on an unbridled horse covered with a lion's skin, her hair carefully arranged in the shape of a tower, we breathe an entirely new atmosphere. This is not Jerome's *sancta superbia*, nor Cassian's monk with the gleam of madness in his eyes. She is the forerunner of all renaissance pride as she cavorts against the infidel virtues, and we hardly believe Prudentius when he goes on to explain how Fraud dug a ditch for her and Hope offered Humility the sword with which Superbia's head was cut off. We know this has to be, but it is not important; and Superbia while she lives is superb beyond all conscience. Nothing quite like this had ever happened before. In *The Shepherd of Hermas* the vices were dark-robed women with uncovered shoulders and hair streaming. Now at last pride is a gleaming thing, even though evil.

Throughout the Middle Ages in church carvings, on playing cards and in paintings pride was to remain the delectable warrior, riding her charger, glorious in her insolence. But why on horseback? The sons of God came down and knew the daughters of men and begot the Titans who had "members of horses", says Enoch. There may have been other reasons. Prudentius was a Spaniard and he must have known of the Arab custom of taking into the midst of the fighting men the most beautiful virgin of the tribe, in a howdah decorated with scarlet and blue tassels and waving plumes of ostrich feathers. From this high place she would taunt the warriors and accuse them of being laggards. Certainly there is an oriental flavour about her, the flavour not only of the Amazons but of Tomyris, *reyne des Massagetes en Scythie*, who defeated the great Cyrus, and hurled his head into a vessel full of blood, saying scornfully, "Now thou shalt be satiated with blood, who for thirty years hast persevered insatiably." Orosius and Dante both respected her, and half delighted in her revenge. We may never know why Superbia has at last become a Queen, but it is certain that the purely intellectual concept of pride, the pride that ravaged the souls of the anchorites in the desert, fades as she appears. *Accessit homo ad cor altum, id est, cor secretum*, Augustine had written, but now the secret and proud heart was to be displayed openly in the shape of a woman, brandishing her spears, like Joan of Arc, who was herself condemned to death, not for her *contumelia* towards the King, but for her pride against God.

Perhaps it was the weather of the soul, which changes unaccountably through the centuries. An image grows, acquires accretions from foreign sources, twists and turns within the changing contours of the times, and by acquiring so many accretions and so many changes becomes another image entirely. The great images by which people live are of this kind: God, love, the soul, space, time, the sense of death, the awareness of life. They do not grow as plants grow. Every man's thought subtly changes them, and all experience, and every voyage made by every man, and every shock of grief or love makes its minute accretion to the theme. Superbia becomes a warrior goddess for the same reason that God in thirteenth-century France became the Virgin Mary—men desired it so, and made this image of their desire. Synesius, the Christian Bishop of Ptolemais and pupil of Hypatia, said once that the spiritual essence (*anima spiritualis*) was "both God and idol and demon of every shape—herein also does the soul receive its punishment." These are the dangerous images by which we live, and all the history we can ever know is the history of these images.

Unhappily for the historian these images are continually changing. It is not only that we never know whether they are God, idols or demons, but the confusion implacably increases when the images themselves possess a kind of magical instinct for change. When Avitus, in his *De Spiritalis Historiae Gestis*, says that the Devil can assume the form of a bird or of a voluptuous woman, he is saying only that the Devil is the fallen angel (who resembles a bird) or a beautiful woman (who offers the greatest temptation of all). But the Devil could assume still other disguises: the history of pride is largely a history of the Devil's assumed disguises. And because these disguises are inevitably reflected in the characters of men, we can never say like Rousseau's *Emile* that the natural man is wholly himself, an integral unity, an absolute whole: he is coloured by the conflicting images and dreams of all who have preceded him, and all who live with him, and perhaps even of all those who come after him.

There are therefore two levels on which the history of pride can be written: there is the scriptural level devoid of all images, the level at which the great fathers thundered their accusing anathemas, or the psychological level where we are confronted with images and portraits and the delicate perceptions of those who attempt to uncover causes and ends. When St. John Climacus thunders against pride because it is "the renouncement of God, the invention of the Devil and the contempt of man, the sure sign of the soul's sterility, the promoter of spiritual epilepsy, a rigorous creditor and an inexorable judge," and says that pride falls only "before the gift of tears," he is pronouncing a scriptural thesis, which is of incalculable importance because it offers us a measure of man's freedom and abuse of freedom during this time. But when Prudentius describes the cavorting horse, or an illuminator paints the portrait of pride, or St. Augustine wrestles with the pride of his own flesh, we are closer to an understanding of them. One is the scriptural text, the other provides the brilliant illuminations. But neither can be completely evaluated: there is no measurement by which we can measure the soul's power at any time.

As time goes on, we are conscious that we are moving towards a completer definition of pride. The shining facets have been held to the light; all have been found disappointing. Now it is necessary that we should step back and see the whole object as it is. One cannot touch it; one can only describe it, as though it was a man walking; and the difficulty for the medieval scholars lay in the fact that the proud man had no place in Christian theology. Jove could be dethroned, but Christ could not; and against the love of God pride becomes a meaningless and impotent weapon. There had arisen with the Christian Church a new conception of love which was entirely foreign to Jews and the Greeks. Love rules, said the Christians, but Lucifer indisputably remained; there were powers that challenged God's love; and all Augustine's desperate efforts to solve the problem of unique love challenged by the will of man led to despair. Gradually the portrait of the challenger of God begins to take shape. He is not Cassian's lunatic priest, nor is he Heron, and least of all is he Queen Superbia, though all these have their place in him, suggest some facet of him, belong to his birth. When we meet the tragic hero of Christian pride for the first time it is in the pages of Gregory the Great, in one single startling sentence whose reverberations can be heard down the centuries, a sentence which comes surprisingly at the end of a disquisition which does not substantially differ from many that have gone before. In the great *Commentary on Job* Gregory rages against pride with the scholar's fervour, but even as he writes we are conscious that he is trembling on the edge of some kind of revelation:

Pride, which we have called the root of vices, far from being satisfied with the extinction of one virtue, raises it up against all the members of the soul, and like some universal and deadly disease corrupts the whole body. When pride assaults the mind a kind of tyrant closely invests, as it were a besieged city: and the wealthier are those whom he seizes, the more harshly he rises up in his authority, because the more largely the business of virtue is transacted without humility, the more widely does pride exercise its sway. He who with enslaved mind admits this tyranny within himself suffers the first greatest loss, for the eye of his heart being closed, he loses calm of judgment. Then it comes about that all the good things of others become displeasing to him, and the things he has done himself, even when they are mistaken, alone please him. Now he always looks down on the doings of others and admires only his own actions; because whatever he has done, he believes he

has done with singular skill; and for that which he performs
for desire of glory, he favours himself in his thought; and when
he thinks he surpasses others in all things, he walks with himself along the broad spaces of his thought and silently utters
his own praises.   (MORALIA, XXIV, 48)

In these lines of Gregory the Great the proud man has come at
last to his maturity. He will change inevitably; there will be more
impassioned discourses on the nature of *megalopsychos; a* host of
commentators will follow, and not the least of them will be Baudelaire and Dostoievsky; but already we observe the lineaments of
the mature image in "the man who walks with himself along the
broad spaces of his thought and silently utters his own praises."
Gregory was never to accomplish the portrait of *megalopsychos*
again with such accuracy. He wrote in another part of the *Commentary on Job:* "Leviathan in order to fall smote himself with
pride alone, for he could not wither up those many branches of
sins, had he not first through this become rotten at the root." The
rage is only too evident, but there is not enough light, we do not
know what is happening among those entangled roots, and we are
left neither with a complete image nor an effective rebuke. Leviathan
is Ahab's whale, but he fails to make us shudder, fails to suggest
power. Gregory is more explicit when he says that "the proud
man is not content to destroy one virtue: pride rises against all
the members of the soul, like a disease which corrupts the whole
physical body." But the portrait of the proud man wandering along
the broad spaces of his thought, like Hamlet wandering the ramparts
of Elsinore, is fixed forever.

From now on the portrait is to suffer only the faintest modi-
fication. Behind Ivan Karamazov, behind Pascal's mathematician,
Dante's *terribiltà*, there is this brooding hero, wandering alone in
a climate which is not our climate, uncertain of his ends and certain only of his praises. He has a majesty which is denied to Satan,
and never possessed by the fallen angels, or even by Prometheus.
He lives in a world of distinctions, of perfect self-limitations, and
there is beauty in the conventions he employs, and rigour in the
intrigue, but it is an intrigue without any purpose, for if the proud
man comes close to God, he loses his stake, and if he moves further

away, he is no longer proud. Herder will echo Gregory's phrase when he speaks of God living "in the great inane of primeval eternity in a little corner (*Räumchen*) where he contemplates himself," but the theory of God's delight in his own self-contemplation springs from sources which have helped to bring about the portrait of pride. In one sense Gregory failed. He showed neither the causes of pride, nor how so majestic and terrifying a figure could be saved. The palpable thing he had seen for a moment in his mind and projected on to the page is caught on the wing, sketched hurriedly, as with a flash of lightning, and then he was gone.

Isidore of Seville, a contemporary of Gregory, the author of the immense *Etymologicum Magnum*, says somewhere that the word Satan means "falling downward", and the name was given to him because he despised the peace of Heaven, and thereupon he fell out of Heaven, "dragged down by the weight of his pride." He seems to have been shooting in the dark, and Origen, at the beginning of the Christian Church, was wiser when he said that it means "adversary":

> Now he who in the Hebrew language is called by some Satan and by others Satanus—as being more in conformity with the genius of the Greek language—signifies, when translated into Greek "adversary". . . . With more propriety, however, is he called "adversary", who was the first among those who were leading a peaceful and happy life to lose their wings, and to fall from blessedness; he who, according to Ezekiel, walked faultlessly in all his ways "until iniquity was found in him" and who, being "the seal of resemblance" and "the crown of beauty" in the paradise of God, being filled as it were with good things, fell into destruction, in accordance with the word which was said to him in a mystic sense: "Thou hast fallen into destruction and shall not abide forever."
>
> (CONTRA CELSUM, VI, XLIV)

The wheel has turned full circle. It is significant that the great Alexandrian doctor, Origen, was responsible for the transformation by which the Devil, who had begun by being jealous of man, became proud and in rebellion against God. He believes completely, following the prophecy of Ezekiel, that the Devil has fallen into destruction and shall not abide forever. But by the time of Gregory the Great, four centuries later, we have at least a hint that pride has become indestructible.

The elaborations of the portrait first drawn by Gregory the Great are endless. One scholar sees the hands clearly, another fills in the outlines with memories of the description given by Cassian, and adds further details, still a third pays particular attention to the thrust of the head and the feet. The portrait proceeds by accretions into our own day, when Paul Valéry in his descriptions of Monsieur Teste and Narcisse did hardly more than provide an extended footnote to half a sentence of Gregory. Theodulphus, Bishop of Orleans, offers a portrait which begins as though he was idly copying something out of any one of a hundred manuals, and then suddenly he throws his pen aside, the gaze quickens, for a moment he catches the monster on the wing——

> O hideous is Pride! He has a haggard eye and a crazy laugh, his head is ringed round with vipers and his voice is large. His food and drink form only a mingling of dark poisons; his body is all swollen, his hands calloused and wrinkled, he walks lightly and by fits and starts. Pride advances in jerky motion, flies like a bird, with the daring which allowed it to descend from the celestial heights, and the memory of the crime committed in the heavens forever present in his thoughts, tell him to employ all the cunning tricks which led him to the abysses of Hell.
>
> (CARMINA, V, 158-191)

This is not the monster who walks alone in the solemnity of his pride, but he is built to the same measure; we should have known the calloused hands and the light, jerky gait. The vipers perhaps are only the signs of his earthly origin, for we remember that the Giants had the legs of vipers—is there, in Theodulphus' description, some dim recollection of a serpent's glide when he speaks of the curious walk? Prudentius says the vices, like the Titans, were born of the earth; he calls them *terrigenae phalangae*, earth-born phalanxes, though elsewhere he leaves the matter in some doubt and once he refers to the Devil's habit of asking his companions to believe he had himself created himself, and had even created matter out of his own body. There was something bird-like in him, Theodulphus says. St. Bernard, the famous abbot of Clair-vaux, answers that this is perfectly true, but "he flew on one wing only—the wing of the intellect," which explains perhaps why the flight is jerky.

When St. Bernard comes to describe the proud man he adds almost nothing to Gregory's portrait. He returns to Cassian, only emphasising the peculiar jerkiness of movement which by this time had come to be regarded as an ingrained characteristic of pride:

> Look at that monk you have supposed to be a sensible man. He has now taken to staring about him, whether he is standing up, walking about or sitting down. He thrusts his head for-ward and pricks up his ears. From his outward movements you can clearly see the inward change he has undergone. For it is the forward man who winketh with the eye, presseth with his foot, and speaketh with his finger, and from the unusual movements of his body is seen to have lately contracted a disease of the soul—the careless sluggishness of which in care-ful examination makes it inquisitive about others.
>
> (PATROLOGIA LATINA, CLXXXII, 947)

St. Bernard is not perhaps an unimpeachable witness: he said once of women that "their face is a burning wind and their voice the hissing of serpents." There is the faintest suggestion that the monk is simply bored, and will soon escape from the monastery, to join the wandering scholars whom the churchmen held in such horror that they called them *luciferi*, for they possessed the bookish knowledge of the monks, sang bawdy songs and gave themselves to the delights of the burning winds and the hissing serpents.

When Alanus de Insulis (or de Ryssel) came to write his inter-minable *Complaint of Nature*, which pleased Chaucer so much that he translated some passages of it, the schoolmen had been elaborating upon the proud man for nearly eleven hundred years. A thousand texts were at his service. Alanus adds all the existing portraits together, and almost he gives the impression of laying them one upon the other: to give them body and weight. There is no concision, and never once does he write a memorable line, but he surveys the whole portrait, remembers Jerome's virgins with their upthrust chins, Cassian's fit of the ague, the odd jerky movement described by Theodulphus and even throws his mind back to the days when Aristotle was describing the sources of Greek drama. He should be quoted in full, because he so singularly summarises the medieval tradition:

> Tainted by the fatal contagion of this infirmity, a multitude of men, while they violently exalt themselves above themselves, descend in ruin beneath, detract from themselves in their very arrogance, sink while they bear themselves aloft, destroy themselves in their self-elevation. They speak either with a solemn pomposity or they keep silent, or they show some singularity of behavior, or gesture, or excessive adornment. For some, whom lowliness of servile condition abases, boast of majestic liberty. Others, while they are of common stock and plebeian race, in word at least pretend themselves distinguished by some excellence of blood. Others, while they cry in the cradles of dramatic art and are suckled at its breasts, profess the height of Aristotelian subtlety. Others, though numb with the ague fits of a frightened hare, by the single remedy of verbosity present the courageous front of a lion. There are others who plainly reveal, by a silence merely external, what the pride of inner indignation keeps close-shut. For they disdain to grant a share of mutual conversation to others, whether these lie in the lower walks of life, or resemble themselves in the equality of worth, or sway in more exalted eminence or dignity. If one requests word from them, the reply is separated from the question by such a great interval of silence that it seems unrelated to it by any tie. Others, who take pleasure in individualising their actions, try everywhere to be lonely in a crowd, peculiar among the general, opposed to the universal, diverse in the midst of unity. For while others engage in conversation, they give themselves up to the pleasure of silence; while others relax in pleasures, they seem to be involved with serious matters; while others are taken up with religious celebrations, they enjoy their ease in wanton pleasures; while others are bright of face with joyous humour, their countenances present a very tempest of malevolent severity. Others, with external peculiarity of deportment, betoken an inner demeanour

of pride. These, as if they despised everything earthy, with heads thrown back look up to the things of Heaven, indignantly turn aside their eyes, lift their eyebrows markedly, turn up their chins superciliously, and hold their arms as stiff as a bow; their feet graze the ground on tiptoe only. Others make their bodies too effeminate by means of woman's attire. They quiet, with the aid of a comb, the assembly of their hairs in such peace that no breeze can lift them; by the help of scissors they clip the fringes of their dense eyebrows, or pluck them up or root them out from the over-full wood; they bring to bear on the stripling beard the frequent treachery of the razor, that it may not dare to sprout ever so little; their arms cry out against the lightness of gloves, and their feet are imprisoned in narrow shoes. Alas, whence this arrogance, this pride in men? Their birth is fraught with sorrow, trouble and pain consume their life, and the still more painful necessity of death ends even that pain. With them, being is a moment, life is a shipwreck, the world a banishment.   (DE PLANCTU NATURAE, VII, 5-66)

St. Bernard states that there are three states of mystical experience: vision, dreams and *pura mens;* this belongs to none of them. Alanus de Insulis did not capture the proud man as Gregory captured him, or as Blake caught the superhuman image of the Flea. The arrows of vainglory, which St. Bernard appears to have invented, are also absent; there is nothing barbed, nothing that a proud man might be afraid of, no mirror of perfect lucidity in which we can gaze at the Devil confronting himself, no abyss. The mysterious mountains of the mind are wholly absent. Anselm said in one of his sermons that the Devil sinned in his pride when there was yet no punishment for his sin, and in a surprising passage of his meditations Bernard says simply: *Superbia in coelo nata*. At such moments we wake up. Alanus de Insulis sends us to sleep. Yet he is worth examining. He has drawn a curious portrait where vainglory, pride and arrogance are all hopelessly confused, he has no real understanding of the forces that make pride, he is the poet continually looking over the shoulders of others, and yet the final impression is a memorable one, a picture such as men believed in at the time.

More violent battles, more deliberate attempts to outline the shape of pride were to be made in the eleventh and twelfth centuries, but by then the Devil had become almost the mathematical symbol of the individual will. There were some, however, who believed that the sin by which the angels fell was not a *peccatum superbiae*, but a *peccatum luxuriae*. It was Duns Scotus who sought to give life to the Devil by attributing to him a kind of spiritual voluptuousness. There are traces in these centuries of the belief to be found in the Koran that the first man was created a more perfect creature than the angels. The schools were coming into greater prominence; more and more schoolmen began to suffer from the stings of pride. ἡ γνῶσις φυσιοῖ; knowledge puffeth up. It was written in the school manuals, and repeated by the professors, but there were young dialecticians like Peter Lombard and Abailard who showed that they possessed some of that wanton insolence in themselves. Pride was changing direction. The obsessions of St. Augustine and St. Jerome were becoming curiously out-dated, and when Hugo of St. Victor speaks of pride, he tells the story in a way which suggests a gentle mockery rather than a desperate evil. He explains that God placed the Devil in the bottom-most pits of Hell, because this was the Devil's own choice. God commands that the Devil shall have all that he desires, and says: "Lest it happen that thou shouldst accuse my violence in judgment, or my avarice in offering, whatsoever thine eye seest, that shall I give unto thee." The Devil lifts up his eyes to the high mountains, the yawning chasms, the great wildernesses. "These I shall have," he answers. God smiles and says: "Thou praisest that which thou seest, and I, that which I see. Thou art in the depths, and therefore nothing is open unto thine eyes but that which is high. As for myself, I look down from above and see the pleasantness of lowly things, and my inheritance is good unto me." We are aware that God has played a delightful trick, such a trick as Echo may have played on Narcissus; and though Hugo of St. Victor, with his French delicacy, approves of God, he gives the Devil his due, and confirms him in his powers. Once Augustine had written of the seacoast: "Men draw thither to admire the heights of the mountain and the powerful waves of the sea, and to turn away from themselves." Dimly already Hugo of St. Victor realises that by gazing fondly on the high mountains men may enter more deeply into themselves.

It was the time of the breaking up of the Holy Roman Empire. There came perhaps from the deserts of Arabia the measureless impulse for freedom, coming through Spain with the advent of the first lyric songs, for the most perfect expression of European freedom has always been reflected in the songsters. The years of servility towards the Church and the State were over; Roger Bacon was writing of the undiscovered worlds of the future; a new hope arose in men. Once already the desert had altered the course of European history; now there came, as though from a great distance, subtly reflecting the colours of the Orient, virtues and values which had never made their appearance before on European soil. God Triumphant, the *Kosmokrator* of the Byzantines, gave place in France to the Virgin Mary clothed in cloth of gold, holding the Christ-child with a caressing abandonment to the joys of this world. The discovery of the Virgin in twelfth-century Europe may be compared with the discovery of the goddess Isis in first-century Rome: it announced the end of an era. All traditional values were displaced. The motives by which men lived, their hopes, their prayers were directed to different ends; and the greatest of all ends was the contemplation of the beauty and charity of a young girl.

It was the time of the *troubadors*, the *albas* and the courts of love. In these courts, pardoning the sins of the body, granting her miraculous grace to all men, the Virgin reigned supreme; and pride, though it survived, took on a form which did not demand the thunderbolts of Jove-*Kosmokrator*. The Virgin dressed simply in a blue and white gown, and hated ostentation; yet she was ostentatious herself in her beauty and her disarming smile. Her triumphs were among the people. Her grace was an almost tangible thing, like a flower dropped from her hands; and all her oriental jewellery shines through the rose window of Chartres.

Now since all were proud, the sting of pride was gone. Did not the Roman Mass speak of "the dignity of human nature wonderfully fashioned by God"? As though deliberately reflecting the changing atmosphere of the times, Duns Scotus makes excuses for pride, and all the thundering of the desert fathers is in vain when confronted with the new dignity of man affirming himself once more. For Duns Scotus pride is hardly a sin; it is "the shadow of a virtue":

> For no vice is found but is the shadow of some virtue. Pride is only a perversion of a true sense of power—in good men it takes the form of a love of heavenly excellence and a contempt of earthly weakness—and it was from pride that the sin of man began. (DE DIVINA NATURA, I, 68)

Duns Scotus gently reproves, but even the reproof is an afterthought. Pride, in the sense of men's pride in their human dignity, had come to stay. Had not St. Thomas Aquinas said, in his famous sermon on the Blessed Sacrament, that "the son of God became man in order that men should be like gods." At the turn of the thirteenth century, while the new sap flooded men's veins, to be godlike was simply to exist, and so many excuses were made for the existence of the human will that when the poets of the Spanish *renacimento* came to speak of honour, their poetry derived directly from the scholastic arguments of an earlier age. Even honour itself was of little importance compared to the "new love" that had entered the European stage:

> *O, o, totus floreo*
> *iam amore virginali,*
> *totus ardeo,*
> *novus novus amor*
> *est, quod pereo.*

> I am wholly in flower
> With the love of a maid.
> I am wholly on fire
> With new love, new love.
> Of this I perish.

> (CARMINA BURANA, 140)

To flower wholly in a maid's love, to burn wholly in a new love and to perish became desirable ends, and the Virgin herself could be expected to give her blessing on lovers whose sacrament had nothing whatsoever to do with the Church, for the *novus amor* defied all the principles of scholasticism and rejected the claims of the priests. Nor was it only the love between the sexes which was suddenly raised to the height of passionate worship; the comradeship of the Crusaders had become so exquisite a thing that the aims of the Crusades could be forgotten in the excitement of living in camp. In the late *Jouvencel* of Jean de Bueil, the emotions of previous centuries are crystallised:

> For war is a joyous thing. You love your comrades so in war. When you see that your quarrel is just and your blood is fighting well, tears rise to your eyes and a great sweet feeling of loyalty and pity fill your heart as you see your friend prepared to execute and accomplish the command of the Creator by exposing himself to danger; and then you prepare to go and die or live with him, and for love not to abandon him. And out of that there arises so great a delectation that he who has not tasted it is not fit to speak of delight. Do you think that a man who does this fears death? Not at all, for he feels so strengthened, so elated, that he does not know where he is, and truly he is afraid of nothing.   (JOUVENCEL, III, XIV)

It was the old cry of Solomon's lover—love is stronger than death; but love was also stronger than God, than all the churchmen and all their warnings. When Richard the Lion-Heart went into battle, his oriflamme was woven with the legend: *O Splendor Dei;* but it was the splendour of man which he celebrated in the Crusades, and the wandering minstrels who accompanied the Crusades returned to celebrate the beauty and the virtues of the Syrian maids. Men speak of love as though they had discovered it for the first time; the *novus amor* is so new that men are almost delirious with delight in discovering it, in wandering on the virgin territory:

> *Si me dignetur quam desidero,*
> *felicitate Iovem supero.*
> *Nocte cum illa si dormiero,*
> *si sua labra semel suxero,*
> *mortem subire,*
> *placenter obire,*
> *vitamque finire,*

libens potero,
hei potero, hei potero, hei potero,
tanta si gaudia recepero.

If she whom I desire would stoop to love me,
I would be above Jove in felicity.
If for one night I could lie with her
And kiss both her lips,
Then I would die
And pleasantly vanish
And put life behind me,
Drinking contentedly,
O content, content, content,
To have such delights!

(CARMINA BURANA, 167)

"To be above great Jove in felicity" is something that even Augustine had never dreamed possible. There were secrets withheld from the desert fathers, who desired to attain a perfection granted to every lover and his girl. An invisible Augustine could rage against the worship of the *civitas terrena* and the *civitas amoris,* and the Church could still speak of all love-making as a concert of the Devil unless it was performed for the sake of producing children, but the times spoke otherwise; the dignity of men demanded that they should take pleasure from one another, even though, like Paolo and Francesca, they would be consigned to Hell. Hell had no terrors for lovers. It was a friendly place, as Nicolette had observed long ago, where one met one's friends in friendly converse. The medieval monument was crumbling. Out of it there stepped, majestic in their nakedness, the new Adam and Eve, having anointed the place where the serpent bit them with oriental unguents, and guarded, not by angels with fiery swords, but by the blue-robed Virgin who would not suffer them to suffer, but would give them a grace for the asking.

It was a dangerous world, and they were hardly conscious of the dangers. They were to grow old and bent; there was to come upon them sometimes an impatience against restraint, an intolerance of all the careful walls which had been erected for their own safety. There were times when they were to become strangely insecure, desiring above everything else to return to the monument they had destroyed so wilfully, and with such delight. The Church continued to offer its warnings, but once its temporal power was broken by the emergence of nationalism, there could be no return. Once again, as so many times in the past, men went out of the garden in search of their freedom.

At this point the pride of man changes direction. For ten centuries pride had been an accursed thing; now pride became the instrument of science, the thing men lived for, their delight in life. As the temporal power of the Pope declined, the nations took as their symbols the fierce animals which had been the symbols of pride; and Queen Superbia rode at the head of her armies everywhere. Each nation developed a national pride; and the pride of Italy becomes a thing which can be distinguished from the pride of Germany, France, Spain or England. Each have their own characteristics; and though the self maintains an identity of its own, we shall see that it is coloured by the characteristics of the race. The *terribiltà* of the Italians, the *honor* of the Spaniards, the *moi* of the French were born at the time of the separation of the Church's temporal and spiritual powers; and just as men grow and suffer constant transformations while remaining recognisably the same, so the pride of nations suffers transformations yet remains recognisably similar. The nymph Hubris, chained by the Church, now breaks away from her chains and wanders freely over the world, tempting men wherever she finds them—Pandora's box has opened and the superb Prometheus once again claims the gift of fire from Heaven.

The Terribiltà

WHEN Dante Alighieri was born, according to Boccaccio, his mother dreamed of giving birth to him in a meadow where he fed on laurel-berries; then, to her horror, a strange transformation took place. First the boy became a shepherd, then he became a peacock. The strange and brooding poet is presented to us from the beginning as a demon of pride, rejoicing in the heights of his genius, the *altezza d'ingeno*, contemptuous of man and deliberately separate from God; like Farinata he seems to hold all Hell in scorn.

We approach him with alarm. The fierce passions which worked in him have oddly northern features. When we remember the ferocity of his rage against the Florentines, who sent him into exile, and his desire to destroy root and branch the city of his own birth, the German claim that he came originally from Teutonic stock need not surprise us. The pride of Leonardo was gentler, softer, closer to the earth. Where Dante hurls himself out among the stars, Leonardo patiently explores the world of the earth; and where Leonardo appears to us as someone continually in command of himself, Dante's feverish rages and illuminations suggest that he was continually beside himself with anguished terror at the vision of perfect beauty. There is a cold, remorseless deliberation in Dante, and when he spoke of "the angels that were not rebels, unfaithful to God, faithful only to themselves":

> *Angeli che non furon ribelli,*
> *Nè fur fedeli a Dio, ma per sè foro.*
>
> (INFERNO, III, 38)

we suspect that he may be half-hinting at his own presence among them.

The rage of his intellectual pride is something that hardly existed before in Europe, and nothing comparable to it has been known since, for in *The Divine Comedy* he assumed in himself the powers of the Pontiff and in *De Monarchia* he assumed the powers of the Emperor. Once Leonardo spoke with envy and approval of the eastern Kings who showed themselves only when hidden by masks and veils; with Dante, we feel we are in the presence of someone who is continually veiled, whose features are never revealed, a titanic intellect so proud that we are almost surprised that he did not meet himself and curse himself during his voyage through Hell. We track him to earth at last, perhaps, in the *Pietra Sestina*, where the misery of unsatisfied love turns into calculated bitterness and despair.

Machiavelli, in his life of Castruccio Castracani, that violent red-headed youth who made himself for a while master of northern Italy, remembered odd fragments of conversation spoken by the tyrant. Among them, embedded among anecdotes of his prowess with women and his rudeness—at one time Castruccio was taken into an exquisitely furnished house, and wanting to spit, he spat in his host's face, because "he could have spit nowhere to have offended his host less"—there comes, almost by accident, the portrait of the Renaissance hero in all his panoply. It is a simple portrait. Where Aristotle takes many folio pages to describe the *megalopsychos*, Castruccio says all that need be said of the *megalopsychos* of his time in a single sentence: "Men ought to try all things and be terrified at nothing; for it is clear God Almighty is a lover of courage, because he has made valiant men the ministers of His judgments and corrected the poor-spirited by them." But two centuries previously it had been said of Dante that he feared nothing in Heaven, Purgatory or Hell, and therefore he could write about them.

Dante tried all things and was terrified by none. He was the wanderer in search of a Kingdom until the day he died. While he lived he could look on all things without flinching: with steadfast gaze he looked upon the Virgin in her glory, as he had looked upon the devils in Hell, and he reported faithfully what he had seen; in neither case was he blinded. In the famous letter to Can Grande he explained why it was necessary to wander through Hell: *Poeta agit de inferno isto, in quo, peregrinando ut viatores, mereri et demereri possumus.* "The poet is dealing with that hell wherein, as we walk as travellers, we can acquire or lose merit." All that he ever wrote was concerned with merits and demerits: the idea of glory seems to have been planted in him from the beginning, from the days when, as a young apothecary, he learnt the trade of the Orient and dealt with jewels, spices and strange drugs. At one time—so violent are those visions he describes minutely—he may have drunk infusions of Indian hemp.

Sometimes, of course, the immense pride crumbles. Nothing is so moving as the moment when Matilda draws Dante through the streams of Lethe, and throwing her arms round him cries: *"Tiemmi, tiemmi"* (hold me, hold me). Here and there, breaking through the solemnity of the interminable canzone, there is heard another voice, the voice of a desperate lost child who babbles nonsense or cries out in alarm, and though the words are placed in the mouths of others, they are recognisably Dante's own. *"Ben sem, ben sem, Beatrice."* It is the cry of pride which seems to go back to childhood, and yet it is not far removed from that other cry, uttered by Capaneus, who blasphemed against God and was struck down with a thunderbolt: *"Buono Vulcano, aiuta, aiuta."* There is desperate pleading behind the jewelled verses. *L'uomo universale* is not always in command of himself, and not always under Virgil's protection. There are moments when the great edifice cracks, and he seems to be on the verge of Pascal's abyss, darker and more mysterious than the host of abysses he described.

He placed himself *sesto fra cotanto sermo*, and declared himself openly superior to his contemporaries in style and the favourite of God. He thirsted after glory, and in *De Monarchia* he admits casually that he wished to set forth the idea of monarchy not only in order to be useful to the world, but also *ut palmam tanti bravii primus in meam gloriam adipiscar*. When he comes to describe the proud, the violent against God and nature, those who have attempted to scale the uttermost heights, there is always something curiously relenting. He seems half to forgive pride, and all his fury is directed upon "Cupidigia" or Covetousness, "the evil that possesses the whole world". More curiously still, when he comes to describe the Titans in the ninth circle of Hell they are unrealised and formless shapes, and all he can speak about is their immensity. The proud rebellious Nephilim, "the mighty men who were of old", who made open war upon Heaven, are seen in the fading light like distant fortress towers, higher than St. Peter's at Rome. Dante is full of a shuddering horror as he confronts them, and also of shame. The huge giants are embedded in rock up to the waist, "for where the argument of the mind is joined to the evil will and to great powers, men cannot defend themselves against it," and therefore, like Prometheus, they must be chained to the rock; and Dante gazes upon them with something of the expression of Zeus after chaining the Titans. He is relieved at their captivity, yet the shuddering fear does not leave him. Nimrod babbles some words. Dante even copies them down: they are perhaps the only authentic words heard from the lips of a Titan: "*Rafel mai amech zabi almi*." It may mean: "Raphael has taken away from me my soul," but it may mean nothing at all. So he goes on, leaving Nimrod to confront the giant Ephialtes, who attempted to pile Ossa on Olympus and Pelion on Ossa, whose right arm is pinioned behind him and who is chained from the neck downward by nine chains, but only five are visible, because from the waist downward he, too, is imprisoned in rock. It is all smoke and darkness, and it is still misty, with the sound of storks tapping on the ice, as he passes through the hell reserved for the traitors; then at last he comes into the presence of Satan himself, "*lo imperador del doloroso regno*," and he too is half submerged in the ice. Immensely high above him, Dante sees the three satanic faces, one red, one "middling white and yellow" and the other jet back as an Ethiopian. We wonder at the significance of the colours until we remember that St. Bernard amused himself by giving colours to some of the vices: "*Superbia rubet; kenodoxia albet; invidia pallet*." "Pride red; vainglory white; envy yellow." Dante throws in black for good measure, and combines vainglory and envy into a single colour-scheme. Then there is Judas with his head between his legs, and the great journey through Hell is over.

But it is not among the Titans or in the presence of Lucifer that Dante comes to grips with the proud. There is no special circle where the proud are damned, for they are scattered through the *Inferno* and the *Purgatorio*. By some strange mischance the Titans and Lucifer, who appear at the end of the circuit of Hell, also appear in purgatory beside the heathen oppressors of Israel and with the proud sinners of Greek legend. Besides the Giants and Lucifer Dante chooses, as examples of the congregation of the proud, Niobe, Saul, Arachne, Rehoboam, Eriphyle, Sennacherib, Cyrus, Holofernes and the city of Troy, Virgil's *superbum Ilium*. Surely there was never such a strange company of fallen angels! One wonders why Niobe and Eriphyle are among the chosen, when there were so many other Greek heroines who suffered from a greater pride. No explanations are given. The poet seems determined to pass quickly through this place, gazing mechanically at these figures who are depicted on the pavement in sculptured images, and the coldness of his treatment of them is only equalled by the cold and impassioned verse. It is when we look at the verse-form itself that Dante begins to reveal his secrets. The first group of four sinners is delineated in four *terzine*, beginning with *Vedea;* the second group also has four *terzine* beginning with O; similarly the third group consists of four *terzine* each beginning with *Mostrava*. The inference is inescapable that the initial letters have for Dante a profound significance. The proud, who have been selected with such studied carelessness, are indicated hermetically by the initials of tragedy, VOM or UOM, i.e. man. All mankind is assailed. None shall escape pride, he seems to be saying. And as though he was desperately anxious to keep his sombre secret, and at the same time to reveal it, Dante goes on immediately to lament the folly of the proud:

> *O superbite, e via col viso altiero,*
> *Figliuoli d'Eva, e non chinate il volto.*
>
> (PURGATORIO, XII, 70)

Dante comes closest to the *megalopsychos* in his portrait of Farinata degli Uberti, who half rises from the fiery tomb, showing no more of himself than the Titans showed, and as the sinner glances haughtily around him, showing scorn of Hell—*come avesse lo inferno in gran dispitto*—his first question to the poet is the immemorial question of great princes when confronted with poor poets: "Who are your ancestors?" Farinata boasts of his success in preventing Florence from being razed to the ground and utters a mysterious prophecy, but no more is needed: the portrait of the proud man is fixed indelibly in our minds. The clear-cut vision returns again when Dante reaches the edge of the third ring of the seventh circle and sees the plain of scorching sand, where the fire-flakes continually descend and the naked writhe in their agony, "ever restless with the dance of their miserable hands", as they attempt to shake off the burning. There he finds Capaneus, and now for the first and last time Dante puts into the mouth of Virgil the name of the fit punishment of pride:

> O Capaneus, because thy pride remains unquenched,
> Thou shalt be punished more; it is not torture,
> But thine own furious raving shall be thy punishment.
>
> (INFERNO, XIV, 63-65)

Afterwards Virgil is heard muttering:

> As I have told him, his scornful words
> Are ornaments that will befit his breast.
>
> (INFERNO, XIV, 71-72)

Why ornaments? It seems so unimaginably gentle a word. Dante himself is rarely gentle. His rage against Boniface VIII is a personal and relentless thing. Other Popes please him more. He is gentle to Adrian V, who, in Dante's own statement, raised him up and said: "I am thy fellow-servant, and of thy brethren that have the testimony of Jesus." It means only that Dante approves of Adrian V. Dante's pride is sometimes outrageous, as when he places in the mouth of Peter his own essential hatred against the abuses of the papal court. There are times when his pride reaches towards the end of madness, becomes a palpable and terrifying thing. The grotesque punishments of the damned, his passionate singularity and delight in fallen magnificence, suggests that he was given over to pride. It is not necessary to codify his grouping of the sinners in order to discover why he chooses to place one sinner in one group and not in another, for the proud are everywhere in *The Divine Comedy*, and often enough they are described, not in terms of pride only, but of raging pride—*furor*. Dante shows no mercy;

to the weak he demonstrates his conscious superiority. When Filippo Argenti rises out of the slime and approaches him, saying: "Who art thou, who comest before his time?" Dante replies: "If I come, it is not to remain. But thou, who art thou, who hast become so foul with slime?" Filippo Argenti answers: "Thou seest I am weeping." Virgil approves of Dante's arrogance, saying: "Indignant soul, blessed is she that bore thee." Pride and indignation have become virtues.

So it is throughout *The Divine Comedy:* here is the *terribiltà* which feeds on its own misfortunes, and on the misfortunes of others. Gregory had spoken of the man "who walks with himself along the broad spaces of his thought, and silently utters his own praises." With Dante we meet him in the flresh for the first time.

Perhaps he could hardly help himself. There was a vertigo in the air. The most astonishing claims were being made by the man who seemed in Dante's eyes the least worthy of all. Boniface VIII had proclaimed by a papal bull that "all Kings, Emperors and other Sovereigns, whoever they may be, are subject like all other men to be summoned before the apostolic court, for every sort of cause; for we, by the permission of God, command the whole universe." Nor was this all. In 1300, the year of *The Divine Comedy* and of the great celebrations of the Jubilee, the pilgrims who flocked to Rome were privileged to see the Pope sitting on his throne with the diadem of Constantine on his head, and in his right hand there was a drawn sword. With an almost maniacal laugh, the Pope, supreme arbiter of Christendom, commander of the whole universe, was crying: "Am I not Pope? I, I am Emperor!" It was Dante's task to put this madness to an end; he could hardly be blamed if the urgency and despair of the task made him seethe with an indignation bordering on madness. He, who called himself *exul immeritus*, the undeserved exile, was conscious of a role to be played quite as great as the role played by Boniface VIII. If we accuse him of pride, it is at some peril, for he may have possessed more than a consciousness of his own significance to the world; a divinity seems to flow from him; when he rages, it is as a god rages. Against this wanderer, like another Oedipus in search of his home, neither the fury of the Florentines who sentenced him to death nor the anathemas of the Pope who sentenced him to eternal damnation are of any avail. Where his predecessors had been content to call themselves "Vicars of Peter" Innocent III claimed for himself the title of "Vicar of Christ". So Dante might claim that in a sense he was the mediator between the antique world of Rome and the present; and it is not Dante only who unlocks the gate of Hell in the company of Virgil, but Dante clothed in the shadow of Christ—his claims for himself are sometimes terrifying in their audacity. `

It was the time of the *terribiltà*, that untranslatable and most menacing of Italian words, for it implies the most arbitrary rule, the most violent gestures, the absence of all pity and even of understanding. A Cardinal writing in late Hohenstaufen times maintained that he who seeks to rule the Romans must show them: *et gestus magnificos et verbia tonantia et facta terribilia*. All these are present in *The Divine Comedy*, made deliberately present to the imagination, presented with a clear and menacing purpose. In this sense *The Divine Comedy* is pure tragedy, even when it recounts the purposes of paradise and even when it shines with the splendour of Beatrice's smile.

Dante was writing at a period when the city states were emerging against the arbitrary power of the princes. There could be no question that the power was purely arbitrary, and had fallen too often into the hands of those whose lust for power had driven them insane. So Boniface VIII died insane at Anagni, tormented by French soldiers and broken-hearted because his power was taken from him. Frederick II, who died only fifteen years before the birth of Dante, emulated the Pantocrator, desiring to possess not only men's bodies but their souls; and for this reason, but with unaccountable gentleness, only hinting at his presence, Dante placed him in Hell. This new type of Emperor had been enthroned in Palermo, in Aix, in Worms, in Mainz and in Jerusalem. His heart beat with no other purpose than to be lord and master of the whole world, whispered Brunetto Latini; and he had come to this position by persecuting the representatives of free municipal life, by ruthlessly opposing all opposition and by reigning as a purely arbitrary prince, killing those who, like Piero delle Vigne, ultimately opposed his will. His superb will fought against the superb will of Boniface VIII, who cursed him and was himself cursed. Of both of them it might have been said, as Christ says to the Pope in the *Revelationes* of St. Brigit: "*Tu autem pejor es Lucifero.*" "Thou art worse than Lucifer."

In this dialogue of wills Dante had his solemn place; his was the third will. There were other wills: there was the will of the city states, long forgotten, the one destined to survive longest, and against this too Dante raged with hopeless and passionate abandon. Against the march of the advancing world Dante sets himself sternly, standing at the *ultima poste*, the final frontier of his pride, the most imposing, because the most enduring, among modern men, of those whom Kierkegaard called the *Enkelte*, the individuals conscious of their sin and of their power.

With Frederick II we come for the first time into the presence of the *terribiltà* robed in the costume of the Emperor. Dante is naked and weaponless; Frederick wears the dalmatic, carries the Lance, the Golden Apple and the Eagles, and steps out into the full light of day like some miraculous and portentous sign of man's dominance and challenging powers over the elements, *stupor mundi et immutator mirabilis*. Henry IV had knelt in penitence at Canossa, Barbarossa had flung himself at the feet of the Pope at Venice; Frederick humiliated himself before no one. It was not only that he wrested Jerusalem from the enemy, assumed the crown in the Church of the Holy Sepulchre and employed Saracen mercenaries against the Pope, but he was cultivated and learned in six languages, wrote poetry so admirable that Dante, though he placed Frederick in Hell among the heresiarchs, was compelled to commend him. Frederick possessed so great an intellectual tolerance that he allowed Jews, Arabs, Englishmen and Frenchmen to hold high positions in his court, protected scholars, introduced the first university examinations, and even amused himself by introducing a form of democratic government into Sicily. He was the prime exemplar of *uomo universale in tutte le cose*, the most gifted of heresiarchs, and physically the most endowed of the princes of his time. Yet his crimes were so numerous that the Church had no alternative but to anathematise him, and the dread ceremony in which the anathema was pronounced—to the clanging of discordant bells, the Cardinals beating out their torches against the flagstones while the Pope uttered the final malediction: "So be the fortune and glory of the Emperor extinguished upon this earth"—was worthy of his own terrible and exact sense of vengeance.

He was not the only prince gifted with the power of *terribiltà*. Others were to come after him in their floods, as merciless as the black-winged furies of the Greeks, strange men with wild and insatiable passions, who arose from nowhere and passed into no obscurity, for they left behind them monuments of their prowess. As the papal power weakened and Italy split into princely states, each one vieing with others for supremacy, there arose the tribe of the *condottiere*, adventurers in search of splendour, and not all of them were warriors in search of kingdoms to conquer. When Plutarch wrote in his letter to posterity: "In others I perceived pride, not in myself, *et cum parvus fuerim, semper minor judicio meo fui*, for kings and princes cherished me, I know not why, and I was with some of them as if they were rather with me," he was mapping out the spiritual landscape of the time; it was in this way, discreetly but with all the panoply of adoration, that men desired to be remembered. The *persona* emerges, the masks are stripped off, and there must be some significance in the year 1430 when the first statue of a naked man was made by an Italian artist. As the clothed and archaic Apollo emerged from the rock to become the naked Peirithoös ruling over the Temple of Olympia, so Donatello's bronze David, negligently holding a sword, with one foot on the head of Goliath, comes to rule over the Florentine scene. Men came to feel that they possessed a kind of unity of being, using that term as Dante used it in the *Convito* when he compared heavenly beauty to a perfectly proportioned human body. The splendour of Pindar's world was returning, heaven and earth were drawing together for mutual delight, it was a time when lordship implied more than temporal dominance: it suggested at least a stake in heaven. Virtù, the old ἀρετή of the Athenians, had returned to delight men with their own powers.

At such a time there could be nothing strange in the fact that boys of fourteen became cardinals. Great artists were employed to paint the furious energy of the age. The Christ on the altar-wall of the Sistine Chapel is the brother of the young David in Florence as he prepares to throw his stone; both are omnipotently calm and arrayed in divine nakedness, both breathe the air of the heights, both challenge and take joy in being superhuman champions. Vasari trembled before the visions of Michelangelo. "His imagination was so stupendous," he wrote, "that his hands were unable to shape the immense and terrible figures, the ideas he had conceived in his mind, and therefore he often relinquished his work or rather spoiled many of them." Stupendous, terrible, immense. . . . They are the adjectives of a lawless time.

Lawlessness ruled. It was not only the Popes and their daughters who were lawless. Sigismundo Malatesta strangled one wife and poisoned another, then he married the celebrated Isotta degli Atti and built a temple to celebrate her divinity. He denied God and the immortality of the soul, and when the reigning Pope pronounced sentence of excommunication he enquired pleasantly whether the excommunicated enjoyed the flavour of good bread and wine.

It was more than tyranny; it was an exaltation of the self beyond all barriers and beyond all decencies. When Pope Julius II arrived in Perugia without an army, escorted only by his cardinals and a small baggage-train, Machiavelli is thunderstruck because the tyrant Giovan Paolo Baglioni did not seize him and slit his throat. He asks himself why the Pope was enabled to return to Rome unharmed:

> It could neither be goodness nor conscience that constrained the tyrant, since no pious respect could have a place in the bosom of a guilt-stained man who had seduced his own sister, and murdered his cousins and nephews in order to reign; but they arrived at the conclusion that men did not know how to be honourably bad, or perfectly good; and as a completely wicked act has some greatness or some element of generosity, so they cannot perform it. Thus Giovan-pagalo, who had not shrunk from incest and public parricide, could not, or rather dared not, even on a public occasion, accomplish an enterprise for which everyone would have admired his courage, and which would have procured him eternal remembrance as the first man to show prelates of how little account are those who live and rule after their fashion, and who would thereby have done a deed whose greatness would have surpassed every infamy, and every danger that might have ensued from it.

(DISCORSI, I, XXVII)

Through the works of Machiavelli there breathes the spirit of the times, rude, insolent, depraved, impelled by paradoxes—*honourable frauds, generous cruelties, glorious crimes*. The tyrant must be exalted, the people must be enslaved, the *terribiltà* is alone worthy of worship. Michelangelo could inveigh against *la dura vergogna*, the bitter shame of those times, but he was a voice crying in the wilderness and his genius was placed at the service of the Popes who committed the same "honourable frauds, generous cruelties, glorious crimes" as the tyrants of the Italian states. That power was deadly, could kill by a look and had its origin in an exalted conception of honour is admitted by Guicciardini, whose *uomo individuale* professes to see treason in every slight and in the attainmen of honour the only *virtù*.

Machiavelli has no illusions on *virtù*. In the famous seventh chapter of *The Prince* he performs the difficult task of absolving Cesare Borgia from all taint of crime. He even approves of Oliverotto da Fermo, who asked his uncle if he could enter the city "in order to show his splendour", and at once set out, with the hundred knights under his command, to exterminate his uncle and his uncle's party. "Experience has proved in our time that the princes who have achieved great deeds," says Machiavelli happily, "are those who have held good faith of little account, and have known how to bewilder men's brains by cunning, and in the end have succeeded better than those whose actions have been ruled by honour." The confusion is everywhere in Machiavelli: honour is to acquire power by every means, but it is also what we understand by virtue. "Clearchus, the tyrant of Heraclea, when placed between the fury of the people and of the patricians hated by the people, murdered the latter and then satisfied the former." Machiavelli passes on, gracefully and impenitently, to consider ever more serious, even more honourable crimes. It is the apathy of the surgeon, looking at the compulsive and nervous movements of a dying man's agony, but aware that at the moment of agony the dying man is superbly and terribly conscious of himself. Machiavelli admires the force and energy of the mind which knows and dares all things; he glorifies energy, even when it is at the service of the bad, and is impatient of the humanists who desire an end to warfare, "for where then shall men be able to assert their honour?"

Where, indeed? Savonarola hinted at the secret in his sermon on All Soul's Day, 1496, when he spoke of death hovering overhead, bearing in one hand the illuminated scroll inscribed: *"Ego sum,"* and in the other hand holding a scythe. In *L'Arte del Ben Morire* Death is drawn magnificently as he flies over the desolate landscape, a bishop, a nun and two youths lying in Death's shadow. He was the last to attempt to found a spiritual empire, but he too had fallen into the dangerous disease of pride and exasperated the citizens of Florence with his desire to destroy all that they prized most—their precious silks, paintings and even their monuments. His militia of children, *militia sacra*, was no answer to the rise of tyrannical forces; his loathing of the papacy—"the cardinal's hat is a smear of blood"—placed him in danger of the vengeance of the only power that might, under different stars, have protected him. Tyranny, a purely earthly tyranny, was to run its course to the end, throwing up its Napoleons and Mussolinis centuries later as a mark of its survival, glorifying man and murder in the same breath, resolute against all opponents, cherishing above everything else a strange conception of honour.

Pico della Mirandola, "the earl of Mirandolle and lord of Italy", stated the case for honour with the utmost purity. Savonarola's *"Ego sum,"* the watchword of death, becomes transformed into the most delicate virtuosity, and if he placed man higher than the angels, it was with no intention to make him a tyrant. He was intent only upon breaking up "some seals which none had touched before," as Vaughan says in his poem *Vanity of Spirit*, in a curious mingling of intellectual pride and spiritual humility. In his *Very Elegant Speech on the Dignity of Man* Pico della Mirandola, employing the imagery of fire derived from Dionysius the Areopagite, sees man as a living flame, which shines superbly through the dark night of this world. Ascribing to a mysterious and imaginary Abdul the Saracen the words that were uttered by Sophocles in the great chorus of the *Antigone*, he repeats that nothing is more wonderful than man, and then hurries towards his conclusions. The case, he says, is wonderful beyond belief. The Great Artificer made man to admire His handiwork, for He desired "that there should be someone to reckon up the ratio and reason of such a great work, to love its beauty, and to wonder at its greatness".

"Therefore He took up man as being, without limitations, a work of mirroring, and placed him in the mid-point of the world." The Creator speaks to man:

> I have set thee at the centre of the world, that from there thou mayest more conveniently look around and see whatsoever is in the world. I have made thee neither heavenly nor earthly, neither mortal nor immortal; and like a judge appointed for being honourable thou art made the moulder and maker of thyself; thou mayest knead thyself into whatsoever shape thou desirest. Thou mayest sink into a beast, and be born anew to a divine likeness. The brutes bring from the mother's body what they will carry with them as long as they live; the higher spirits are from the beginning, or soon after, what they will be for ever. To thee alone is given a growth and a development depending on thine own free will. Thou bearest in thee the germs of a universal life.
>
> (ORATIO ELEGENTISSIMO DE DIGNITATE HOMINIS)

The extraordinary challenge of God to man involves, as we might have expected, dangers of sheer brutishness and of intellectual pride. As for those who have become like the brutes, Pico contents himself with the remark that "they are not men which you see." Neither is the proud man a man, for "if you see anyone blinded by the illusions of his empty and Calypso-like imagination, tarred with the tickling allurement, and delivered over to the senses, it is a brute not a man which you see." Only the contemplator, "in pure contemplation, ignorant of the body, banished to the innermost places of the mind," belongs to the heavenly order; and of him it may be said that he is "more superbly a divine presence robed with human flesh." He quotes the unknown prophet Asaph, who said: "Ye are all gods, and the most high sons, unless by abusing the very indulgent liberality of the Father, we make a free choice harmful to us, instead of helping towards salvation," and then he reverts to Jerome's holy pride, *sacra superbia*, and it is at this point that the great fire-images of Dionysius return in their splendour:

> Let a certain holy ambition invade the mind, so that we

may not be content with mean things but may aspire to the highest things and strive with all our strength to attain them; for if we will to, we can. Let us spurn earthly things; let us struggle towards the heavenly. Let us put in last place whatever is of the world; and let us fly beyond the chambers of the world to the chamber nearest the most lofty godhead. . . . There the seraph burns with the fire of charity; the cherub shines with the radiance of intelligence; the throne stands in steadfastness of judgment, and there we shall flame altogether with cherubic light. . . . On these heights is the peace of God, which the angels descending to earth announced to men of good will, that by this peace men themselves may ascend to heaven and become angels. Let us desire this peace for our friends, for this age.

In the most unpeaceful of ages Pico della Mirandola made his generous plea. The slight and slender youth with the steady grey eyes and yellow hair of Botticelli's portrait seems, as we read him, to be about to make the dizzy ascent to the heavens he describes with such loving care, the sanctuary where the philosopher-priests "contemplate the many-coloured, star-constellated royal decorations of the higher realm of God". There is no confusion; he employs all the resources of his imagination to construct the simple flight and the simple vision, taking his evidence from Job as gratefully as he imitates the dialectics of Empedocles. The fervour comes from gratitude for life, an intense and unavailing *veneratio vitae*, for he died too young to have enjoyed life to the full. "By gazing at the sempiternal beauty of those things, we shall be prophets of Phoebus, his lovers with wings, and shall finally, like the burning Seraphim, be learned in that inexpressible charity like a furnace, and shall be placed outside ourselves." For him, speaking from Florence in an age of undisguised disgrace and tyranny the dignity of man lies in his being and in his power, and both are like flames, burning with seraphic intelligence. "The elementary fire burns, the heavenly fire vivifies, the supercelestial fire loves."

It is perfectly possible to disbelieve everything Pico della Mirandola says; to say, for example, that he has borrowed so widely and invented so broadly that nothing he says has any value in itself. This quotation comes from the *Kabbala*, that from the *Timaeus*, another from Dionysius the Areopagite; and indeed, from the *Divine Hierarchies* of Dionysius, which once "ranne like a deere" through England, and laid the foundations of English devotional poetry, he borrows most; but what Dionysius says of the angels, Pico della Mirandola says with infinite good sense of men. Though every sentence may be criticised, the whole shines with the living flame of the youth who graced Florence by his presence, and spoke (in a speech composed for a philosophical tournament) of the dignity of man as no one else before him. Long before Bacon wrote his classic text that "man is a little world, in which we may discern a body mixed with earthly elements and ethereal breath, and the vegetable life of plants, and the senses of the lower animals, and reason, and the intelligence of angels, and a likeness to God", Pico della Mirandola had stated it better, and with considerably more beauty of expression.

Pico della Mirandola left his mark on the times; no one else had been capable of making so high a synthesis of the knowledge of his age. He was bookish and learned, and towards the end of his brief life fell under the influence of Savonarola, and even desired to be buried in San Marco shrouded in a Dominican habit. Thoughts of damnation came too late to prevent him from publishing his essay in celebration of man's dignity; and it was perhaps easier then than now to believe in man's infinite potentialities, for the world was still a limited place, bounded by crystal walls, a painted toy for children to play with on the shores of time.

Something of the remarkable serenity of Pico della Mirandola was retained in the high Renaissance. We are accustomed to see in the fevers of Leonardo and the terrible shapes which Michelangelo hewed out of marble the conscious terrors of the *terribiltà*. Yet Michelangelo's sonnets are filled with the same sunlit fervour as Pico della Mirandola's prose, and when Leonardo complains against the heavenly sun, he is talking like someone who has been deceived by the Florentine youth and has desired to follow him:

O false light, how many you have deceived miserably in times past, as you have deceived me! If I would see the light, should I not distinguish between the Sun and the false burning of a smoky tallow?   (CODEX ATLANTICUS, 67)

So he returns, in loneliness and despair, to the contemplation of his own glory, and in one fragment of his inverted handwriting makes a boast more proud than any in recorded history—the boast that he would be the first of all men to fly; for there can be no doubt that the *grande uccello* refers to himself:

> The great bird will take the first flight mounted on a great swan, filling the universe with stupor and filling all writings with its glory: praise eternal to the nest in which it was born.
> (SUL VOLO, 2R)

Pride, a very secret and self-considering pride, tormented him. Here and there in his note-books, scattered in the unlikeliest places, there are warnings that seem to be addressed to himself. *Si tu sarai solo sarai tutto tuo.* "If you are alone, you belong entirely to yourself," he wrote once, but on another page he wrote that he hated cages and cage-keepers, and thought they bred self-love and hypocrisy; and he seems to have known that to be completely alone is to invent for oneself the most adamantine of cages. Molinos wrote once that there were three kinds of silence, the first of words, the second of desires, the third of thoughts. The first was perfect, the second more perfect, the third most perfect. As Paul Valéry described Leonardo in his *Introduction to the Method of Leonardo da Vinci*, Leonardo was possessed of all these silences and all these perfections, and his art was, as it were, the accidental breaking of these deliberate silences. "Those who search for the impossible are chastised by melancholy and despair," Leonardo wrote, and in his essay on painting he describes the artist as alone possessing mastery; the painter is the lord of everything he desires, almost God-like in his power of creation and equal to God in the power of his imagination:

> For if the painter desires to see beautiful things that awaken love in him, then he is their lord and can create them; and if he desires to see a terrifying monster, or a grotesque or ridiculous or touching thing, he is their lord and God. If he wants to create landscapes and wildernesses, or shady or cool places on

hot days, he has only to represent them; and so, too, he can represent warm places on cold days. If he desires to see valleys before him, if he desires to see a wide landscape spreading out from high mountains, he is their lord, also.   (TRATTATO, 13)

It was an enviable position for Leonardo, but the dangers were only too manifest. So great a lordship implies a load of responsibility as heavy as the earth. In him the bright passion of Pico della Mirandola is becoming sicklied over with thought; to stimulate himself he must adventure into the regions of the bizarre, the hermaphroditic, the tormented. The fatality of the proud obsessed him, and once again he seems to be writing of himself when he speaks of the water in the sea:

> The water in the superb sea which is its element took delight in mounting high into the air. There, aided by the fiery particle, it climbed in subtle vapours, relying on the lightness of the air. Then, when it reached higher, it came to an even rarer air where there was greater cold, and here it was abandoned by the fire. Its molecules there drew together, combining and growing heavier, and its pride was converted into sudden descent; and so it falls and is drunk by the dry earth, and deep in the earth it is imprisoned, paying penitence for its sin.
> (FORSTER MS. III, 2R)

The symbolism is clear: Leonardo is speaking of himself. In a life of restless wandering, desperate ambitions never realised, Leonardo comes at last to see himself as a drop of water sparkling in the sunlight, whose pride must be converted "into sudden descent". He reverts to the theme of pride at greater length in the mysterious letters addressed to the strange Diodor of Syria, letters written in his notebook as though they were the fragmentary notes for an unfinished autobiographical novel. Here he describes the Flood and the Fire, the end of the world, the manner in which he came to the white mountain of Asia Minor, climbed towards its peak and survived the cataclysm. Reading his powerful prose, or seeing the illustrations of the Flood and the Fire, we seem to see not the mountain, but the towering figure of Leonardo himself, assailed by the fire beneath the waist, but eternal in the summits of the mind.

Only once did he seem to fear his own dissolution; this was when he drew himself as an old, beautiful and bearded god, but the beard is like a wave in which the face slowly dissolves.

Something of the same pride occurred in the greatest conquistador of all—Christopher Columbus, who believed that the world was about to come to an end and on him devolved the burden of the mystery by which the world would be saved by the discovery of a lost Atlantis. The tumultuous notes written by him in the *Libro de la profezie* testify to the calm acceptance of his own unerring mission in the world:

> It was by no means mathematics, nor the charts of the ancient geographers, nor the deductions of reason which helped me to accomplish that which I did accomplish; but solely the prophecy of Isaiah about a new heaven and a new earth.

It may be that this was the explanation of why men behaved with such singularity in the Renaissance; the hope of "a new heaven and a new earth" was almost within their grasp. In this new heaven there was perfect freedom; everything could be dared; the wisest were those who dared to the uttermost. In this world, where men partook of the qualities of gods, pride was no longer a sin; pride was simply the state of being oneself. Of these proud men, Dante, who was among the proudest, wrote the superb epitaph:

> Heaven chased them forth to keep its beauty fresh,
> And the deep hell refused to have them there:
> For the wicked would have some glory in them.
>
> (INFERNO, III, 40-42)

The Spanish Interlude

WHEN Don Quixote on his travels came upon a waggoner on his way from Oran to Madrid, with a cart containing a caged lion, he decided to face the lion in chivalrous combat, ordered the cage to be opened and approached on foot. Thereupon the lion yawned, opened its huge mouth, thrust out half a yard of broad tongue, licked the dust out of its eyes and face and stared menacingly at Don Quixote. The lion, however, did not attack the knight, but instead turned round contentedly, showing its immense posterior. Don Quixote commanded the waggoner to rouse the lion with a pole. This the waggoner refused to do, explaining that no man was obliged to do more than challenge the enemy; if the enemy does not show himself, then the honour belongs to the challenger. To this astonishing statement Don Quixote replies:

> "Come then, shut the cage door, my honest friend, and give me a certificate under thy hand, in the amplest form thou canst devise, of what thou hast seen me perform; how thou didst open the cage for the lion; how I expected his coming, and he did not come; how, upon his not coming, I staid his own time, and instead of meeting me, he turned tail and lay down. I am obliged to do no more. So, enchantments, avaunt! and heaven prosper truth, justice and knight-errantry. Shut the door as I bid thee!"   (DON QUIXOTE, II, LVI)

Having explained his own position in relation to the enchantments of honour, the wandering knight turns to Sancho Panza, as he recovers from his fright, and says: "What dost thou think of this?

Can enchantment prevail over true fortitude? No, these magicians may rob me of success, but never of my invincible greatness of mind."

Here, indeed, is the whole theme of *Don Quixote*: the invincible greatness of mind faced with the enchantments of the world. The famous certificate of the waggoner, like the ticket which Ivan Karamazov gives back to God, is the tangible passport to honour. What is needed above all by the proud man is that a certificate should exist, and even if the certificate is not accurate, nothing is lost, and perhaps even something is gained: a completely accurate certificate would be terrifying. Through all his adventures Don Quixote is demanding his certificate of honour, and never receiving it until the last moment, and then it is too late; the words on the tombstone written by the bachelor Carrasco formed the epitaph he had desired throughout his life:

> The body of a knight lies here,
>   So brave that, to his latest breath,
> Immortal glory was his care,
>   And made him triumph over death.
>
> (DON QUIXOTE, II, LXXIV)

In default of this certificate (signed by whom?), Don Quixote must pile adventure upon adventure, rage hither and thither across the Kingdom of Spain, the eternal *desdichado* in quest of fame, finding no solace in the journeying: all is terror, the smell of straw in ancient inn-yards, discomfort, darkness and stray gleams of sunlight. He enters the magical caves, sees the heroes on their tombs, discusses the fortunes of the world with talking apes, and there is something of Swift's *saeva indignatio* under the serene aspect with which he confronts the world. His attempts to disenchant the enchanted world, to discover the Archimedean lever, all these are subtle disguises: what he is after is the discovery of himself. Guile, irony, savagery and courtesy, all these are employed in the insane pursuit; the very intensity of the chase suggests that *Don Quixote* is as serious as exposition of the landscape of pride as anything to be seen in any literature. Irony abounds; there is the faintest smile of understanding as the proud man watches himself. He is Aristotle's *megalopsychos* magically translated to La Mancha. "It is characteristic of the high-souled man," says Aristotle, "never to ask help from others, or only with reluctance, and to render aid willingly; to be haughty towards men of position and fortune, but courteous towards those of moderate station. He will not compete for the common objects of ambition, and he will be idle and slow to act, except when pursuing some high object or endeavour; and he will not engage in many undertakings, but only in such as are important and distinguished. He likes to own beautiful and useless things, and you will recognise him by his slow gait, his deep voice and deliberate utterance." It is almost as though Cervantes had the *Nicomachean Ethics* under his eyes as he wrote, in the prison darkness, the account of a hero entrapped by his own heroism.

For it is necessary to observe that only in the widest sense can *Don Quixote* be regarded as a caricature of the heroic impulse and the relentless search for glory; the real, the tangible glory eludes the hero, but his quest is as deliberate as Lancelot's or Perceval's; and if he is the fool of God, he is also the authentic hero in love with the name of honour, and the honour of God. We understand Don Quixote better when we listen to the majestic speech of the Demon in Calderón's *El Mágico Prodigioso*:

> Chastised, I know
> The depth to which ambition falls; too mad
> Was the attempt, and yet more mad than now
> Repentance of the irrevocable deed:
> Therefore I chose this ruin with the glory
> Of not to be subdued.

The parallel goes no further. The Demon speaks with a greater authority than Don Quixote if only because he is closer to the sources of power. It is power which eludes Don Quixote, who is never so mystified as when his heroic acts produce no visible glory, no certificate, no breath of sunlight leaping up to Heaven, no deliberate reward. The equations are forfeit. In the world of Don Quixote, as in the world of Dostoievsky's prison, one and two together makes less than one; and how this should come about, why the earthly enchantment is so strong, is something as bewildering to him as it is bewildering to Kafka, who wanders forlornly to his

Castle, enraged by heavenly bureaucrats as Don Quixote is enraged by the absence of divine laws.

A divine absence plagues Don Quixote, as it plagued John Donne. In one of the most extraordinary passages of the whole work, a passage where all the twisted strands of meaning are suddenly gathered together into a single strand, Don Quixote explains to Sancho Panza, who has been sleeping, why it is necessary to keep awake through the long night:

> "Sancho," said the knight, after he had pulled the squire till he had waked him, "I am amazed at the insensibility of thy temper. Thou art certainly made of marble or brass, thou liest so without either motion or feeling. Thou sleepest while I wake: thou singest while I mourn; and while I am ready to faint for want of sustenance, thou art lazy and unwieldy with mere gluttony. It is the part of the good servant to share in the afflictions of the master. Observe the stillness of the night, and the solitary place we are in. It is a pity such an opportunity should be lost in sloth and inactive rest; rouse for shame, step a little aside, and with a good grace and a cheerful heart score me up some three or four hundred lashes upon thy back, towards the disenchanting of Dulcinea. Thus I make my earnest request, being resolved never to be rough with thee again upon this account; for I must confess thou canst lay a heavy hand on a man upon occasion. When that performance is over, we will pass the remainder of the night in chanting, I of *absence*, and thou of constancy, and so begin those pastoral exercises which are to be our employment at home."
>
> (DON QUIXOTE, II, LXVIII)

This passage, towards the end of the book, with its strangely evocative reminiscences of the passion at Gethsemane, is even more elucidating than the great speeches of Don Quixote when, having given Sancho Panza power over the island, he exhorts him to give obedience only to God. The rage for victory has died down; in its place there is only the contemplative's delight in seeing the world as it is. The illusions have not entirely perished; there are still veils between himself and the world, but they are growing so thin that in a moment he will pierce through them, discovering not the great knight-errant Don Quixote de la Mancha, but Alonzo Quixano, "the same whom the world, for his fair behaviour, has been formerly pleased to call *The Good*". At this moment the single word "absence" comes like the sound of a distant carillon of bells, not explaining anything, but giving a blessedness to all that has passed; and as we follow the story to the end we are conscious that the proud man has turned away from pride, not because his pride was folly, but because it enabled him to understand the world as it is; he who tilted at the world has become at last king of himself.

The point of honour, which is the obsession of Don Quixote, is also the obsession of nearly all Spanish drama. Isidore of Seville thundered against it; Prudentius raged against it; the story of the Cid is no more than the story of the working out of a prodigious debt of honour. Pride turns inward and becomes reflective in *Don Quixote*, where the windmills take the place of mirrors; but it is in the drama of the golden age, in the impassioned triumphs of Lope de Vega, Calderón and Tirso de Molina that we see pride most resolute, most fierce and most completely equipped for the contest, just as it is in the great Spanish mystics that we see the same battle fought more decorously, more quietly, in the stillness of the soul.

Partly, of course, it springs from some elemental rage within the Spanish soul. The anarchists who went to their deaths singing "*Viva la Muerte*" were as defiant as El Compreador; and it is not only St. Teresa who complains of the *violencias de singularidad*, for every Spanish peasant is a prey to the temptations that assaulted Anthony. The fury, the sense of sin, the fever that springs from the deserts of Spain, the sense of implacable forces to be placated whatever the cost, the deliberate austerity and the gaiety in the presence of death, all these are elements which we associate with spiritual pride, but the genius of the Spanish people suffers from the more wanton and physical pride that rises from a deeply engrained conception of masculine honour. Arturo Barea has related that he once quoted the famous lines of Lorca describing a gypsy's love for an unfaithful wife:

> Her thighs slipped from me
> Like surprised fishes,

Half filled with fire,
And half with ice.
On this night I rode
The best of all roads
Astride a pearly mare
Without bridle or stirrups.
Being a man I shall not tell
The things she told me. . . .
I behaved like what I am,
Like the true gypsies.
I gave her a large basket
Of straw-coloured satin,
And refused to fall in love,
For she had a husband:
She told me she was a maid
When I took her by the river.

(LA CASADA INFIEL)

An illiterate boy from Jaén, who overheard the poem, exclaimed: "That's right. The bitch! Why did she want to deceive him?" For the boy it was simple, though at least four different aspects of honour were involved. There was the code of honour by which the lover refuses to divulge the words of the woman; the brutal triumph of the gypsy is itself a point of honour; the woman, by offering herself to the man, compelled him to fulfill his honour, and her refusal to say she was already married was a crime of honour. The honour of the married husband is also inextricably involved. The complexities are endless, but there are no subtleties among them: everything is sharply defined. It is a clear-cut world, where the debts shine as brightly as swords; and in that feast of honour which is the Spanish scene there is a complete mingling of Saracenic, Visigothic and Roman codes.

"I behaved like what I am." *Me porté como quien soy*. It is a cry that can be heard throughout Spanish poetry, as insistent as grief, as alarming as passion; and indeed there is a passionate grief concealed within the effortless and devilish appeal to singularity. There is no relief from the tension. The scholastic axiom that two contrary wills cannot possess a single aim is denied, not only by the Demon in *El Mágico Prodigioso*. Pride moves in Spain to all extremes, to the greatest loss and the greatest gains, so that the greatest surrender of power may itself be a form of pride, as when Decius discovers that he is loved by Zenobia in Calderón's *Zenobia*, and exclaims:

> *Cielos, luego tú me quieres?*
> *Perdiera cien mil victorias,*
> *Volviérame. . . .*

> Heavens, so then you love me?
> For this shall I sacrifice a hundred thousand victories,
> And flee before the enemy.

It is not surprising that the words of Decius should have been among the favourites of Schopenhauer, for here at last Spanish pride comes closest to the German. But no Spanish Don Juan would cry like Lenau's Don Juan: "I shall rely on my human strength, and with bold courage break down the solid gates of Eden, massacring the angels on guard." The Germanic terror of pride, which obliterates all things within its path, is foreign to the Spanish, who prefer their rages to assume comprehensible aims; and if the tornado destroys, it destroys without ambiguity, cleanly, according to a pattern which has been already evolved by a code of honour handed down through the centuries. "My honour is my only master," says Busto Tabera in *La Estrella de Sevilla*, and it is this boast which we hear more than any other.

Yet, though the boast is simple, there are strange overtones, sudden startling changes of direction, extraordinary accretions. The legend of Don Juan seems to have been born in Andalusia, the last battlefield of two races and two religions. Don Juan is never simple; he balances a hundred interpretations of honour in the air even by the time of Tirso de Molina, but it is significant that when we meet him first he is an arrogant youth who finds a skull in his path and kicks it aside with a gesture of mockery, begging it to dine with him. The skull accepts the invitation. The youth's arrogant pride is punished with death. Here pride is closely associated with the raising of the dead; it is death which is the enemy, and only death. But the skull, by one of those transformations peculiar to the landscape of pride, becomes the Stone Guest, and once more we are confronted with the survival of the Titans "painted over with mystic gypsum". Thereupon the battle begins, not on a single front, but on all fronts: the battle against death and against virtue, the battle which ensures the greatest accumulation of honour in all its forms. "There are a thousand ways of entering and of being oneself," says St. Teresa; and something of the mirage brightness of the Spanish scene is reflected in Don Juan's titanic struggle for survival, entering himself and being himself in a thousand different ways, till he becomes at last no more than a portrait of pride in all its forms, a strange amalgam of Cid, spiritual Don Quixote, seducer and *matamore*, that comic trumpeter and descendant of the *miles gloriosus* from ancient Spanish comedy who boasted of imaginary victories. Cyprian and the Demon in *El Mágico Prodigioso* speak alternately as though they were Don Juan, but the Demon glitters with the light which shone once on the Son of the Morning. His disguises are endless. He becomes ship, lynx, pirate and tempest:

> Then I sailed
> Over the mighty fabric of the world,
> A pirate ambushed in its pathless sands,
> A lynx crouched watchfully among its caves
> And craggy shores: and I have wandered over
> The expanse of these wide wildernesses
> In this great ship, whose bulk is now dissolved
> In the light breathings of the invisible wind,
> And which the sea has made a dustless ruin,
> Seeking ever a mountain through whose forests
> I seek a man, whom I must now compel
> To keep his word with me. I came arrayed
> In tempest. . . .
>
> (EL MÁGICO PRODIGIOSO, II. SHELLEY'S TRANSLATION)

We do not believe him, but the magical boasting goes on. "You are not to wonder that I appear as a tempest. Why, I can put out the light of the sun if I choose. I have pierced the flaming circles of the spheres!" The boasts are prodigious and delightful, but it is significant that the most wonderful boast of all suggests the wild woods of Arcadia where Hubris was born:

> Let it not seem to thee
> That I boast vainly: wouldst thou that I work
> A charm over this wild and savage wood,
> This Babylon of crags and agéd trees,
> Filling its leafy coverts with a horror
> Thrilling and strange? I am the friendless guest
> Of these wild oaks and pines.

It is only then that we realise he is of Pan's company, and not far removed from brotherhood with the Stone Guest. He rejoices in his honour, and he has an instinct for stealing it from others. Yet all through the play, and in nearly all the other honour-admiring plays of the time, we are obsessed with the thought of something left unsaid. How real are these victories? "All is a dream; let us consider our pride and our hatred in order never to return to that particular dream." It is the last saving grace, but the Spaniards are not satisfied even with this solution of their affairs, for even withdrawal from a dream may be a dream, and a dream itself may be a dream of a dream. It is only occasionally that we cut through the veils. Once, in Tirso de Molina's *El Condenado por Desconfiado*, the hermit has to go to Hell for doubting his salvation and Enrico, the brigand and assassin, goes to Paradise. Then it seems, though all values have been transformed, we are on safer ground. In *Belshazzar's Feast* thought in the abstract is assigned the comic role. There, too, the pagan good sense of the Spanish wins its victories.

It is among the contemplatives that the inconsistencies of the proud soul become dangerously confusing. Some hint of the essential confusion is given by St. Teresa herself when she speaks of the soul's conquests. "I seem to be announcing an extravagance," she says when relating the allegory of the Castle, "for if the castle is the soul, then it is clear that the soul cannot enter into it; one cannot enter the place where one is." Even St. John of the Cross, the most humble and most gentle of saints, will sometimes speak as though he were Lucifer, playing the game of identity which was played by Angelus Silesius, but oblivious of the dangers, so gentle indeed that all the glory of the heavens which he assumes for himself seems no more than a passing dream:

> *Míos son los cielos, y mía la tierra, mías son los gentes, los justos son míos, y míos los peccadores: los ángeles son míos, y la Madre de Dios y todas las cosas son mías y el mismo Dios es mío y para mí porque Xro es mío y todo para mí. Pues que pides y buscas, alma mía, tuyo es todo esto y todo es para ti.*

> Mine are the heavens, and mine is the earth, mine are men, the just and the sinners are both mine; the angels are mine, and the Mother of God, and all things are mine, and God himself is mine; for Christ is mine and all for me. Well then, my soul, what dost thou search and yearn for, since all is thine and all is for thee?

The ancient colloquy with the soul continues in the soul of this prince of saints, whose aphorisms provide a commentary to his own commentaries on his great poems. Once he wrote in his commentary to *The Dark Night of the Soul* a faintly menacing threat against pride, saying: "There are some who are occasionally desirous that others should perceive their spirituality and devotion, and for that end they give outward tokens by movements, sighs and divers ceremonies." But there are inward tokens, unuttered sighs and ceremonies which the soul alone partakes in, and of these, in his great joy with God, he is not entirely innocent. In another of his delightful aphorisms, he wrote:

> *No te pongas en menos ni repares en meajes que se caen de la mesa de tu Padre; sal fuera y glóriate en tu gloria, escóndete en ella y goça y alcançares las peticiones de tu raçon.*

> Do not in any way make yourself small, and do not stop with the crumbs which fall from your Father's table; but go from yourself and glorify yourself in your glory; hide and rejoice in it, and you shall receive all the demands of your heart.*

* I owe these quotations to Jean Baruzi, *Aphorismes de Saint Jean de la Croix*, Paris, 1924, p. 14.

Once again we see the lover gazing at himself in the mirror, Narcissus and the lake, but the mirror has taken upon itself the aspect of Christ. With the utmost gentleness the lover and the beloved confront one another, till the time comes when they become each other; and St. John lost in the gaze of Christ is Christ indeed. But if the accents are the accents of pride and the skyrocketing soul, there is implicit in the texture of so great a love a humility which goes beyond humility, into a world where neither humility nor pride have any meaning. There, love speaking to itself of love remains the final glory.

Something of that final glory is revealed in the *Spiritual Canticle*, surely the most amazing of all love poems. It is significant that at the moment of consummation St. John of the Cross invokes the symbols of earthly pride, the lions, the purple and the shields of gold:

> *Nuestro lecho flórido,*
> *De cuevas de leones enlazado,*
> *En púrpura tendido,*
> *De paz edificado,*
> *De mil escudos de oro coronado. . . .*

> Here on our flowering bed,
> Ringed round by lions
> And hung with purple,
> Builded with peace,
> Crowned with a thousand shields of gold.

> By the trace of thy footsteps
> The virgins reveal the way:
> At the touch of a flame,
> At the taste of spiced wine,
> Flows divine balsam.

> I have drunk at the inner cellar
> Of my beloved, and when
> I went forth over these meadows,
> I knew nothing——

I had lost the flock I knew long ago.

Then he gave me his breast,
He taught me the delectable ways.
I also surrendered myself,
Reserving nothing for myself,
And promised to be his bride.

My soul has employed itself,
And all my possesions are in his service:
Now I guard no flock,
Nor have any offices——
My exercise is love for him alone.

(CANCIONES ENTRE EL ALMA Y EL ESPOSO)

But the blaze of glory announced by the bride in the first five lines vanishes, to reappear for a moment in the spiced wine—the images are all oriental—and thereafter there is only the contemplation and love of the beloved. It is the inevitable progress: to pass through glory, or pass through the dark night of the soul. At the end of the *buele de espiritu* there is peace.

Even there it is the quality of honour that rules—all the oriental imagery is employed only to increase the honour of the lover; the lover claims the love of God by *dignidad*. It is nearly always the same in Spain, a personal honour, a personal scorn, something so deeply rooted in the Spaniard himself that he is unaware of its existence outside the man. No Spaniard would have said, like Fichte in his *Anweisungen zum seligen Leben:* "I am eternal and defy your (World, Time, History) might." World, Time and History would mean nothing; the pure might of the heavens would be regarded as a thing above man's dignity to assault. His pride is not rooted in absolutes, but in human relations; and indeed he never regards pride as the worst of his sins. Prudentius, the Spanish poet, when he made his catalogue of vices in the *Psychomachia* did not place pride last or at the beginning; he placed it squarely in the middle, giving the first place to the respect men possessed for the ancient gods (*veterum cultura deorum*); then came sodomy and anger; it was only after anger that there appeared the four

vices of pride—*superbia, luxuria, avaritio* and *discordia*. "Discord"
meant "heresy", and with his list of vices he rounded the circle.
Nor is there in Spain that violent belief in the powers of the dis-
embodied will which arose perhaps from that odd and infinitely
dangerous phrase of St. Thomas—"the will which moves itself"
(*movet se ipsum*). What they believed, with profound faith and
incalculable resource of love, was that man was the highest of all
things, and each man was to be approached like a god. "There is
nothing higher than man," wrote Gregory Palamas. Calderón
wrote: "The laws of honour are more than the divine laws."
"*Leyes de honor son más que divinas leyes.*" Here the Byzantine
and the Spaniard meet.

The implications of Spanish honour were endless. Corneille and
Goethe both drew their inspiration from the theme of Spanish
pride, and Faust is the direct descendant of Don Juan by way of
the Jesuit play *Leontius* which was performed all over Germany
in the late Middle Ages. But somehow the simple pride of the
Spanish people was forgotten, and this was always more astonishing than the poetry men made out of their pride, for every
Spaniard is a Cid and a Don Juan combined, and more than any
people in Europe the Spanish gaze at themselves and see themselves
gazing at themselves in the mirror of the mind.

When the Emperor Charles V was dying in the monastery at
Yuste, having abdicated all his powers, he ordered the celebration
of his own obsequies while he was still alive. He ordered his
private chapel to be hung with black and lit with tapers. Below
the altar lay his coffin, and while the monks observed the celebrations for the dead, the Emperor in a black mantle moved among
them. He heard all they said and sang. He lit a taper, wept openly
and prayed at his own death. From the tomb at Yuste came orders
to the very last: "Tell the Grand Inquisitor and his Council from
me to be at their posts." It was the most typically Spanish of all
his actions—to have observed and taken pride in his own death.

Beelzebub

WHEN Dean Swift addressed the Parliament of Ireland, taking as his text the whole problem of pride, he said: "Gentlemen, there are three kinds of pride: pride of place, pride of spirit, and pride of birth. As for the second, since no one in this august assembly can be accused of it, I shall not give myself the pleasure of referring to it."

One wonders why. If any man of his time could have expatiated on spiritual pride, it was Dean Swift, whose Gulliver is a monument to man's hovering trajectory between the extremes of pride and humility. Pride threatened him, and in the end drove him insane. "The little bacillus which is made of the air in a mirror" confronted him continually, and as he lay dying he was heard to mutter, "I am what I am, I am what I am," in a supreme effort to discover his own identity. Once he was seen threatening his own ravaged image in a mirror. "We walk through ourselves . . . always meeting ourselves," says Joyce in *Ulysses*. When Swift went on his travels, he met himself at all the corners of the world.

But when we speak of pride in England, all the delicacy of French self-communing, all the feats of strength and desolate annihilating visions of the Germans, all the *saeva indignatio* of the Irish and the magnanimous causes of honour among the Spanish seem to be absent. Instead, there is an odd indifference, a sullen determination not to take the proud man at his own evaluation, a repugnance and a kind of awkward horror at the thing. The English seem to feel instinctively that the naked human rage for superiority cannot be disguised, and is not pretty when its wrap-

pings of politeness slip down and leave it bare. When they hate
it, they hate it with a raw and furious hatred, as Richard Baxter
did when he wrote on "How the proud do hinder peace":

> They are the "turbines", the hurricanes or whirlwinds of
> the world, whose work is to overturn and to rule. He that
> cannot command the putrid vapours of his veins, nor the
> worms out of his bowels, nor will he be able to forbid them
> shortly to crawl or feed upon his face, will now damn his soul
> and shed man's blood, to obtain the predomination of his will.
>
> (RICHARD BAXTER, PRACTICAL WORKS, VI, 265)

In almost the same tones Pride speaks through the voice of
Christopher Marlowe:

> I am Pride. I disdain to have any parents. I am like to Ovid's
> flea; I can creep into every corner of a wench; sometimes,
> like a perriwig, I sit upon her brow; or, like a fan of feathers,
> I kiss her lips; indeed, I do—what do I not? But fie, what a
> scent is here! I'll not speak another word, except the ground
> were perfumed, and covered with cloth of arras.
>
> (THE TRAGICAL HISTORY OF DR. FAUSTUS, VI)

The passion behind these words springs from disgust, a contempt for pride so deep that it becomes another kind of pride
altogether, and one that it is not easy to describe, only because
it is rough-edged, hardy and not in the least vainglorious. Something of scholastic hatred survives, but there are subtle changes.
Burke said of the English that they were a fierce people, and
they were never more fierce than when confronted with the evidence of pride. Their ferocity shows itself in a deliberate effort
to make the proud man savagely ridiculous, as when the mirrors
which the devils wear in their hair in the old mystery plays—
mirrors which descend from the coloured sky-reflecting crystals
in the well of Le Romaunt de la Rose and the pool of Narcissus
—become a dripping pan:

> In comes I, Beelzebub;
> In my hands I carries club,
> On my head a dripping pan,
> And don't you think I'm a funny old man?

We do; it is one of the deliberate resources of the English that they vulgarise the things they hate, either making them more lovable or commonplace, or dismissing them with a rude word. We know the funny old man; his club is now a clown's sausage; there is still a dripping pan on his head, but his clown's clothes are prinked out with sequins and he is no longer old, for he has no age at all—he is Charlie Chaplin, Grock, the pantomime dame, and he leers at us still, and like the figure of Superbia who arose from the youth Narcissus, he can change his sex at will, *Filius Terrae*, the grotesquely joking son of the earth, as old as Pan, and therefore close to the obscure goddess Hubris who gave him birth. So he remains—the laughing and faintly sinister barroom jester, who is older than the hills.

Pride rides for a fall when it comes to England. Though Donne and Milton rave about spiritual pride, they have derived their excitement from Italian sources, and we are conscious that they write of something foreign to ourselves. Burton will annotate the degrees of *philautia* till the head swims with the calculated mystery he has borrowed from half the *incunabula* of Europe, but the proud man has little enough place in English literature. In a hundred figures Corneille has described the life of the overweening soul, but Shakespeare only once attempted the task. Hamlet is not proud, nor Anthony, nor Prospero; they do not grapple against fate; they make whatever fate they like; they are masters of their magical destiny. Only Lear, descendant of the Titans, and Caliban, descendant of Beelzebub, show lingering traces of the pride that rejoices in its own downfall. Of all English authors there is only Shelley who will speak with the authentic accents of the European tradition of pride, borrowing his substance from half a dozen sources. Marlowe's *Doctor Faustus*, the scholar who felt his soul ravished by Aristotle, who eased a thousand remedies with Galen, and mastered all the *Institutes* of Justinian—this proud soul in league with the Devil can perform no prouder miracle than to bring a bunch of grapes to the Duchess of Vanholt in January. Even Mephistopheles, entering a London hostelry in a moment of time from Constantinople, crying that he is monarch of Hell, and the greatest potentates kneel before his "black survey", is greeted by Robin with English sauce: "How, from Constantinople! you have had a great journey: will you take sixpence in your purse to pay for your supper and be gone?" When Mephistopheles threatens, for his presumption, to change him into an ape, Robin answers sagely enough: "How into an ape! that's brave: I'll have fine sport with the boys; I'll get nuts and apples enow."

Perhaps it is that there is no room for the proud in a small island where everyone is stepping on everyone else's toes. The great conquests take place overseas, and are half imaginary. When Fancy says, in Skelton's *Magnyfycence*, on the entry of Cloked Colusyon:

> By Cockes harte, he loketh hye,
> He hawketh, me thynke, for a butterfle,

he has stated the English case: all conquests, all the high-leaping antics of the proud man, all his singular collusions and deceits lead to nothing more rewarding than a butterfly or a gnat. In *Wisdom*, a fifteenth-century morality play, Lucifer speaks of "the grete drede" there is in following the contemplative life, where men have wasted themselves by abstinence:

> Then febyll ther wyttis and fallen to fondness,
> Sum into despeyer and sum to madnes,
> Who clymyt hye, hys fall grete ys.

Nothing could be simpler: the problem of pride is reduced to a common denominator, the world well lost if one can go about one's own quiet tasks. In this sense the English are closer to the Chinese than to any race in Europe. It is not, of course, that they have a passion for walking the middle way—it has never occurred to them that there is any justice in the golden rule—but the world to them is as it is; they do not dream of an unattainable Atlantis; they are familiar with tables and chairs, meadows and streams, and take their glory in them. Blake wrote on the fly-leaf of *Divine Love and Wisdom*: "There is no good will. Will is always evil." So Shakespeare will put into the mouth of Julius Cæsar the words: "The Cause is my Will," and he will put the same words into the mouth of Shylock in *The Merchant of Venice*: but both are foreigners. When an English King speaks of pride, he will do so sorrowfully, regretting that he should have dared so much and so inevitably created his own downfall:

> I have ventur'd,
> Like little wanton boys that swim on bladders,
> These many summers in a sea of glory;
> But far beyond my depth: my high-blown pride
> At length broke under me; and now has left me,
> Weary and old with service, to the mercy
> Of a rude stream that must forever hide me.
>
> (HENRY VIII, III, 2)

This is not the proud voice of the fallen Titan or of a Mephistopheles flaming down the skies; there is sickness in it, and not too much consciousness of guilt. Life has been evil and hard—we heard the same note in the complaints of the Anglo-Saxon minstrels, and they too remember their services. It is the world seen with a steady gaze after misfortunes, and a passing glance at the misfortunes of others, and a real care for people and sorrow over one's own fate. A world where men know that all the pomp of pride is utterly unavailing, since we all come to a common dust.

Perhaps it is for this reason that the English pay so little attention to the complexities and the nuances of pride, which so fascinated the Italians and the French. The unknown author of the *Ancren Riwle*, a treatise on the rules of the monastic life in the thirteenth century, is obviously bored by the complex symptoms he has read in the books of St. Isidore of Seville. He begins well enough; he promises to examine the whole problem patiently, but half-way through a kind of nausea overcomes him, and we can almost see him throwing up his hands and smiling wryly:

> The Lion of pride hath a great number of whelps, Vainglory, Indignation, Hypocrisy, Presumption, Disobedience, Loquacity, Blasphemy, Impatience, Contumacy. There are many others that are derived from wealth and prosperity, high descent, fine clothes, wit, beauty, strength: pride groweth even out of ordinary piety and pure morals. Many more whelps than I have named hath the Lion of pride whelped; but think and meditate very seriously on these, for I pass lightly over

and only name them. But wheresoever I go most quickly forward, dwell ye the longer; for where I touch lightly upon one, there are ten or twelve. Whosoever hath any of these vices which I have named before, or any like them, she certainly hath pride. In whatsoever fashion her kirtle is shaped or served, she is the Lion's companion and nourishes his fierce whelps within her breast.   (ANCIEN RIWLE, M. 198)

Thereupon the class is dismissed and the nuns go out to dig potatoes, and behave like ordinary people "with ordinary piety and pure morals". It could hardly be otherwise. The long excursions of St. Isidore do not go well in English; the fine points are lost in translation; and why should one bother, why *should* one bother, with all these strange foreign inventions? What is needed is not the heaven-leaping trapeze-artist, but more assurance, surely, a safer place on the earth. The proud man in Gower's *Confessio Amantis:*

> doth all his things by geese,
> And voideth all sikernesse.*

It is "sikernesse" that is wanted, and Lydgate in *The Fall of Princes* includes a prayer for greater "sikernesse" at the same time that he damns pride heartily:

> Ye that be wise, considreth how the roote
> Of vicis alle is pride, ye may wel see;
> Pullith hym doun and put hym undir foote
> And tak your counseil off humilite:
> And yf ye list to stonde in surete,
> Beeldith in herte for mor sekirnesse
> A tour of vertues groundid on meeknesse.

There is no end to the medieval English sermons on pride. The Early English Text Society publications are full of them, and yet we are almost never conscious of deep feeling. Pride there is—the examples of St. Thomas of Canterbury and of Wolsey and a hundred other princes remain as a warning, but we cannot quite believe that pride is taken seriously. The texts have a curiously

---

* Security.

spurious air, as though they had strayed from somewhere else and were nothing more than translations. When John Myrc, the canon of Lilleshall, who lived about the time when Chaucer was dying, came to write his *poenitentia*, he tells his parishioners they are proud if their voices are "gode and hye", their wit "gode and slye", and if they have a "renabulle tongue" and if they know their bodies are "whyte and clene", and if they take the least pride in these things, then they must seek immediate penitence:

> The forme remedy ys mekenes:
> Oft to knele, and erthe to kys,
> And knowlache wel that erthe he ys,
> And dede mennus bonus ofte to see,
> And thenke that he schal syche be.

> (EETS, INSTRUCTIONS FOR PARISH PRIESTS, P. 14)

We hardly believe it. It is not simply that we refuse to believe a comely girl who has washed herself must seek penitence by contemplating the charnel yard; but we are not even impressed by the catalogue of vices. We would believe John Myrc more if the poetry was not so obviously a translation.

But if the penitences of the early Middle Ages were not so severe as some of the priests would like us to think, glorying in their power to command penitence, there were harsh traditions deriving from the more rigorous religious laws under the Anglo-Saxon kings, when an elaborate scheme of punishments was devised for sinners. At this time no punishment was too great for the proud, since the proud were the deadliest enemies of the Church, and the Church was not yet in complete power over the people and must fight for survival. So it came about that among the punishments for sinners were chains, blows, "pollupas" (prison-darkness), to live among earthworms or swine, and sometimes also there was mutilation of limbs. Occasionally the punishment was death. There are terrible catalogues of punishments enacted under the reign of King Edgar, and the confessions demanded of the proud are extremely detailed. One such confession reads:

> I confess my mind's deadly sins, and perjuries, and enmity and pride, and recklessness of God's commandments. I confess to thee all the sins of my body, of skin, and of flesh, and of

bones, and of sinews, and of veins, and of gristles, and of tongue, and of lips, and of gums, and of teeth, and of hair, and of marrow, and of everything soft or hard, wet or dry.

It was a time of blood-curdling anathemas, where the proud man was lucky to be allowed to live. The punishment of pride, according to the Poenitential of Theodore Archbishop of Canterbury, was three years imprisonment, and this may have been in chains in the dark prison-hole behind the church. For vainglory it was the same, and for lechery it was only a little less. The *Prymer* of the Salisbury Use, composed more than five hundred years later,* shows that the usages of the past have been almost forgotten, and the penitent begs for forgiveness in softer and subtler tones:

> I have synned in pryde of herte, not lowly thankynge God of gyftes and connynge whiche he hath lent me. Also I have synned in pryde of clothynge: in strength: in eloquence: in beaute: in proude wordes—whereof I cry God mercy.

The dread tones we have heard among the Anglo-Saxon poenitentials can be heard again in the *Sollempnitas Sancti Pauli* of the Sarum Missal, where the unknown scholastic demonstrates the fearfulness of the pride of St. Paul before his conversion, and how heavily the hand of God fell upon him; and there breathes in the litany the terrible tones of the fury which the Church brings against her oppressors:

Instigatus furia dirum uirus efflabat strage seuissima membra Christi seuiens torquebat.

Lux etherea quem circumfulgens uisu priuat.

Spiritualem set ei intuitum donat.

Colafizat eum ne superbiat.

Sternit eum, set ruentem reuelat.

Deiectum increpat

Increpans emendat.

---

* Theodore Archbishop of Canterbury ruled *circa* 668-690.
The *Prymer* of the Salisbury Use from which the sinner's appeal is taken was printed at Rouen in 1438, but may have been written many years earlier. The two following quotations are taken from *Monumenta Ecclesiae Anglicae*, edited by William Marshall, London, 1846, II, 272, and *The Sarum Missal*, edited by Wickham Legge, London, 1916, p. 476.

Instigated by fury, he breathed fearful violence and with cruellest
   slaughter tortured the members of Christ.
The light of heaven shone round him, depriving him of sight,
But the light gave him spiritual vision.
Shaking him, lest he should be proud.
It lays him low, but raises him from falling.
Rebukes him when caste down
And heals by rebuking.

It is necessary to give the words in the original Latin, because
the heavenly savagery is wanting in the English. Our language
itself defies the priestly anathemas. It is one of the misfortunes
of the English tongue that we cannot curse roundly or speak with
quite that degree of *gravitas* which is possible in Latin. We say
our weightiest things almost lamely. We are not a grave people,
and when men spoke of pride in those early days there is often
a curious awareness that the dreaded adversary is not so dreaded
after all, may even be a likeable fellow, though he comes from a
foreign land. So William of Shoreham sings a little song where all
gravity has gone, and we are compelled to a kind of admiration
by the delicate vision which could see pride instantaneously in a
flowering garden, in the courts of princes and among the beggars:

> Prede suweth in floures
>   Of wysdom and of wyt,
> Amang leuedys in boures
>   The foule pride sizt.

> Under couele and cope
>   The foule prede lythe;
> Thez man go gert wyth rope,
>   That prede to him swyth.

> Prede syzt under ragge
>   Wel nobel and wel bald;
> That kepeth wordes bragge
>   And countenaunces chald.

(EETS, WILLIAM OF SHOREHAM, P. 107)

We can almost sing the tune. Nothing could be simpler, and nothing could be more passionless. The anathemas of the Church do not enter here, nor do they enter into the amazing delicacies of the fifteenth-century *Jacob's Well*, a book of contemplative mysticism, where pride is seen as an enemy, but the victories of lowliness are so certain that pride is almost dismissed with a cavalier shrug of the shoulders. "Great fishes are taken in the net and slain, but small fishes escape through the net in the water and live. Proud folk are taken in the fiend's net, and are slain in pain of death; small folk, in lowliness, escape through the fiend's net of temptation into the water of grace, and shall live in bliss." We know this country. It has all the grace and decorum we associate with the humble folk of *Piers Plowman*, and it does not surprise us in the least when the monkish author turns in his mind for an example of pride which will be intelligible to his congregation, and suddenly finds himself thinking of a wrestling match, and the champion lifting the foot of the village bully hurls him to the ground. "Right so does the fiend, when he may lift the foot of thine affection up to pride he casteth thee down to sin and to damnation. The higher he raiseth thee up to pride, the lower and the fouler fall thou shalt have at thine end in the pit of hell." But who else, except in England, would look for the uplifted "foot of thine affection"? No, the victories are so demonstrably those of lowliness that the battle is won before it is ever engaged, and the gentle prayer for lowliness contained in *Jacob's Well* has nothing whatsoever to do with the atmosphere of pride. It was in the weather of lowliness that the poor folk of the time lived, taking themselves not too seriously, and serene in misfortune; for certainly this little hymn seems to spring direct from the people's heart:

> This lownes, here in oure lyuyng,
> that we mowe be heyghed in heuen, in oure endyng,
> graunte vs he
> that for vs deyed on rode tre.

(EETS, JACOB'S WELL, P. 76)

It is gentleness, the simplest of psalms, the quietest outpouring of emotion; and it springs from the same people who could think of pride with a wry and comic intimacy, understanding it well enough, but regarding it as so much waste of good time. In *Nature*, a play by Henry Medwall written at the end of the fifteenth century, the character Pride complains solemnly that all pride is useless and it is like doing one's hair:

> I knyt yt up all the nyght
> And the day tyme kemb yt down ryght.

Why be proud? they seem to be saying: only the cuckoo loves to sing for himself alone. Why be a tree that is blasted down? Why overleap oneself when it is pleasant enough to walk? To live in peace—this is the pleasant plea they make to God:

> To lyve in ease, thy lawes to kepe,
> Graunt me grace, lorde in blys soo bryght,
> That I neuer in that caban crepe
> Ther lucifer ys lokyn with-outyn light.

The poetry walks; there is no fine frenzy of religious feeling. God is somewhere near, and you converse with him on almost equal terms, neighbour to neighbour, and if sometimes a note of intensity enters, it comes quietly, hardly knowing it is there, as when Lydgate conjures up the high waves of pride and instantly we are transported to the sea-coast:

> And lyk as foom amyd the se
> Ys reysed hihe with a wave,
> And sodeynly ys efft with-drawe,
> That men sen ther-off ryht nowht,
> Ryght so the waves of my thouht
> By pryde reysed hih a-loffte,
> With unwar wynd be chaungyd be.

But it lasts only for a moment, and never reaches these heights again. For the space of seven lines he moves with Gregory's splendid elegance, and then for four hundred lines he continues to describe pride with an aimless fidelity to the French of Guillaume de Deguilleville's *Pilgrimage in the Life of Man*, which is one of the longest pilgrimages ever made. We sigh for colour, and Lydgate never gives it to us—not for a moment is there an exclamation like Dekker's quiet prayer at the end of *Foure Birds of Noah's Ark:* "When man is proud, it is a great miserie; but when God is humble, it is a greater mercie." But then, there are not many Dekkers in English literature.

As we follow the course of pride through early English literature, it is all soft low-land, with pastures and shady woods; no eminences; only occasional knolls. The people are going about their business, and it would hardly occur to them to be anything but humble. Not for them is the thirst of Farinata degli Uberti as he entertains his scorn of Hell. Somewhere, lost in the gentle depths of their minds, there may have been recollections of the Anglo-Saxon forebears, of the Thorgils and the Thorgeirs, "who are afraid of nothing at all". They fear God, but they fear him gently. If Cardinal Manning told them, as he told a later generation, that the effect of a mortal sin was to strike the soul dead, they would have nodded their heads and passed on to other things. If they hated pride, what they hated chiefly was foppishness in dress, decorated cod-pieces and skin-tight trousers. Chaucer's Parson inveighs against all these, and also against a certain proud misuse of nakedness:

> Allas! some of hem shewen the boce of hir shap, and the horrible swollen membres, that semeth lyk the maladie of hirnia, in the wrappynge of hir hoses; and eck the buttokes of hem faren as it were the hyndre part of a she-ape in the fulle of the moone. And moore-over, the wrecched swollen membres that they shewe thrugh the disgysinge, in departinge of hir hoses in whyt and reed, semeth that half hir shameful privee membres weren flayen.   (THE PARSON'S TALE, 420)

This was one kind of pride; there were many others. In the *Hous of Fame* Chaucer hurls himself into an invention concerning spiritual pride, following at a great distance a story already told in the Babylonian inscription describing the ascent of Etana to the sun. Etana desired to make love to the goddess Ishtar, who reposed in the sun, so he fashioned for himself a basket glued to an eagle's wing. The eagle led him to the heights, but when he looked down at the earth from his perch in mid-air, he saw it no larger than a lake, then no larger than a date-seed, and gradually he grew dizzy. He never reached the sun, for when the eagle came close to the sun's rays, the glue melted and the basket fell to the earth.

Chaucer follows the ancient story closely. There is a similar basket, a similar goddess and a similar eagle. The poet mounts into the basket, sees the earth dwindling, wonders at his own pride, and describes the journey in almost the same words as those used by Etana millenniums before. He enters a strange landscape. Down below is the zodiac, the Milky Way, clouds, mist, snow, rain and winds. He hears the words of Fame sounding like the waves beating against the rocks of heaven. This heaven is all of ice, and somewhere at the top there is a house—the house of Fame, made of beryl and full of windows, with minstrels playing near. There are jugglers and conjurors and golden gates, and then his eyes fall on the towering goddess before him. She had seemed like a dwarf, but now she reached from heaven to earth. She had crisp and wavy hair that shone like burned gold:

> Hir heer, that oundy was and crips,
> As burned gold hit shoon to see.
> And soth to tellen, also she
> Had also fele up-stondyng eres
> And tongues, as on bestes heres;
> And on hir feet wexen, saugh I,
> Partriches winges redely.
>
> (THE HOUS OF FAME, 1386)

She stands in the high hall among the iron pillars, and we suddenly remember that we have seen her before, for this immense goddess was present to Keats when he wrote the second Hyperion, and indeed Keats knew Chaucer's *Hous of Fame* well. She is Moneta, the Titan goddess, who gazes down among the fallen rocks upon the supplicant, her face "bright-blanch'd by an immortal sickness that kills not". There are echoes of Chaucer's poem throughout the second Hyperion; there can be no doubt of the identity. And so it is that across the centuries the Babylonian shepherd, Chaucer and Keats meet by a miracle of accident.

The figure of the immense goddess in the icy House of Fame is not Superbia; the pride lies in the poet who dared to make the imaginary journey. He was reasonably proud of his adventure, and said so: the tremendous leap is accomplished alone and with a complete absence of any religious scruple: it is an essentially pagan work, full of a fresh, bubbling coarseness, as when there comes to the goddess people demanding the rewards of fame and she commands Eolus to blow on his brass trumpet:

> And swiche a smoke gan out-wende
> Out of his foule trumpes ende,
> Blak, blo, grenissh, swartish reed,
> As doth wher that men melte lead.
>
> (THE HOUS OF FAME, 1645)

One does not write such attempts to unveil the mansions of heaven with impunity, and when Chaucer leaves the House of Fame and finds himself confronted with a mysterious "man of greet auctorite", the poem comes to an abrupt end. Goethe, Hölderlin and Keats were to break off in dismay when confronted with the princes of heaven, their poems broken and their eyes dazzled.

So far we have followed the lowland plains, where a few dark-robed priests move among green fields and the peasants pray to the sound of the angelus. Caedmon had written of the "Angel of presumption" and seen him bathed in a lake of fire, and during the time of the early Anglo-Saxon kings pride had been a power to be reckoned with; but in the early Middle Ages man's presumption was for the most part tamed by a natural humility in England. Now gradually there arise the steep outcroppings of the great mountain which gleams with a fiery light, and then vanishes.

Suddenly, and for no reason that can be traced, there appears in English poety an explosion of pride so colourful that it is breathtaking. It is as though all the pent-up emotions of the lowly peasants were released in a fury of astonishment and delight. Chaucer had written the majestic line which suggest the coming of this delight. *Hyde, Absolon, thy gilte tresses clere*. There are other occasional lines among his work which have the same resonance, but there is nothing in the whole of English poetry up to the time of Marlowe which gleams and glitters with the feverish pride of Herod in the York play. Why it should be Herod and not Lucifer, no one knows. Why there should be put into the mouth of Herod a boast more glorious than any boast of Tamburlaine's remains a mystery. It was one of the more disarming qualities of the English that they could never take pride seriously, and they had none of that tenderness for the soul's image of itself which characterises the French. But here, written for a performance at Candlemas and paid for by the masons of York, is all the soul's sweetness and pride in its own discovery, and every kind of boasting. Herod advances to the centre of the stage, throws up his hands, and while pretending to show his power over the infant Jesus, he sings in a language which is strange to us now but well worth the effort to discover his meanings:

> The clowdes clapped in clerenes that ther clematis in-closis
> Jubiter and Jouis, Martis & Mercury emyde,
> Raykand ouere my rialte on rawe me reioyces,
> Blonderande ther blastis, to blaw when I bidde.
> Saturne my subgett, that sotilly is hidde,
> I list at my likyng and laies hym full lowe;
> The rakke of the rede skye full rappely I ridde,
> Thondres full thrallye by thousandes I thrawe when me likis;
> Venus his voice to me awe
> That princes to play in him pikis.
> The prince of planetis that proudely is pight
> Sall brace furth his bemes that oure belde blithes,
> The mone at my myght he mosteres his myght;
> And kayssaris in castellis grete kyndynes me kythes,
> Lordis and ladis loo luffely me lithes,
> For I am fairer of face and fressher on folde
> (The soth yf I saie sall) seuene and sexti sithis,
> Than glorius gulles at gayer than golde in price.
>
> (THE COMING OF THE THREE KINGS TO HEROD)

The self-praise of Herod is of a kind that had never appeared before in poetry. The clear clouds trailing one behind the other above his realm rejoice him, the thunder is his to throw, he can "rapely ride the rack of the red sky", and speaking of his own beauty he does not say in the conventional phrase of the Townely Herod—"clear-shapen, hide and hair, without lack"—but with a soaring simile which paints a picture of wide, wheeling sunlit wings: "I am fairer than glorious gulls that are gayer than gold." It was something that even Marlowe, shouting of the pampered shades of Asia, was never to accomplish. The authentic accent is here: this is the pride that makes the Church tremble, for it embraces the heavens and the earth and all the sweetness between them in the shape of a towering sunlit bird—the skylark; the nightingale will follow, but none will sing with such delight in itself. But this is not quite the end. In the same play Lucifer speaks in almost the same tone:

> In a glorius gle my gleteryng it glemes,
> I am so mightly made my mirthe my noghte mys,
> As sall I byde in this blys thorowe brightnes of bemes
> Me nedes noghte of noy for to heven,
> All welth in my welde haue I weledande,
> Abowne thit sall I beeldand,
> On heghte in the hyeste of hewuen
> Ther sall I set my selfe, full semely to seyghte,
> To ressayve my reuerence thorowe righte o renowne,
> I sall be lyke unto hym that es hyeste on heghte.

> (THE CREATION AND THE FALL OF LUCIFER)

Yet it is not the same: something precious has gone: the same voice speaks, but it is becoming wearied with the strain of upholding pride. What Bunyan called "the holds of Defiance, mid-night hold and sweet-sin-hold" have disappeared. Why it should have gone, why the note was never again to be so sustained, is clear: such notes tremble on the edge of poetry into something else—into pure breath. In a moment Herod, like Narcissus, will be drowned in the well of self-love.

We hear Herod's voice again in another miracle play. There is power in it, but not that trembling power:

> I am king of all mankinde,
> I bid, I beat, I loose, I bynde,
> I maister the Moon; take this in mynde,
>   That I am most of myghte.
> I am the greatest above degree,
> That is or was or ever shall be.
> The Sonne it dare not shyne on me,
>   As I bid hym goe downe.

No rain to fall shall now be free;
Nor no Lord have that Liberty,
That dare abide, and I bid flee,
But I shall cracke his crowne.

(ADORATION OF THE MAGI)

But it is in the Chester Play of *The Fall of Lucifer* that we come
closest to the original impetus that made the York Herod what
he is. Here once more, in the words of Sir Thomas Browne, we
hear how "the Devil, like an insolent champion, beholds with
pride the Spoyles and Trophies of his Victory in Adam", but the
irregularity of Herod's verse gave pith and substance to the matter,
as it does in Shakespeare, and this new Lucifer, though free, is
bound by rhyme and metre:

Lucifer

Aha! that I am wounderous brighte,
Amonge you all shynning full cleare;
Of all heaven I beare the lighte,
Though God hym selfe and he were heare.
All in this throne yf that I were,
Then shulde I be as wyse as hee . . .
Destres! I commaunde you for to cease,
And see the bewtye that I beare;
All heaven shines through my brightnes,
For God hym selfe shines not so cleare.

Lichtborne

In fayth, brother, yett you shall
Sitte in this throne, that is cleane and cleare,
That ye mighte be as wise withall
As God hym selfe, yf he were heare;
Therfore you shalbe sette here,
That all heaven may you beholde,
That brightnes of youer bodye cleare
Is brighter then God a thousande foulde.

Potestates

Alas! that pryde is the walle of bewtye,

That tornes youer thoughte to greate offence:
The brightnes of youer fayer bodye
Will make you to goe hense.

Lucifer

Goe hense! behoulde, seniors, one everye syde,
And unto me you caste youer eyne:
I charge you, angelles, in this tyde
Behoulde and see nowe what I meane.
Above greate God I will me guyde,
And sette my selfe heare as I wene;
I am pearles and prince of pryde,
For God hym selfe shines not so shene.

God

A! pryde! why mighte thou not barste in towe?
Why did the that, why did the thus?
Behoulde, my angelles, pryde in youer fooe,
All sorowe shall shew wher soe ever yt is.

(THE FALL OF LUCIFER)

In the cry of *Potestates* there is one of the great quatrains of
English poetry, the immediate ancestor of Nashe's *In Time of
Pestilence*. It is astonishing enough that Lucifer should speak as he
does, having in spite of the tight rhymes the breathlessness in-
separable from the exercise of glory in high altitudes, but there is
no flash of unbearable brilliance: it burns with a slow fire. We are
left to wonder why it is Herod who should have all the poetry, as
he does again in another fragment of another mystery play:

Of plesaunt prosperyte I lakke non at all;
Fortune I fynde, that she is not my foo. . . .
My grett goddes I gloryfye with gladnesse,
And to honoure them I kneel on my knee;
For thei have sett me in solas from all sadnesse,
That no conqueroure nor knyght is compiared to me.

(HEROD'S KILLING OF THE CHILDREN)

The first line rings majestically, but the rest is a wayward coasting downhill. After the great explosion of the York play nothing comparable follows. There are other treasures to be found in the mysteries, but the exaltation of human pride is not one of them. For a moment, in the Coventry play called *The Council of the Jews*, we have a gleam of the Englishman's sardonic attitude to fine clothes, when Satan harangues his lieges and counsels Poverty to arrest Pride for wearing a goodly pair of long-peaked shoes, made of Cordovan leather, hose of crimson cloth, very costly, with a dozen points of kid leather, the tags of fine silver; a shirt of fine holland, a stomacher of clear Reynes cloth, the best purchasable; Cadiz wool to stuff a doublet; two small legs and a great body. The trap is sprung in the last seven words, but we are far away from the golden bird hovering in the sunlight in "the rack of the red sky".

Marlowe and Milton follow. They are giants, but it is permissible to ask whether either could have written without the discoveries made by the unknown poets of the mysteries. The true satanic fumes and witches' brews were prepared before their coming. Even

> That perfect bliss and sole felicity,
> The sweet fruition of an earthly crown

is pale compared with Herod's dreams of power. Though spiritual pride is derided by the hostlers in *Doctor Faustus*, there is evidence enough of it in *Tamburlaine*, in the giant murderer who

> Scalds his soul in the Tartarian streams,
> And feeds upon the baneful tree of Hell,
> That Zoacum, that fruit of bitterness,
> That in the midst of fire is engraffed,
> Yet flourishes as Flora in her pride.
>
> (TAMBURLAINE THE GREAT, II, II, 3)

and in a hundred other trumpet-flourishes in the great plays, but the most remarkable portrait of pride which Marlowe left behind is in the portrait of Hero the faire,

> Whom young Apollo courted for her haire,
> And offred as a dower his burning throne,

> Where she should sit for men to gaze upon.
> The outside of her garments was of lawne,
> The lining purple silke, with guilt starres drawne,
> Her wide sleeves grene, and bordered with a grove,
> Where Venus in her naked glory strove. . . .
>
> (HERO AND LEANDER, I)

And so it goes on, a poem written in endless pursuit of the process of glory at a time when men were stepping forth and glorying in themselves, in their beauty, their fierce and untrammelled powers to exert themselves to the uttermost, but in a sense the trump-card was still held by the Church—these overweening powers condemned themselves.

The image of the Titans, however, returns with King Lear, who raves amid the lightning-strokes and calls in despair for the whole world to crack wide open:

> Blow windes, and crack your cheeks; Rage, blow;
> You cataracts and Hurricano's, spout,
> Till you have drench'd our Steeples, drownd the Cockes.
> You Sulpherous and Thought-executing fires,
> Vaunt-curriors to Oake-cleaving Thunderbolts,
> Sindge my white head. And thou all-shaking Thunder
> Smite flat the thicke Rotundity of the world,
> Cracke Nature's moulds, all germaines spill at once
> That make ingratefull Man.
>
> (KING LEAR, III, 2)

It is one of the great explosions of consciousness—so Zeus might have spoken in his rage against Cronus, and indeed there are overtones from Hesiod in the tragedy. There are also overtones from an unexpected source: so great a desire for destruction is only to be found outside *King Lear* in the *Nibelungenlied*. When the Gentleman describes Lear in his utmost misery, the wild thirst of the defeated will reaches its heights. Lear tears his white hair, and in "the night wherein the cub-drawne Beare would crouch, the Lyon, and the belly-pinched Wolfe keep their furre dry, unbonneted he runnes, and bids what take all." It is not till Melville that we shall hear that cry again.

Elizabethan pride never recaptured the first glory of Herod's speech. Chapman's Bussy d'Ambois will exercise the elements and pull himself up on buskins till he has the stature of a god, but once more we are made conscious of a foreign source. Except in *King Lear* Shakespeare, superbly humble, did not paint pride, perhaps because he could not. There is Anthony enthroned in the market-place, sitting alone. There is Cæsar conscious of his fate like a hero of Corneille, but their pride seems to be something not of themselves, but placed around them. *The Phœnix and Turtle* states the debate of pride, the two faces confronting themselves in the mirror, but it states so many other things that pride is lost in the witchcraft and the subtleties. If we are to find the note of authentic pride again in the Elizabethan circle, we must look for Calantha, the king's daughter in John Ford's *The Broken Heart:*

> O, my lords,
> I but deceiv'd your eyes with antique gesture,
> When one news straight came huddling on another
> Of death, and death, and death: still, I danc'd forward;
> But it struck home, and here, and in an instant.
> Be such mere women, who with shrieks and outcries
> Can vow a present end to all their sorrows,
> Yet live to vow new pleasures, and outlive them.
> They are the silent griefs which cut the heart-string.
> Let me die smiling.

This is not a *Medea superest*, but something far more complex: a grief which turns into a triumph, a solemn vow to endure and to die dancing. It is one of the supreme moments of our poetry, and puts Milton's roaring Satan to shame.

Milton's Satan marches to the brass bands of the Cromwellian Republic of England. This perverse and petulant *miles gloriosus* is the only one of the characters who never comes adequately to life. When he appears the action sags, the scenery sways, and the violent flames are no more than painted bunting stretched over the stage. It is not sufficient to state the fact of rebellion. There should be a recognisable voice belonging to the truly rebellious soul, and this voice is not heard:

> . . . before that cloudy van,
> On the rough edge of battle ere it joined,
> Satan with vast and haughty strides advanced,
> Came towering, armed in adamant and gold.
>
> (PARADISE LOST, VI, 107-110)

We would be happier if we believed it was real adamant and real gold, if Satan spoke even once with the voice of delirious, self-conscious freedom, if he was not so obedient to Milton's purposes. He is too calculated a figure, too innocent of real harm, and when in the seventh book we see him as one

> whom now transcendant glory raised
> Above his fellows with monarchial pride
> Conscious of highest worth,
>
> (PARADISE LOST, II, 428-431)

only to find him in the tenth book a monstrous serpent on belly prone, we are not convinced: the pasteboard is only too evident, the fall from heaven has been no more than a fall from a stage ladder.

This is not in any way to underestimate the sense of pride which informed Milton himself. His desire for supremacy, even a kind of ultimate supremacy, derived either from his Italian journey or something innate in himself. The Church wisely regards profound scholars with suspicion; and Milton possessed a more intricate scholarship than the famous doctor of Wittenberg. His phenomenal rages, his desolate hatreds, the fury of his invective and his sudden lapses into the extremes of weariness, all these are indications of a personal pride so great that it approaches to madness, and even to self-destruction, for there can be no doubt that in *Samson Agonistes* Milton drew a portrait of himself. Like Dante he was so full of pride that he was not convincing when he described the proud; by hints and by other signs we recognise the guilt. But here and there, occasionally and then only for the briefest moments, he reveals the secret, as in the great reverberating phrase which seems to hold itself separate from the rest:

> So clomb this first grand Thief into God's fold.
>
> (PARADISE LOST, IV, 192)

It is enough; we hear the beating of the eagle's wings.

"Milton," said Blake, "was of the Devil's party without knowing it." Milton almost admits the charge. He said of himself that he had "reasonings, together with a certain niceness of nature, an honest haughtiness, and self-esteem either of what I was or what I might be (which let envy call pride)."

With John Donne we are on firmer ground. He too had gone to Italy and returned an Italianate Englishman, vicious according to his fashion. There is a fierce pride in his letters till grief ended it; thereafter, seeing the metaphysical heaven through gaps of brightness, he charms God out of Heaven by his poetry and in the great hymns orders the saints and even God about with delightful effrontery, which is not pride, but rather the result of impatience in his natural heart.

When Donne talks of pride, he denies himself, and makes poetry out of the denial. He begins his famous sermon on Pride with the statement that "Solitude is not the scene of Pride; the danger of pride is in company, when we meet to look upon another," then proves the contrary. For he goes on a little later: "Nay, we gather Pride, not only out of those things, which mend and improve us (God's blessings and mercies), but out of those actions of our own, that demolish us, and ruin us, we gather pride; sins overthrow us, demolish us, destroy and ruin us, and yet we are proud of our sins." He remembers St. Augustine's reproach on the pride of men who boast not of their virtues but of their vices, and pounces upon the text: *Sequere, Follow, come after*, and plays with it proudly, but with a delicacy that makes us tremble at the enchantment of the dialogue between himself and pride. He admits to the sin. He almost delights in admitting to its universality, and despairs gracefully because even children strive for place and precedence—"Mothers are ready to go to the Heralds to know how Cradles shall be ranked, which Cradle shall have the highest place; Nay, even in the womb, there was contention for precedency: *Jacob* took hold of his brother *Esau's* heel, and would have been born before him." There is pride at birth; there is also pride at death; and he remembers Jerome when he speaks of those with a holy pride who desire to be buried close to the martyrs' graves, even though they had never been to church in their lives, or if they came to church it was only for the sake of being seen. And this is not the end of it: there must be large annuities for the up-keep of the grave, perpetuities "for new painting of the tombs, and for new flags, and scrutcheons, every certain number of years."

So far the sermon is playful enough; there is no bite to the words: Donne is engaged in being seriously amused by human follies. Then suddenly, from the heart, there comes the cry against the evil of pride, a cry which is more lyrical than his litanies, so single in its purpose that it is like a note of music rising and falling into grief.

> O the earliness! O the lateness! how early a Spring, and no Autumn! how fast a growth, and no declination, of this branch of this sin Pride, against which, this first word of ours, *Sequere, Follow* come after, is opposed! this love of place and pre-cedency, it rocks us in our Cradles, it lies down with us in our graves.

It is an extraordinary achievement to have complained of pride so urgently that we hear across the centuries the voice of the complaint, the very timbres of his urgency. The *spontanea insania* and *voluntarius daemon*, the wilful madness and demon of pride, are not castigated, but soared above, outreached, almost defied in the brief prayer which ends his sermon. So it is, too, in the famous sermon concerning the tolling of the bell—he is better at his con-clusions than in his beginnings, and indeed the beginnings seem to have been often only an excuse for those lyrical and enchanting songs which conclude them. When he puts on his singing robes and composes against pride a litany, he becomes hardly better than any hymn-writer:

> From thinking us all soul, neglecting thus
> Our mutual duties, Lord, deliver us.

We feel the passion; but it is the passion of weariness, and even of artifice. We are left in no doubt of the elementary meaning: the mind does not take flame as it does when he cries out against the mysterious earliness and lateness, which somehow, by some trick of rhythm and phrasing, seem to include between them the whole human condition. But the delicacy and artificiality of the metaphysical poets should never blind us to the depth of feeling in their poetry: they are often most desperate when they conceal their most intimate thoughts in lace. In *Epithalamium* Crashaw forces an entrance into the heart of pride with exquisite gentleness:

> A fine thin negative thing it was,
>   a nothing with a dainty name,
> which preened her plumes in self-love's glass
>   made up of fancy and fond fame;
>   within the shade
>   of its own wing
>   it sate and played
>   a self-crowned king,
> a froward flower, whose peevish pride
>   within itself itself did hide,
> flying all things, and even thinking much
>   of its own touch.

Nothing could be more fragile or more delicate, but the splinter of ice is embedded in the heart. It was embedded again when Abraham Cowley wrote of "the slave in *saturnalibus*, who thinks himself a real prince in his masking habit, and deceives too all the foolish part of the spectators." Hobbes, too, played delicately with pride, inventing a dialectic of "the imagination of power", but it was too tenuous to take root. Vaughan, in his strange *Vanity of the Spirit*, sees pride clearly and then disengages himself from the struggle:

> I summon'd Nature; pierc'd through all her store;
> Broke up some seales, which none had touch'd before;
>   Her wombe, her bosome, and her head,
>   Where all her secrets lay a bed,
>   I rifled quite; and having past
>   Through all the creatures, came at last
>   To search myselfe, where I did finde
>   Traces, and sounds of a strange kind.
> Here of this mighty spring I found some drills,
> With ecchoes beaten from th' eternal hills.
>   Weak beames and fires flash'd to my sight,

> Like a young East, or moon-shine night
> Which shew'd me in a nook cast by
> A peece of much antiquity,
> With hyeroglyphicks quite dismembered,
> And broken letters scarce remembered. . . .

Here the passion of pride, and the failure of pride, are seen and understood. But generally in England the experience has been rare. When Hume writes of pride in *A Treatise of Human Nature*, he is like a man scrambling for shell-fish among the rocks:

> It is evident that pride and humility, though directly contrary, have yet the same object. This object is self or that succession of related ideas and impressions, of which we have intimate memory or consciousness. But though that connected succession of perceptions, which we call the *self*, be always the object of these two passions, 'tis impossible it can be their cause, or be sufficient alone to excite them. . . . Beauty, considered merely as such, unless placed upon something related to us, never produces any pride or vanity.

Such dullness reminds us again that the English have failed to understand pride through most of their history. When Theodulf, Archbishop of Canterbury before the Norman Conquest, made a list of the capital sins, he placed them in the following order. First gluttony, then lust, then acedia, avarice, vainglory, envy, anger and pride. St. Aldhelm slightly changed the order by placing gluttony first and drunkenness second. Even Pope, who suffered abominably from the vice, is hardly convincing when he describes it:

> Of all the Causes that conspire to blind
> Man's erring judgment and misguide the mind,
> What the weak head with strangest bias rules
> Is *Pride*, the never-ending voice of fools.
> Whatever Nature has in worth denied,
> She gives in large recruits of needful pride. . . .
>
> (AN ESSAY ON CRITICISM, 201-206)

But twice at least Englishmen have written superbly concerning Pride. There was Richard Hooker whose *Learned Sermon on the Nature of Pride*, based upon the text of Habakkuk: "His mind swelleth, and is not right in him; but the first by his faith shall live," moves at times with quite extraordinary grandeur. It is not a perfect sermon; it wanders from its subject, and Hooker himself is haunted by his own digressions; but the stately sixteenth-century prose trembles with indignation which is not the less moving because Hooker seems to be seeing continual evidence of the sin in himself. He is more like Gregory than Jerome; he butts his head against the wall, and dares not play with the thing he abhors, that "token of the very imminent breach and of inevitable destruction". He determines to examine the cause of the sin and the dangers which arise from it, and already at the beginning he seems to choke at the throat, held to his purpose only by the immensity of the *crimen laesae maiestatis*, which it is his purpose to punish in words, for pride is

> a vice which cleaveth so fast unto the hearts of men, that if we were to strip ourselves of all faults one by one, we should undoubtedly find it the very last and hardest to put off. But I am not here to touch that secret itching humour of vanity, wherewith men are generally touched. It was a thing more than meanly immoderate, wherewith the Babylonians did swell. Which that we may both the better conceive, and the more easily reap profit by, the nature of this vice, which setteth the whole world out of course, and has put so many even of the wisest besides themselves is first of all to be enquired into: secondly, the dangers which it draweth inevitably after, being not cured: and last of all the way to cure it.
>
> (HOOKER: WORKS, 551)

But there are almost no ways to cure it. He sees it like a continual thundercloud which never moves away, trickling down into men's hearts, perpetually darkening their souls. "For, as Judas's care for the poor was mere covetousness; and that frank-hearted wastefulness spoken of in the gospel, thrift; so there is no doubt but that going in rags may be pride, and thrones be challenged by unfeigned humility." He can see no use for pride; its horror is only too manifest. Like Christopher Smart, who wrote in *Rejoice in the Lamb:* "Let Huldah bless with the silkworm—the ornaments of the Proud are from the bowels from their betters," he sees pride as something on the edge of scatology; there are terrible dark areas where the mind cannot move, one goes by one's senses and everything turns blood-red. Virtue and vice in these regions are equally deplorable. In a paragraph which Coleridge copied out entire in *Aids to Reflection* Hooker snarls majestically at the whole creation of elaborate vice and elaborate virtue: there is no way out. His prose jerks like the desperate cries of Dostoievsky's epileptics:

> What is Virtue but a Medicine, and Vice but a Wound? Yea, we have so often deeply wounded ourselves with Medicine that God hath been fain to make wounds medicinable; to secure by vice where virtue has stricken; to suffer the just man to fall, that being raised he may be taught what power it was which upheld him standing. I am not afraid to affirm it boldly with St. Augustine, that Men puffed up with a proud Opinion of their own Sanctity and Holiness received a benefit at the hands of God, and are assisted with his Grace when with his Grace they are *not* assisted, but permitted (and that grievously) to transgress. Whereby, as they were through overgreat Liking of themselves supplanted (*tripped up*), so the dislike of that which did supplant them may establish them afterwards the surer. Ask the very soul of PETER, and it shall undoubtedly itself make you this answer. My eager protestations made in the glory of my spiritual strength I am ashamed of. But my shame and the Tears, with which my Presumption and my Weakness were bewailed, recur in the songs of my Thanksgiving. My Strength had been my Ruin, my Fall hath proved my stay.   (HOOKER: WORKS, 556)

No more dangerous *devise* could be found than in the last bold words in which Hooker had impenitently attempted to justify his error. Coleridge approved of it, because it sang with romantic resonance; it was the eternal cry of the fallen Titans, still thinking themselves in heaven. Even Hobbes, who delighted in kingship and the ordered hierarchies, could say of pride only that "it was a passion, whose violence or continuance, maketh madness." It was, he said, a great disorder of the mind, and once started upon, could have no end. Hooker goes on his own way, one of the few Englishmen who have battered their heads against that wall and out of the encounter derived a kind of strength. In *Piers Plowman* pride is dismissed in nine lines of humble pleading; envy has over a hundred, and avarice still more. It seems as though Langland had no heart to describe pride; it was something beyond him, though he will complain against the presumption of those who wear finery. The English are always complaining about pride; they hardly know, though, what they are complaining about. When Pythagoras, according to Plutarch, passed among the people assembled at the Olympic games, he showed them his golden thigh; the Englishman would have done no such thing, but would probably have complained about the weather and the price of entry to the games.

There is something almost mysterious in the Englishman's refusal to take pride seriously. Once in an old Anglo-Saxon play, again in the York play and once in the heavy pondering of Hooker he saw it plain. He pretended to see it, or rather Spenser pretended to see it in Orgoglioso and the Palace of Pride which raises its obscure bulk in the *Faerie Queene*, but this pretence deceived no one; the rare metal is not present; even Queen Lucifera and her six sage counsellors, who together make up the seven deadly sins, are decorative stuff, too flimsy to survive—a mere breath can blow them off the stage. So it is nearly everywhere else in English poetry. To find pride described perfectly again, though negatively, we must got to the great poet of our own times who wrote in Italy after the war:

> Pull down thy vanity, I say pull down.
> Learn of the green world what can be thy place
> In scaled invention or true artistry,
> Pull down thy vanity,
>   Paquin pull down!
> The green casque has outdone your elegance.
>
> "Master thyself, then others shall thee beare"
>   Pull down thy vanity
> Thou art a beaten dog beneath the hail,

A swollen magpie in a fitful sun,
Half black half white
Nor knowst'ou wing from tail
Pull down thy vanity
           How mean thy hates
Fostered in falsity,
           Pull down thy vanity,
Rathe to destroy, niggard in charity,
           I say pull down.

(PISAN CANTOS, LXXXI)

But even when Ezra Pound, the last of the Italianate English-men, more English than the English by being American, speaks of a subject he knows well, we are aware of no hidden meanings and few subtleties. Pride is "fostered in falsity", "a swollen mag-pie in a fitful sun", and there is an end to it. The magpie will die a natural death, and soon enough pride is forgotten, abandoned, left to rot. It had little enough part in the English scene.

The German Agony

IF A Greek dramatist had been alive during the years of the war against Hitler, he would have been able to watch a typical Greek tragedy staged against an arena which embraced the whole world. Once again, as so often before, overweening Hubris was to be confronted with implacable Nemesis. It was one of the axioms of the Attic stage that the innocent should suffer; it was also an axiom, broken only once by Sophocles, that the tragic hero should die in a blaze of agony. Germany was the blind hero who, by his overweening pride, brought destruction upon himself.

The German sense of pride went deeper than the Italian; there were dragons in the German soul. For the Italians pride was nearly always young, a thing of leaping astonishment even to the Italians themselves: the Germans took no delight in their pride, for they knew its fatal tendencies from the beginning. Siegfried must kill the dragon and bathe in its blood. Kriemhild must treacherously fire the palace where her closest friends are asleep. At the end of the *Nibelungenlied* Kriemhild unsheathes the sword of Siegfried and kills Hagen, and she in turn is killed by Hilde-brand—*diu vil michel ere was da gelegen tot.* "The very great glory there lay dead." Always, at the end of the German road, there was the vision of the World Destruction called the *Muspilli*, the avenging flames, the very great glory lying dead.

The story of German pride begins perhaps with the Anglo-Saxon epic of *Beowulf*. On the sea-coast of Schleswig, where the sea-caves were deepest, there rises the monster Grendel. Who is Grendel? There are few clues. She is never fully described. She belongs to the past, to some previous dispensation, and she has about her something of the archaic fury of the Flood in the *Iliad*. She is all the released forces of chaos, before civilisation had acquired its empire over men; and she is also the beast that tempts men's pride. Almost Beowulf is Achilles. Achilles bore a shield; Beowulf carries a sword on which was engraved "the origin of the primeval quarrel, when the Flood, the rushing Ocean, destroyed the giant's brood". Somewhere behind the legend of Beowulf there is another legend of the Titans' overthrow. And in fact pride, the fall of the Titans and the heaven-leaping aspirations of the hero have a cardinal place in the epic; Hrothgar's famous speech on pride lies somewhere at the centre of the whole legend.

It is a strange speech, for it carries echoes of Aristotle, Sophocles, and even of St. Gregory: not all of them can have been accidental echoes. This is not Greece: there are no gold helms flashing, no oiled and naked Achilles in the bright sunlight. All is grey and cloudy, and Hrothgar's great warning sermon comes like thunder out of the darkening storm:

> Here was a man who became great, not for the pleasure of the Skyldings, but for the sake of mortal combat and the giving of death-blows to the Danish leeds. He, in his ungoverned fury, crushed his closest companions, the people of his body, till at last he wandered forth alone, the great King, away from the companionship of men, even though Almighty God had with the attractions of strength and power exalted him above men. Nevertheless, within his soul there grew a bloodthirsty passion: he was not of those who give presents of rings to the Danes according to their deserts. So he went on, apart from human joy, suffering the penalty of the outrage in the face of his people's hate for him.
>
> Therefore take warning of this: know well the ornaments of man. It is about thee that I, now old in years, relate this story.
>
> Wonderful it is how Almighty God with large understanding dispenses the intelligences of men, giving them position and powers to hold the dispositions of places. Sometimes He

allows the purpose of men of noble race to turn towards possession, giving them earthly joy on His estate, to hold the citadel of men, assigning him regions of the world so extensive, a kingdom so wide that he in his unwisdom is not able to carry his thought to the end; he dwells in prosperity, nor does anything torment him, nor does age and sickness and deep care darken his spirit; he has no quarrels, nor any feuds; the whole world moves to his mind; he knows no reverses.

Then at last within the man himself something of arrogance grows: then sleeps his guardian, the soul's keeper; his sleep were too fast and deep, the assassin is near who from his arrow-bow shoots in malice. Then the helmeted man is smitten in the breast with the bitter shaft: he cannot defend himself from the crooked demanding counsels of the damned spirit; all that he has enjoyed, he fancies too small: with covetousness and malice he is; he no longer glories in the pomp of bestowing gold; he forgets the ends; he considers too lightly how God, who dispenses glory, once gave him his dignity. In the end it comes to this: the shrunken body falls away, life drips from him, another takes his place. Guard thee, O beloved Beowulf, from this course.   (BEOWULF, 1709-1759)

No one would ever have dared to speak to the great heroes of the *Grettis Saga* in this way. Thorgils says: "Thormod fears God, and Grettir is so afraid of the dark he would not stir, but I do not know that Thorgeir, my kinsman, is afraid of anything." Beowulf's pride is humbled, but it is humbled as the pride of Œdipus was humbled. There is still the Dragon to be fought. He must go on, all his humility set aside as he confronts the final blaze of destruction, caught up in the toils of an ineluctable power greater than himself. It is wholly German, this final surrender to destruction against "deadly scorching fire, blast and poison", the three elements of the concentration camps. Beowulf says:

In my youth I fought many wars, and now again will I, the aged keeper of the people, seek strife and do famously, if the terrible beast from the earthy cave will come forth to meet me. I would not bear sword or weapon against the Dragon, if I knew how I could otherwise maintain my pledge against the monster, as once before against Grendel. I expect deadly scorching fire, blast and poison. It is for this reason that I carry sword and shield. I will not flee away from the Keeper of the Mountain—not a single foot; and it shall be decided between us on this mountain, as fate allows, the governor of all men.

I am in spirit so eager for action that I cut short boasting against the winged warrior. Wait for me on the mountain with your shields about you, O warriors, and see which of us after mortal combat shall survive his wounds. This is not your task, nor any man's, but mine alone to strive against the monster and achieve glory. I must with daring conquer gold, or else war will bear me away, pitiless death carrying away your lord.   (BEOWULF, 2512-2537)

This is not the fierce boasting of the sagas: it is more reasoned and compassionate, but with the terrible compassion of the German soul in sorrow over itself, knowing that the end is vain, and all the spirit's perturbations end only in nightmare. Against this defeated triumph the ceremony of his burial on Hrothness comes as an anti-climax to the epic which had begun with the unbelievably beautiful burial of another hero, Scaef, in the dead of winter, on a ship covered with icicles, golden shields flashing in the winter sun. Beowulf has failed because he is compelled to pit himself against his own dread; for the same reason the heroes of the sagas spend their energies against trees and rocks when there is no living adversary within reach; and so Gudrun in the *Nibelungensaga* takes vengeance on her husband and gives him the blood of her own children to drink before stabbing him in his bed, and so Hadubrand in the *Hildebrandslied* must inevitably slay his father. In this world of grey smoke, encircled by serpents, enormous heroes who come out of the dusk clothed in the mist-cap, the *Tarnkappe* which makes its wearer invisible and gives him the strength of twelve men, everything has the strange distorted look of nightmare. Are the swords real? Is the blood real? Is the final destruction, to which so many of the authors look forward as though it provided a moment of rest at the end of a journey, more real than the struggles on earth? There is a split in the soul somewhere, and Walther von der Vogelweide, the most enchanting of the songsters, saw the darkness and the brightness of the German soul long before Hitler revealed it for us:

> *Diu welt ist uzen schoene, wiz gruen unde rot,*
> *und innan swarzer varwe, vinster sam der tot.*

> The world is fair to look on, white and green and red,
> but inwardly it is black of hue, and dismal as the dead.

"Rot", "tot"—it is the inevitable rhyme in German, life pouring into death the tribute of their resemblance; and what is strange is not that the Germans were perfectly aware from the beginning of the split in the soul, but that they failed entirely through the centuries to heal it. For the Germans the *persona* of authority was nearly always the anarchic hero, saying like Kleist's Penthesilea: "I should go mad if I did not attempt all that is within the bounds of possibility." But it was not only the possible that was attempted; the Faustian magus sees God and desires to shine with His splendour, but at the same time he desires to live in the apocalyptic moment of the world's end. The two are probably irreconcilable.

It was the fashion in the Middle Ages to make drawings of the seven capital sins. By some curious fate no sufficient iconography of the deadly sins was ever attempted; the goddess Superbia walks under an infinity of disguises, and nowhere is she more completely disguised than in the early German engravings. Now she is a woman riding on a dromedary, with a peacock crest, an eagle shield and a banner showing a crowned lion; at another time all her splendour has been taken from her, and she is an old and naked woman glaring at herself in the mirror. Superb engravings of her were to be made by Altdorfer and Landenspelder, but she changes with every artist. The artists were remote from the theological quarrels and the theological visions. When St. Hildegaard of Bingen in one of her visions comes upon Pride face to face, she is at her wits' end to describe what she has seen, and combines a kind of glory with the most extraordinary distaste: the thing is seen to be unclean, yet she cannot entirely prevent herself from a wistful note of admiration. In execrable dog-Latin she describes the awful mud-spattered, winged and truncated thing:

> For this first image seemed to possess the face of a woman, whose eyes were of fire, whose nose was spattered with mud, and whose mouth was closed (*cujus oculi ignei, et nasus luto aspersus, et os clausum fuit*). She possessed neither forearms nor hands, but at the upper arms there were attached wings like bats' wings, the right wing facing the east and the left the west. She had the breast of a man, and her feet and legs were like those of locusts, and there was neither stomach nor back to her. Nor was there any hair on her head or on the rest of her body, nor could I see any clothing over her, except that which derived from dark shadows; but there was a kind of rope, like a golden circle, which passed through the top of her jawbones and through her chin.
>
> (ANALECTA SANCTAE HILDEGARDIS
> SPICILEGIO SOLESMENSI PARATA, VIII, 106)

Almost we can believe in the vision! Nothing like this animal had ever appeared in literature before; its bonelessness brings it perilously close to the famous *nyedotichomka* of Gogol, which possessed only a slit for a nose and a hole for a mouth. The golden ring, which fastens the mouth, derives from the scholastic belief that the mouth of Satan opened so wide that it extended from heaven to earth. The mud-spattered nose, at first so perplexing, is no more than an abstruse insult, for the nose, because of its position in the middle of the face, possessed a peculiar importance in medieval times from the superstition that its blessed position was ordained by God, and was most like to Him, and possessed a peculiar resemblance to the genital organ; and for a husband to smash in his wife's nose was therefore taken as the supreme punishment. The bats' wings belong to the earliest iconography of the devil; the locusts appear to have been invented by the visionary saint without any foreign assistance. The terrible beast of pride no longer frightens us, but it is conceivable that to Hildegaard of Bingen the vision was as terrifying as Blake's ghost of a Flea.

This extraordinary portrait of pride might be compared with

the Superbia of Cesare Ripa's *Iconologia* which appeared during the full flood of the high Renaissance:

> She is a beautiful and wanton lady, nobly gowned in red, crowned with a gold crown inlaid with innumerable gems, her right hand holding a peacock and her left a mirror in which she admires and contemplates herself; and she is robed in red because pride finds itself most particularly among choleric and sanguine men. . . .   (ICONOLOGIA, V, 255)

Red faces, red robes. . . . The red robe of Beatrice. . . . It is a delightful portrait, and belongs wholly to the Renaissance, while Hildegaard's portrait belongs still to the world of Grendel, to the creeping things of the earth. The German thirst for the sunlight of Italy is explained by the confrontation of the two portraits.

But if the Italians possessed a *terribiltà* of their own, there were occasions when the German *terribiltà* had a curiously Italian flavour. When Meister Eckhardt assails God, he performs this act of supreme defiance with something of the boldness of Frederick II assailing the Pope. For him there is nothing of what Savonarola was later to call a *"subtilli soperbia"*; all is harshness, defiance, the spirit leaping for the assault. He makes his famous defence of sin:

> For God mostly sends the burden of sin to people for whom He has provided a higher destiny. See, who was dearer to our Lord or more intimate with him than His apostles? None of them but fell into mortal sin, and all were mortal sinners.

Eckhardt delights in his contraries, insists upon them and uses them as weapons with which to assault the heavenly fortress. Nearly all the twenty-four statements for which he was excommunicated can be read as examples of spiritual pride, and most terrible of all in the sight of the papal chancellery must have been the statement that "the eye with which I see God is the same as the eye with which God sees me." His will was formidable. He wrote once: "I would stake my life upon the fact that by strength of will a man may pierce a wall of steel." At another time he wrote: "Even God cannot thwart the humble soul that has towering ambitions," but in the most devout of his sermons he admits the futility of pride: "If thou seekest ought of thy own, thou wilt never find God, for thou art not seeking God merely. Thou art seeking something with God, thou art making a candle of God, as it were, with which to find something, and then having found it thou throwest the candle away." He is always complex, and continually denies his premises, for "God is in oneself," but "one must stand aside from God to find God." It is almost Fichte's "I am absolutely because I am," a philosophy without laws and therefore without system, but expressed continually in the most violent and rugged prose. The divine wings have broken against his head; he holds himself proudly and urges all men to so hold themselves:

> You are whatever you love. Do you love the earth? Then you become the earth. Do you love God? Then you are divine. But if I love God, do I become God? I do not say this, but I refer you to the Scriptures which say: "You are gods and the sons of the Almighty."

The evasion, which has all the appearance at first of being delicate, may also be regarded as a fierce side-stepping to avoid the charge of heresy. In the most characteristic of his stories he is heretical to the last degree. He tells of coming upon a poor man. He bids good-day to this man, asks about his health and where he has come from. The poor man answers that he has come from God, like all other creatures. "Who are you?" "I am a King." "Where is your kingdom?" "In my soul: for I rule over my senses in such a way that all my desires are at the mercy of my soul." "And who led you to this perfection? How did you become so holy?" "By my silence, my high thoughts and my union with God." There is no equivocation: "*Das tat mein Stillesitzen und meine hohen Gedanken und meine Vereinigung mit Gott—das hat mich in den Himmel gezogen.*" The road to Heaven was never so easily traversed.

Eckhardt is heady wine, and part of the reason lies in the perpetual indefiniteness of his vocabulary. He was compelled to give words more meaning than they could bear; and his conception of spiritual honour and spiritual nobility, which was to have a lasting influence on German theology, leads him into statements where honour and nobility acquire a dubious meaning. "The very great glory there lay dead" of the *Nibelungenlied* is resurrected in his work, and he speaks as often of *der edele Mensch* as Kierkegaard, less ambiguously, speaks of the Knight of the Spirit. But on the flinty landscape of his imagination he sometimes strikes sparks that turns into explosions of lightning, as when he speaks of Paul's cry, "I would that I were cut off from God for my friends' sake," as the greatest example of God's love demonstrated in a human heart, for in saying this "God is surrendered for the sake of God." At this point his own pride seems to double up upon itself, turn itself inside out and then destroy itself utterly: what is left is not pride, devil nor God, but something entirely other.

The furious rage in him is characteristic of German theology; the will is employed as a battering-ram against the fastnesses of Heaven. The desire to invade heaven is so strong, the temptations of earth are so weak and the *persona* of authority in the shape of the Heavenly Father is so heroic that the contest is never completely fought out; and in the process it is heaven that is destroyed, not man. The severity of German theology, and even its brutality, are witnessed by Luther, whose characteristic cry was: "*Hier stehe ich und kann nicht anders.*" For Luther God was a heroic and overmastering warrior, dauntless and beyond the laws of chivalry. "Yea, he is more terrible and frightful than the Devil; for he dealeth with us, and bringeth us to ruin with power, smiteth and hammereth us and payeth no heed to us." Or again: "God in his majesty is a consuming fire." It is all daemonic, grotesque and full of strange pride. In the commentary on the Epistle to the Romans, an epistle to which German theologians are continually returning, Luther says: "*Blasphemiae . . . aliquanto sonant gratiores in aure Dei quam ipsum Alleluja vel quaecumque laudis jubilatio. Quanto enim horriblior et foedior est blasphemia, tanto est Deo gratior.*" "Blasphemy sometimes sounds in God's ears more agreeable than Allelujahs or solemn hymns of praise; and the more frightful and repulsive the blasphemy, the more agreeable it is to God." One wonders why.

Luther lives in a strange, unapproachable world of the heaven-storming will. The existence of such a world had been suggested by Plato in the *Theætetus:* "All things are to be dared. What if we essayed to cast modesty aside?" Luther, indeed, has no qualms: he will cast modesty aside, renounce the Church, see no good in man, who is only *Stock, Stein, Eisen, Teufel, hart*—stick, stone, iron, devilish, hard. He despises man, and desires Heaven. "It is not permissible to man to soar into the height of majesty," he says, and immediately soars. There is paradox everywhere. He throws his ink-pot at the Devil and blasphemes at God and denies good works, though his own translation of the Bible is the most formidable of good works.

With the contemplative mystic Boehme we are on more humble ground, yet here again we can hardly breathe for the fierce smoke of the alembics and anthanors from which he pours the coloured liquids signifying evil and good. He speaks of "the Divine Mercury, or Snowy Splendour, the Celestial Body drawn from the beams of the Sun and Moon," and this Mercury has its counterpart in the earthly Mercury. He explains that the earthly Mercury is pride. At all costs the "heart of the poisonful Mercury" must be destroyed, but as he continues his experiments, the poisonful Mercury always seems to remain. He explains how the will of the poisonful Mercury went out from the will of the divine-speaking Word into its own self-will, and so falls into "the centre of the pregnatress of all essences, that is, into anguish, poison and death, where God's anger took possession of it." But what then? Only God's love and the complete alteration of the will by love is of any avail:

> God must become man, man must become God, heaven must become one thing with the earth, the earth must be turned into heaven. If you will make heaven out of the earth, then give the earth the heaven's food, that the earth may obtain the will of heaven, that the will of the wrathful Mercury may give itself in unto the will of the heavenly Mercury.

There is no other hope: the self-will must be clothed with God's love, but first it must enter into Sulphur, "the first mother which brought it forth". There are no terms too hard for pride. It is "the contrary will, the desire of the abominate, the lust of death". The lust must die, the mother must thrust her child back in the womb, the darkness of pride must be extinguished by a greater darkness. Like Luther assaulting God, Boehme assaults the devil

of pride; and sometimes he stumbles wildly in the assault, there
are confused roars among the alembics, the smoke drifts from the
anthanors, the Greek Lion of the alchemists seems about to engulf
them all in its maw; then the cloud clears, and the poetic voice of
Boehme is heard above the tumult, a voice like an organ, full of
despair and at the same time full of majesty. In the *Aurora*, the
first and most beautiful of his works, he describes the Devil in his
toils:

> Now being that he was so beauteously and gloriously
> Imagined or formed as a King in Nature, his beauteous form
> and feature tickled him, and so he thought with himself,
> *I am now God;* and formed or framed out of God; who can
> vanquish me? or who can alter or change me? I *my selfe* will
> be Lord; and with my sharpnesse rule in all things; and my
> *Body* shall be the image which shall be worshipped; I will
> prepare and erect for myself a new Kingdom; for the whole
> Circumference Extent or Region is mine, *I am God alone,* and
> none else. . . . And in his pride he struck and smote himself
> with darkness and blindness, and made himself a *Devill,* and
> that he must be and abide for *Eternally.* . . . He wrestled
> with the Salliter of God in the flash of fire and anxiety.
>
> (AURORA, XV)

The superb coda adds nothing to our knowledge of the conflict
of pride, but it brings us closer to the coloured liquids in the
intricate vials. Boehme is rarely revealing in his paragraphs; it is
the odd sentences, thrown off in the heat of his strenuous conflicts,
which reveal the nature of the strange hermetical chemistry he
proposes to describe. He returns to the theme in *The Threefold
Life of Man,* and nearly everything is told in another superb sentence: "For the fierce power of the Fire delighted him more than
the meekness of the still habitation." It is in these regions that we
find ourselves convinced. Why did all this happen? he asks himself, and invents, or borrows from hermetical sources, the image
of the fiery mirror:

> Thou askest, what was that which did cause it in himself?
> Answer, his great beauty and glory. Because the will beheld

what itself was in the fiery mirror, this lustrous glance did move and affect him, so that he did eagerly reach after the properties of the centre, which forthwith began effectually to work.   (MYSTERIUM MAGNUM, IX)

The astonishing simplification, the transmutation of the cool lake in which Narcissus admired himself into a blazing mirror, deriving perhaps across the centuries from the bronze mirrors of the bronze age, the clarion note of certainty and of careful deliberation, all these raise Boehme to the position where it can be said of him that he fought the Devil with arms worthy of the contest, but always he returns to the death which Mercury must suffer, the thrusting back "into the dark Matrix, into the anguishing Mind, into the sinking down of death".

The dark matrix has many names in Boehme. Sometimes he calls it the *Schraak*, the ancestor of the Kierkegaardian *Angst*. It is the living hell of the mind given over to the contemplation of earthly things. Mercury, according to Lydgate in the *Secrets of old Philosoffres*, "disposethe to chaunge and doublenesse," and no one ever hated Mercury so much as Boehme, and against "that which is called I, this vile selfhood" he waged impenitent and continual war. Blake, who read him avidly, followed in his footsteps, and Boehme even printed the stamp of his own mind on Angelus Silesius, the Cherubinic Wanderer, yet no two men could have been more different. Boehme writes and thinks in terms of long, complicated paragraphs; Angelus Silesius' thought is all clearcut apothegm. It is permissible to doubt whether Boehme was ever completely sure of himself; the self-assurance of Angelus Silesius leaps from the page. Boehme evades issues, returns to them, erects complicated edifices, tumbles them to the ground; Angelus Silesius simply speaks direct from the heart, simply, ecstatically, and without any feeling for nuance. Boehme, living among the fuming liquids of his alembics, sees shadows in the smoke; Angelus Silesius is always in the broad daylight. It is simple to reach heaven, he says: all that is necessary is that men should be thoroughly God-made (*vergottert*). This Catholic of the Counter-Reformation is the least Catholic of men; he announces his own theology. "*Æternitas Esto.*" "Be eternity." "*Sei nicht.*" "Be not!" It is as simple as that. The self-will is the enemy. If he had the least trace of self-will, Christ would have fallen. He uses "will" in all the senses: there is the other will which leads directly to God. Sometimes it is not possible to tell whether he is speaking in tones of overweening pride, or of the greatest humility: the serpent bites its tail, the wheel turns full circle, the ecstatic note in the humility sounds strangely foreign to us, and yet when Angelus Silesius says: "I am as great as God," "I am myself Eternity" "I must be Mary," "God is nothing," we are appalled, as we are with the blasphemies of Luther. The curious and delicate will of Angelus Silesius is like the interior of the baroque churches in which he worshipped: the heaven-reaching Gothic pillars have been transformed into a rose-garden. He is like Blake in his visionary belief in angelic presences around him—the seraphim even cart dung. Once he said: "The dead will rules," "*Der Tote Wille Herrscht*," and then at once he seems to be speaking with a voice of authority, which is the voice of the oracle. Sometimes violence breaks through. "I love and hate myself. I made war upon myself. To get the victory over myself I use force and practise strategy, I batter and kill myself. I do all that I can to be no longer I." Yet we cannot always trust his motives, and it is a singular footnote to his quiet determination to become God and kill the I that, on the occasion of a pilgrimage to a saint's shrine in Trebnitz, he asked and received from the Emperor permission to carry the Cross through the town, wearing the Crown of Thorns "in order that thereby I may become like unto Christ who also carried the Cross through the town, wearing a Crown of Thorns." There is a baroque perversity somewhere in this man who was known among his friends as the possessor of the most feverish and burning eyes, and whose walk was as measured and determined as the walk of *megalopsychos*. There are even moments when he terrifies. He carries Eckhardt's theory of nobility to the edge of the abyss:

> The highest nobility upon this earth is mine.
> I may become Emperor, King, God or anything I will,

and yet the statement is no more than Boehme's: "*So du heiligt ebest, so bist du selber Gott.*" "If thou art become holy, then thou art God Himself." "Now God demands of thee nothing more imperatively than that thou shalt go out of thyself, so far as thou art creaturely, and let God be God in thee." Angelus Silesius plays endless variations on this theme of Eckhardt: and in the most beautiful of these variations, he writes a famous poem of Shelley's three centuries before Shelley wrote it:

> I must myself be the Sun, and with my rays
> Stain the uncoloured Sea with my divinity.

He is continually likening himself to God:

> I flow into God like the streams of Time,
> And become myself the Sea of Endless Holiness.

> The depths of my spirit cry unto God's depths
> With screaming voice: O, who is deeper then?

> I am as rich as God. Dear friend, believe me:
> No particle of dust that is not His and mine.

> I know God cannot live a moment without me:
> If I should come to nothing, God shall cease to be.
>
> (CHERUBINISCHER WANDERSMANN, IV, 146; I, 115;
> IV, 135; I, 68; I, 14; I, 8)

"Was willst du thun, Gott, wenn ich sterbe?" wrote the poet Rainer Maria Rilke. "What wilt thou do, God, when I die?" and Angelus Silesius seems often to be preoccupied with the same problem, but he passes on quickly, there is never any grief, the holiness must be captured in those bright, chiselled and gleaming rhymes, thrown off as effortlessly as a child will throw off a song. But the I remains, gleaming at him with its tigerish eyes. "The Devil without his I would be God," he says simply, but on another occasion he said: "Load a live charge in your gun," and it is hardly possible to believe that the charge is not a charge of will. He is all contradictions, the brightest of antitheses: "Go out—God goeth in; die to thyself—live to God; be not—He is; do naught—His kingdom come." The presentation is often wilful, the glorying in the negative will is often singularly close to a glorying in the positive will, there are even moments when he seems to have

lost his foothold in the Still Wilderness and appears to be about to break out into fierce crying for the *deus absconditus* who was not there after all. Eckhardt wrote once: "Not only does God give birth to me as His Son, he gives birth to me as Himself and Himself as me, He gives birth to me as His own essence and as His own nature." There are times when the simple dialectic seems in danger of failing, when the harsh voice uttered from Eckhardt's pulpit is more convincing than the thinner notes of the cherubinic wanderer. Angelus Silesius is on more fruitful ground when he says that "man himself makes Time, the senses are the machinery of the hours (*das Uhrwerk sind die Sinnen*), and if you could only quieten their rest, then Time is gone." At such moments piety and love take the place of the singular brightness with which he colours the image of the self. He died in 1677, weak and despondent, suffering from a nervous disease of the eyes, only too aware that the fifty-five pamphlets he had composed against the Lutherans were ineffective, and that Catholicism was never to obtain its hold on the Germans as he desired. It is said that he hanged himself.

Less than a hundred years after his death there occurred in Germany the beginnings of the romantic revival, the sudden opening of the flood-gates. The quickening temper of the times demanded a victim; the most august of all victims was authority. The primacy of the individual was upheld. When Angelus Silesius wrote: "The whole world is at my service: how noble I must be," he was already announcing the anarchic axioms of romanticism, and indeed the romantic poets leaned heavily on the German mystics, and the problems which perplexed Boehme and Angelus Silesius are precisely the same problems which perplexed Goethe and the host of smaller romantic poets. Listen to Ludwig Tieck in his novel *William Lovell:*

> My outer self thus rules the material, my inner self, the spiritual world. Everything is subject to my will. I can call every phenomenon, every action whatever I please. The animate and inanimate world are in leading-strings, which are controlled by my mind: my whole life is only a dream, the many forms of which I mould, according to my will. I myself am the only law in all nature, and everything obeys this law.

It is almost Angelus Silesius speaking, but with looser rhythms, a vaguer terminology. God disappears. The will wills itself; the I sees itself; everything obeys the I's law. But does it? We are never quite certain, for everything is dream. Silesius says: "I do as God does," and makes the mystery greater by suggesting a continual interchange of earthly and heavenly affections, for he continues: "God loves me more than He loves Himself, and I love Him more than I love myself: therefore I give Him as much as He gives me of Himself." Among the romantics the affectionate intercourse between man and God give place to an affectionate intercourse between man and Nature, with Nature in the position of being the recipient of man's occasional grace. When Schelling in 1795 proclaimed the I as the principle of philosophy, and commanded that the self should be removed from the circumference and placed at the centre, saying that "the self is nothing different from its own thought, and the thought of the self and the self are absolutely one," he was merely assuming a logical conclusion for the theme which had been insistent in Duns Scotus and in Eckhardt. "The system of Nature is at the same time the system of our spirit," Schelling stated categorically. "Nature is the visible spirit, the spirit is invisible Nature." It was a little too efficient, this transmutation of the elements "I" and "Nature"; and it was accompanied by no birth-pangs. The horrors came later.

In the interval, however, the delights were continual. Man was not only the lord of the universe, he was the universe thinking itself man. It was a universe where poets wandered freely, delighted by the new aspect of things. Angelus Silesius, with disarming contrariety, had gazed down from Heaven at man disguised as God; the romantic poets did not ape Narcissus, confronting his own beauty in the mirror, but preferred to ape the mirror confronting itself in Narcissus. This is by no means an exaggeration, for Novalis in the *Lehrlinge zu Sais* says as much freely:

> At the well of freedom we sit and spy; it is the great magic mirror wherein serene and clear the whole of creation reveals itself; herein bathe the tender spirits and images of all natures, and here we behold all the chambers laid open. And when we wander from this view into Nature herself, all is familiar to us,

and without error we recognize every shape. . . . It is all a great scroll to which we have the key.

Into this miraculous fairy-land, "the Still Wilderness where no one is at home," the romantic poets wandered as though they had come into their heritage, dreaming that the familiar objects were known to them, though in fact they were strangers. Nor did they possess the requisite keys, for the wilderness was guarded and its inhabitants obeyed laws that were entirely different from the laws they thought applicable. Kafka was to stumble into that landscape later, and discover that there were no laws at all. The romantics imagined laws, obeyed them, expected the inhabitants to obey them and were occasionally delighted to discover that they did so, or gave the appearance of doing so; in fact they were deliberately imitating the laws of the invaders for their own safety. The territory was to be mapped by Blake, Hölderlin, Keats and even (though he retired early) by Goethe; but Novalis never penetrated more than a few inches into that no man's land of the imagination. It was not enough to utter magic spells, or to say, as one of Novalis' characters says, almost in the words of Fichte: "Man is lord of the world, and he can reduce all things slowly to the immutable laws of his own being (*die Feste seines Ichs*)." There were traps here, as elsewhere; the appropriate gestures might be forgotten, or the spells might be uttered at the wrong place and time. Even in Novalis, hymning Night as Leonardo da Vinci once hymned the Sun, there is a note of failure even at the beginning; and we feel that he knows his magic landscapes have been borrowed from the Middle Ages. In the interval the real landscape has changed, and his own maps refer to something which no longer exists.

The Alpine guides are sometimes known to point to dangerous pathways, saying they are *nur für Schwindelfrei*—only for those who never suffer from vertigo. Their own vertigo obsessed the romantics; it was not only that they delighted in it, but they acquired from it the sensation that they were in movement towards some familiar end. They had driven the I to its logical conclusions, only to discover that after a certain point, beyond a certain temperature, the I no longer behaves logically. Where there should, according to the theory, have been mastery and the most exquisite enjoyment of the self, dragons appeared; and they were no less terrible because they had also been conjured out of the hot romantic imagination. Jean-Paul Richter, meditating upon Fichte's ego in his *Leibgeber-Schoppe*, discovered a *Döppelganger*, a mysterious Brocken-spectre which beckoned menacingly and accompanied him wherever he went. The ego split in two, and each watched the other, and doubted in the other's credentials. It was discovered too late that in places where the egos begin to split up like parthenogenetic amœbas, distinctions can hardly be verified. More frightening still, the ego sometimes went berserk, and somewhere in the depths of every man's soul there was a masquerader disguised as Nero, who desired to writhe like a beast and perish in the flames. Jean-Paul Richter describes the process in his novel *The Titan:*

> There is in man a callous bold spirit, which asserts its independence of everything, even of virtue. Man chooses virtue if he will; he is its creator, not its creature. . . . Do you believe that the authors of tragedies and novels, or at any rate the geniuses among them, who a thousand times over have aped everything human and divine, are different from me? . . . The apes are the geniuses among the beasts, and geniuses are apes in their æsthetic mimicry, in heartlessness, malignity, sensuality and gaiety.

The apes rule: nothing must be allowed to contradict the fierce will of the ape. "The will will suffer no law superior to itself," says Friedrich Schlegel, "but must expand towards the desired state of limitless satisfaction." Inevitably, the will by becoming lawless became confused. Since everything was possible, where should one begin? No one seemed to know. Hegel attempted a dialectic of the State, transferring the will of the *Ich* into the hands of a remote, imaginary and unfathomable entity called "the Germanic spirit". "The Germanic spirit is the spirit of the new world, whose object is the realisation of absolute truth as endless self-determination of freedom, which has its absolute form itself for content." Absolutes crowd the pages, and a dialectic of the purest nonsense was invented by Hegel in an effort to provide an interpretation of the universe. This dangerous nonsense, revived later by Marx and Hitler, was purely incantatory. Had not Novalis remarked: "The time of incantations has come again," as though incantatory periods were to be expected in cycles? The end comes with Hegel's final discovery that "the function of the true State is so to act that individuals do not exist."

There seems at this late date no way by which the madness can be stopped. "All power to the *Ichheit*," cried Schelling, and almost simultaneously Fichte and Hegel were proclaiming: "All power to the State," which seems to have been considered as a breathing, sentient and conscious thing. Because the romantic philosophers stumbled upon a conception of *Ichheit* which was not humanly valid, but possessed enticing prospects and a dialectic of its own, and because the characteristics of self-consciousness could be assumed to be applicable to political parties, over a hundred million people have met violent deaths. The price of pride has indeed been annihilation.

The fault, perhaps, lay in the times. We can accuse Hegel and Fichte of being responsible for National-Socialism, and Hegel alone can be placed on trial for his furtherance of a conception of the State beloved by the communists; it is more doubtful whether Kant can be accused of the crime of starting a revolution in moral philosophy when he desired to make the will autonomous, instead of making it bow before a law superior to itself. There is a sense in which the most dangerous of all modern statements, more dangerous even than the final verdict of the State elaborated be Hegel, is Kant's dictum in the *Critique of Pure Reason* that "One may therefore say of the thinking I that it does not know itself through the categories, but knows the categories only, and through them all objects, in the absolute unity of apperception, that is through itself." For from this statement spring our present miseries; and for Hegel it was no more than a hair-breadth between "the I knowing all objects through the categories, in the absolute unity of apperception, that is through itself," and the State possessing the same indivisible autonomy; and after Schelling had enunciated the theorem that the self is "*kein Ding, keine Sache*", the State could consider itself (if it could think) as immune from the invasions of the self, since the self possessed no substance. Between

Ludwig Tieck's "I myself am the only law in all nature, and everything obeys this law," and the National-Socialist State under Hitler there was hardly any difference, for in both cases mythologies were speaking; the real and tangible world of human needs and aspirations had been pitchforked clean out of the door.

But there were many who saw the dangers ahead. Kleist, who threw his spirit spinning into the realms of the impossible, returned to admit failure: the vertigo had been too much for him: he had lost himself on the journey. In his *Penthesilea* he speaks stubbornly and angrily about the rewards of the impossible journey:

> *Das Aüsserste, das Menschenkräfte leisten*
> *Hab ich getan, Unmögliches versucht,*
> *Mein Alles hab ich an den Wurf gesetzt:*
> *Der Würfel, der entscheidet, liegt, er liegt:*
> *Begreifen muss ich's—und das ich verlor.*

> The utmost that human powers can do, I've done;
> And I have sought after impossible things:
> I set my all against a throw of the dice,
> The deciding die is cast, is cast,
> And now I must confess, I have lost!

> (PENTHESILEA, IX)

The loaded dice of the will, the desire "to grasp what is lost" —all this was part of the game as it was played by the Germans. "The dead will rules," said Angelus Silesius. It was the "dead will" which led the Germans to their excesses, to their lawlessness and to the rewards of their pride—the dreaded *Muspilli* or World Destruction, the devouring and licking flames. With Hitler the dark self-righteous pride of the Germans reached its term. Quiet, cynical and calm, speaking with the self-assurance of a sleep-walker, Hitler announced that the most terrifying of all wars must be fought only because he was there to lead the Germans to victory. "You must understand that everything depends on me," he said to his generals. "No one will probably ever again have the confidence of the German people as I do. There will probably never again be a man in the future with more authority." It was enough: at that moment the kindling-wood for the *Muspilli* was being fired, and in the flames he was to meet his own death, desiring at the last moment that the whole of Germany should be transformed into a made-desert uninhabitable by men. Hubris had conquered at last the man whose pride had set the world in jeopardy. The tragedy had completed its cycle. These would be a brief intermission. Then once again the tragic actors would take the stage, suffer the same passions and receive the same punishment: for it is the tragic destiny of Germans to suffer from destructive pride.

The Pride of France

THERE is a gentleness in the land of France and a brilliant clear air which sends one dreaming of Greece. Not so long ago the cathedrals shone white above the fields of corn, and only a little later Ronsard wrote that "all France is a green garden", and then another three hundred years passed and a young German poet Friedrich Hölderlin, coming across the Auvergne in winter, suddenly saw himself in Provence face to face with men like Greek gods. To him the French were legendary athletes, unbelievably god-like, the light of life flowed from their limbs and eyes, and merely to watch them was to be exhilarated by these "geniuses of nature". He may have been exaggerating, but what is certain is that the French have preserved many of the qualities we associate with the ancient Greeks: the love for the middle way, for intellect, for clarity, for splendour and for the sun.

Each country has its own characteristic sense of pride. We come to recognise in time the careless pride of the English, we learn the dangers of Spanish *honor*, and from Faust's speech to Mephistopheles we derive a hint of the German's desire to live on the edge of the emotions, and on the edge of destructiveness. With France there are none of these things: the pride is gentler. The unrelieved pain, the endless despair, the horror which wilfully adds to itself means nothing to these people who led the forces of Europe against the Saracens, and learnt from the Saracens how to sing. Vastness, diffuseness, the insane ramblings of heaven-challenging Titans had no appeal for them. Why challenge heaven, they must have asked, when heaven is so like France? But outrageous and overweening pride was theirs. Hardly anyone in the whole history of France made so superb a boast as the authoress of the charming Breton *Lays:* "I will tell my name that I may be remembered. I am called Marie, and I am of France."

The fundamental beliefs of the French were simple. No Frenchman could have said, like Ibsen's *Brand*, that the day would come when the scattered fragments of his soul—those torsos of the spirit, those heads, those hands—would one day make a noble whole. They were already conscious of being whole. The clear daylight shone on them. It is significant that when Rémy de Goncourt came to define pride, thinking perhaps that he was defining it for all time, he defined it as only a Frenchman could—in terms of the *clarté* which is every Frenchman's birthright, as it is the birthright of the gods: "Pride yields as quickly as possible and retires upon itself, proud of what it is and disdainful of what it is not. The pride of the gods is clear-sighted." The clear sight, the desire for excellence, the pursuit of the whole appears in the cry of triumph of Satan in an early mystery play:

> *J'ay tout gaigné, j'ay tout gaigné,*
> *J'ay fait un hault fait, un chef d'oeuvre.*

We shall hear the same note again from the lips of Valéry and indeed from a thousand Frenchmen. French love of self is so quiet that it seems to be delivered always in a whisper: Narcissus confronts himself in the lake, smiles, and there is only the ripple of wind on the water. It is very much what we might have expected. In French cathedrals no huge Pantocrator glares down from the painted dome; there is no frenzy of desire to imitate God, for there is almost no God—instead, the blessed Virgin offers her blessings from the rose windows, as one might offer flowers. So it is that in the whole history of French pride we never hear the shaggy voice of an Angelus Silesius declaiming that he is as great as God, as rich as God, as eternal as eternity. It is simply not the French way. Nor can the French take Lucifer seriously. In *Le Vrai Mystère de la Passion* of Arnoul Greban, Lucifer is so unbelievable in the role of accuser of this world that he is asked why he screams like a famished wolf: why not laugh and cry and smile and sing like any reasonable mortal?

> *Lucifer, roy des ennemis,*
> *Vous hurlez comme ung lou famis,*
> *Quand vous voulez chanter ou rire.*

Lucifer explains that he can only sing unhappy songs, and laments his past beauty, speaking of his beauty in such a way that we are not entirely convinced it has gone from him; and then he goes on to complain that his glory has become only a dolorous rage—*douleureuse rage*—and only his pride remains:

> *Ma noblesse et ma grant beaulté*
> *Est tournée en difformité,*
> *Mon chant en lamentacion,*
> *Mon ris en desolacion,*
> *Ma lumière en tenebre umbrage,*
> *Ma gloire en douleureuse rage,*
> *Ma joye en incurable deuil;*
> *Ne demeure que mon orgueil*
> *Qui ne m'est moue ne changé*
> *Depuis le jour que fus forgé*
> *Lassus au perdurable empire,*
> *Si non que tousjours il empire,*
> *Sans soy diminuer en rien.*

If we are not completely convinced, it is not the fault of Lucifer; he has painted his desolate picture: his pride was forged in the enduring empire of heaven; he is conscious of power: but how mellow is the melancholy, how satisfying the indulgence in a catalogue of departed glories! A little later, all the demons arrive in black clouds to sing him a little song of damnation which might, with the change of a few words, have been a love-song:

> *La dure mort éternelle*
> *C'est la chançon des dampnés;*
> *Bien nous tient à sa cordelle*
> *La dure mort éternelle;*
> *Nous l'avons deservy telle*
> *Et a luy sommes donnés;*
> *La dure mort éternelle*
> *C'est la chançon des dampnés.*

If damnation cannot be feared, neither can pride, neither can death. There is continual gentleness in the face of death, and it is not till Baudelaire orchestrates death, as he orchestrates pride, that we notice any appreciable change. Death is dismissed with a roundelay; pride is conjured away, and in its place there is left a sense of quiet glory. For these incredible people with their hesitant and delighted awareness of life, the self is not sinful, but something to be delicately enjoyed. And if, as occasionally happens, a Pascal emerges to scream of the terrors of pride or a Corneille adapts the *honor* of the Spaniards, with what impeccable style they describe the nightmare! What, for example, could be more delightful than the dialogue between the *Mondaine* and *la Superstitieuse* in the poem of Marguerite de Navarre:

LA MONDAINE
Je leve ma teste,
Et mon corps honneste
A chascun je montre;
Et tenu de tous
Pour bon rencontre.

LA SUPERSTITIEUSE
Vostre corps de chair
Estimez trop cher:
Ce n'est que charogne.
Il te fault mourir:
Qui qu'en parle groigne.

LA MONDAINE
Ha! mes beaulz yeux vers
Norriture a vers
Ne deviendront poinct.

LA SUPERSTITIEUSE
Vous ferez ce sault;
Mourir il vous fault,
C'est le plus seur poinct.

LA MONDAINE
Ceste mort rebelle
Sy jeune et sy belle
Ne m'oserait prendre.

(COMÉDIE JOUÉE AU MONT DE MARSAN)

It is almost a love-song, played to the sound of flutes; no harsh harping on the evil of death, only a most exquisite pride. "Rebellious death would not dare to take me so young and so beautiful." In the same way Aucassin dismisses the fear of hell, saying he has no desire to go to heaven, where there are only old priests and cripples in threadbare cloaks. "I will go down to Hell, since to Hell go the poets and goodly knights slain in tournaments and in great battles—strong archers and good men. There go lovely ladies with their friends and wedded husbands. There too go all the gold and silver and ermine and costly furs and musicians—all the happy folk of the world. With these will I go, if only I have my sweet friend Nicolette by my side."

This French pride speaks with extreme gentleness. The English lacked such delicacy and tact, having a more robust sense of evil. The French, even more than the Italians, delighted in the sense of being—this was their pride. But even more delightful to the French was the sense of being together. So it is that the self-love of the French is often expressed in a dialogue between lovers.

The tenderest of these French dialogues, and the most important for our purposes, occurs in the *De Arrha Animae* of Hugo of St. Victor. In the conversation between *Homo* and *Anima*, the man conversing with his own soul, the peculiar delectations of the self talking to the self are beautifully expressed; and it is exactly as though we had entered the scene at the moment of the birth of awareness.

The Soul says:

Tell me, what is this thing of delight that merely by its memory touches and moves me with such sweetness and violence that I am drawn out of myself and carried away, I know not how? I am suddenly renewed, I am changed, I am plunged in ineffable peace. My mind is full of joy, all misery and pain forgotten. My soul exults. The mind is made clear.

My heart is on fire. My desires are truly gentle and kind. I know not where I am, because my beloved has embraced me. Because my love has embraced me, I am possessed of something and know not what it is, but I try to hold fast to it for fear of losing it. My soul in joy strives never to be separated from that which she desires to hold forever. Exulting in sovereign gladness, seeking nought, desiring nothing, but to rest in this. Is this, then, my beloved? Tell me, that I may know him, and if ever he comes again I may entreat him to leave me not, but stay with me always.

Man says:

It is indeed thy beloved who visits thee, but he comes in invisible shape, he comes disguised, he comes incomprehensibly, he comes to touch thee, not to be seen of thee. He comes not to give himself wholly, but to be tasted by thee: not to fill thy desire, but to lead upward thy affections. He offers a foretaste of his delights, and the earnest of thy betrothal consists chiefly in this, that he who shall afterwards give himself to be seen and possessed by thee perpetually, now permits himself to be sometimes tasted, that thou mayest learn how sweet he is. This shall console thee for his absence, and the savour of his gift shall keep thee from despair.

(PATROLOGIA LATINA, CLXXVI, 970)

How admirable is this conversation between the man and the soul at the moment of awakening consciousness, for it is hardly permissible to believe that the beloved is Christ alone, or even Christ at all; the passion is turned too directly inward, and the Victorine saint is almost in a state of trance. The quiet contemplative ecstasy is wholly French and wholly heretical, for the exultation leaps beyond anything desired by the Church, confounds the self with Christ, confounds love with the self, and speaks of a state of loving on the edge of self-love. "Exulting in sovereign gladness, seeking nought, desiring nothing, but to rest in this."

There is a freshness in the world of Hugo of St. Victor which is absent in his successors. The trembling intimations derive from Franciscan quietism, but nothing comparable to them can be found among the Franciscans of Italy, and most especially are they absent from the great Franciscan poet, Jacopone da Todi, with his frenzied adoration and grief for the death of Christ, and his continual repetitions of the word *amor*, as though he found it necessary to shout the word repeatedly in order to believe that love was possible. In the *De Arrha Animae* we hear the European soul talking to itself perhaps for the first time, and in the history of the European consciousness it is a document as important as Pascal's *Mystère de Jésus*, the savage cry of Corneille's Medea or Hölderlin's *Patmos*. And of this colloquy of the soul to the soul Fénelon provided the perfect commentary when he said: "There is no longer real silence when we listen to ourselves. After having listened, we answer, and in that dialogue a secret self-love silences God." He added, as though his gaze was fixed directly on the Victorine: "Peace for you is a delicate simplicity."

It would be a mistake, however, to regard the dialogue of the self-contemplating soul as the only level where French pride exerts itself. The sense of glory enters with St. Louis. As early as the reign of Louis IX the Sieur de Coucy can be heard saying: "I am not King, nor Prince, nor duke, nor even count: I am the Lord of Coucy." In something of the same tone Jehan Froissart will conclude the introduction to his chronicle: "I am known by those who desire to honour me as Sire Jehan Froissart of the county of Hainault and of the good sweet and beautiful city of Valenciennes." But even here there is a delicacy, a sense of freshness, a delight in invoking the name of some cherished city. There is nothing heaven-shaking in the emergence of personality at this time, and even when the mad king Louis XI, who lived under the influence of a mad barber, inscribed on the collar of the Order of St. Michael the words *immensi tremor oceani* (I make the immense ocean tremble), a boast more proud than any made by his forebears, the kind of boast which would have reduced the saintly Louis IX to shame, there is a curious air of unreality, and we remember Canute. The new energy, the new successes of French arms, the gradual extension of France until she included within her frontiers a kind of protectorate over the Holy Land, Greece and parts of North Africa, the emergence of a national consciousness, all these were to change the form of French awareness, though the contemplative current of the Victorines remained. Till the time of *le Roi Soleil*, descendant of Heliogabalus, this current was to remain, to be shattered for a while only with the advent of Napoleon, who proclaimed that he had widened the bounds of glory, and after the defeat of Italy gazed towards the East like Alexander before him: "Were I to remain here, doing nothing, I would be lost. In this great Babylon everything wears out: my glory has already departed. This little Europe does not supply enough of it for me. I must seek it in the East: all fame comes from there."

Meanwhile the debate of pride continued, and never more delightfully than in those fragments of *Le Romaunt de la Rose* which Chaucer translated. Narcissus comes to the mysterious well in the garden. He gazes at himself tenderly in a landscape of surpassing beauty. It is a magic well, with transparently clear water and little "wawes brighte the montance of two finger highte," and all round the well are wet grasses:

> About the brinkes of these welles,
> And by the stremes over-al elles
> Sprang up the gras, as thikke y-set
> And soft as any veluet,
> On which man mighte his lemman leye,
> As on a featherbed to pleye,
> And therthe was ful softe and swete.
> Through moisture of the welle wete
> Sprang up the sofe grene gras. . . .
>
> (THE ROMAUNT OF THE ROSE, 1417)

It is the landscape of *Christabel* and even of *Kubla Khan*, the sun shining directly overhead into the depths of the well, where two crystals lie glowing with a hundred colours, mirrors of such surpassing efficacy that a man looking at them can see half of the garden reflected within them, himself in the centre. Narcissus goes to the well and communes with himself:

> When he was to that welle y-comen,
> That shadowed was with braunches grene,
> He thoughte of thilke water shene
> To drinke and fresshe him wel withalle;
> And doun on knees he gan to falle,

And forth his heed and nekke out-straughte
To drinken of that well a draughte.
And in the water anoon was sene
His nose, his moth, his yen shene,
And he ther-of was all abasshed;
His owne shadowe had him bitrasshed.
For wel wende he the forme see
    Of a child of greet beautee.

(THE ROMAUNT OF THE ROSE, 1510)

He is so overcome by the vision of youthful beauty that he dies
without uttering a word, as though in a summer's dream, and
we are led to believe that the adorable youth died because there
was so much beauty in him that it was inconceivable that he could
have survived, since he had reached the summit of his own perfection, and with a passing glance at the crystals in the well:

This is the mirour perilous
In which the proude Narcisus
Saw al his face fair and bright,

(THE ROMAUNT OF THE ROSE, 1601)

the poet goes on to discuss something else altogether, forgetting
the "proude-herted Narcissus that was in love so daungerous", for
it was only one of many incidents that took place in the magic
garden. For the French poet the mirror of pride and the fountain
of love were the same. Like Tristan, Narcissus belongs to a world
where honour may be forfeited with impunity, and he holds the
world well lost for love.

The disarming gentleness of the French theme remains: in the
French legends there is nothing which approaches the terrible
close of the *Nibelungenlied* with its picture of a ruthless avenging
nature wiping out the petty attempts of man to assert himself in
opposition to the divine laws; no superhuman gods breathing fire
and terror are revealed: Roland dies a victim, not to the treachery
of Ganelon, but to the pride that forbids him sound the horn for
aid. The greatest of French epics describes a slow and stately re-
treat. When the French came to describe pride in the moralities—
for example, when Nicole Bozon attempted in his moral tales to

describe the terror of pride, the worst he can conjure up is the peacock with the beautiful feathers and the ugly feet: "for when the peacock looks down at its ugly and indecent feet, it sees something so awful that it is immediately humiliated." But one wonders whether it really is humiliated. *L'étrange me sollicite*, wrote André Gide, half-believing he was enunciating something perverse; but all through French poetry there has been this half-delighted awareness of the beauty of strangeness and ugliness—the peacock's feet appear again, disguised, in Baudelaire's famous description of the mud-splattered swan in the streets of Paris.

In much the same way, refusing to take life with the utmost seriousness, Villon enlarges on the gestures of the damned. He has no terrible, haunting sense of self-consciousness. He knows everything, but he does not know himself:

> I know a horse from a mule,
> And Beatrix from Bellet,
> I know the heresy of the Bohemians,
> I know son, valet and man,
> I know all things save myself alone.
>
> (BALLADE DES MENUS PROPOS)

It is the perpetual cry of Montaigne, who acquiesced in the position of *grand seigneur* as Villon acquiesced in being a murderer and a thief. In the *Essays* we come to know the strength of his heart, not the strength of his soul; we are always in the presence of the anecdote, and never in the presence of the hard core of the self. "Know thyself" said the Greeks; Montaigne answers with his courteous remark that what we know is so little that we should be about enjoying ourselves rather than plaguing ourselves with riddles. *Que scais-je?* For him the great problem is not how to know oneself, but how to get along with oneself. "The greatest thing in the world is to know how to belong to oneself." When he wrote that "they do wrong who wish to disjoin our two halves, for our soul must be commanded not to draw aside, not to despise and desert the body," he was expressing the continual French thesis of the identity of the flesh and the spirit. The final happiness for Rabelais and Voltaire was the planting of cabbages; it is unlikely that Montaigne would have disagreed.

Yet there happened occasionally in France as elsewhere Etnaflares of pride which seem to be entirely out of keeping with the French national genius. Gilles de Rais, who went into battle with Joan of Arc, was executed for the murder of 800 children, whose blood he drank; his satanism knew no bounds; he delighted in inflicting misery and in holding black Masses, and when he was executed, he said proudly that there was not a single person on the planet who would have dared as much. Henri Méchinot, who defended him at the trial, had recourse to the argument that he was defenceless against the demons of pride:

> I say that he was invaded by pride and other demons who, well-armed and resolute, assailed his fortress and enlisted it by force, even as the Greeks coming forth from the wooden horse did invade the unhappy country of King Priam. Messire de Rais should not be accounted guilty of the excesses committed by pride and his band, for a city taken by assault was innocent of the depravity, pillaging and cruelty to which it was subjected by its tyrants and unjust possessors.

This is not the world of Montaigne or even of Rabelais, whose *Fais ce que vouldras* did not include the possibility of cutting the throats of 800 young children, watching over their dying agonies and bathing in their blood. This was crime rampant, as was rarely practised in France; and we explain it at our peril if we say that this was the vengeance of an autocrat who had hoped at one time to be King of France. Other forces were at work. Over-leaping ambition, confusion of the spirit, a desperate desire for a sacrifice equal to himself, all these were present in a curious practice of witchcraft; and it was for witchcraft rather than for murder that he was executed.

Joan of Arc was also executed as a witch. Of the charges against her the most formidable was the accusation of spiritual pride. Jean Rogier in his *Mémoires* quotes a letter of the Chancellor of France concerning the arrest of Joan of Arc: *Que Dieu avait souffert prendre Jehanne la Pucelle pour ce qu'el s'estoit constitué an orgueil, et pour les riches habitz qu'el avoit pris,* "That God permitted the arrest of Jehanne the Maid because she suffered from pride, and because of the rich clothes she wore." The rich costumes seem to have been an afterthought; the costume of the Cardinal cannot have been less rich. But just as the crime of Savonarola was that he heard voices, and was accounted to be a heresiarch, so Joan of Arc, by her refusal to admit that the voices were imaginary, placed herself in danger of death; and the classic entry on the papers of her trial—*responsio mortifera*—is the punishment of her spiritual pride. Henry IV in a long letter defended the action of the Church and revealed the atmosphere of the times:

> The fire of Joan's pride, which was in her heart, suddenly burst out into hurtful flames, blown out by the bellows of envy; and incontinent after, she took again all her errors and false opinions by her before judged and revoked. For which causes, according to the judgments and institutions of holy Church, to the intent that she should thereafter not defile any other members of the flock of Our Lord Jesus Christ, she was again exhorted and preached to openly. And because she still was obstinate in her trespasses and villainous offenses, she was delivered to the secular power, the which condemned her to be burned, and consumed her in the fire.

We are no more impressed by these excuses than was the Holy See when it canonised Joan; it was the Church which was proud, vainglorious and determined upon a sacrifice; nor can Joan's burning be put down to English greed. But pride was the enemy: in this desperate letter it is possible to see how much the medieval churchman feared the emergence of pride.

With the coming of St. Francis de Sales the traditional French theology of grace returns. There is more sunlight, a new renaissance of devotion, and St. Francis himself, revelling in worship, with the gentleness of a girl, attacks pride, but gently, and with something of the Victorine graciousness. For him as for Paul Valéry, the enemy is dryness, the spiritual *ennui* which attaches itself to the most devoted of men; like Hugo of St. Victor he addresses himself to a perpetual dialogue of the soul, disguised under the name Philothea. He will flay pride, but gracefully. "Pearls that are conceived and nourished by the wind, or by the noise of thunder, have nothing of substance, but only the outside of the pearl to commend them"—therefore, Philothea, do not be proud. Or else he will say that honours and dignities are like saffron, which "grows more plentifully for being trodden underfoot", and he asks why people should be proud and insolent when they ride on horseback and wear a feather in their hat—surely the proper pride resides in the horse and the feather? He admonishes those who have "curled up moustaches, trimmed beards and soft hands", but it is difficult to believe that he admonishes them severely. He has a passion for images of honey—a precious stone cast in honey becomes more brilliant thereby—and we almost expect another animadversion on the habit of bees, but no, he means by this only that men cast in divine worship attain to sainthood. Once he quotes St. Gregory's terrifying statement that "Lot, who was so chaste in the city, defiled himself in solitude," but he passes on with measured grace to speak of man's aspiration towards a more perfect life. When he speaks of the sin of fornication, he gently reminds his flock that the human body is like a delicate glass vessel, which will crack if brought into too great a proximity with another; and to all the wiles of Satan he suggests only a gracious silence, a look that will disabuse him.

The French absorption in the self is not rebuked as long as it leads to absorption in God. He tells the story of the youth who returned home after a long journey and his mistress came running towards him, saying: "Dost thou not know me? I am really myself." "Yes," answers the youth, "but I am not myself." It is the theme of Valéry's *La Jeune Parque* four centuries later. He will have nothing to do with the patristic theorem that all friendship must be put aside; on the contrary, friendship must be exalted, for did not Jesus love John, Lazarus, Martha and Magdalene, and did not Peter love Petronilla, and St. Paul love Timothy and Thecla? All things are permitted as long as one loves God, he seems to say, and his testimony on pride should be compared with that of Ignatius to see the difference between the fiery Spanish form and the more contemplative pride of France.

But already there were rumblings from abroad. The French wars against the English were over; the wars against the Spanish were beginning. And it was from Spain, from the great figures of the Cid and Don Juan that France acquired for a brief while an entirely new conception of pride. The gentle blessings of St.

Francis de Sales have departed: a cold frost of wilfulness enters the scene. From Spain and the Spanish code of vengeance Corneille derived his trumpet-note:

> *Percé jusques au fond du coeur*
> *D'une attente imprévue aussi bien que mortelle,*
> *Misérable vengeur d'une juste querelle,*
> *Et malheureux objet d'une injuste rigueur,*
> *Je demeure immobile, et mon âme abattue*
> *Cède d'un coup qui me tue.*

(LE CID, I, IV)

The violence of the dying Cid derives from sources so wholly un-French that we read the words almost with incomprehension, rubbing our eyes. The same words—*rigueur, querelle, vengeur*—will be used later by Valéry; but the atmosphere will then be entirely changed, and the words themselves will have acquired a gentler and more philosophical meaning. When Horace kills his sister, he exclaims: "*Ma patience à la raison fait place.*" Then cold reason takes the place of grace, and the will, which had slept since the death of Seneca, rules the stage.

Corneille's first play had been a kind of *Midsummer Night's Dream*, called *L'Illusion*—a play where the will was mocked at, for it could have no place in the fairyland setting of the play. For some reason never sufficiently explained Corneille, reading the Spanish dramas of the time, turned his back on fairyland: his plays thereafter are abstruse dissertations on the Will, and sometimes and inevitably they trespass into the region of the Absurd; but Corneille's absurdity is unlike the absurdity we meet, for example, in Kierkegaard and Kafka, for with him even the most absurd punishments and the most absurd gestures obey a law. Kafka wrote in *The New Attorney*: "No one can ever lead the way to India. Even in Alexander's time the gate to India were beyond reach, but the direction was indicated by the King's sword. Today these gates have been moved somewhere else, farther away and higher up; no one indicates the direction." In the world of Corneille India is at the door-step.

Like Kafka, Corneille borrows an alien law, and with great cunning and violence compels his characters to parade within this law; the recompense, in the words of Mme. de Guion, is *le midi de la gloire*, illimitable honour and glory. And just as in Kafka the most absurd vows are redeemed by senseless accidents, beyond all hope, so Corneille also moves in a world beyond hope, an artificial and abstruse world where the meaningless dance of the swords is the only reality. In "A Dream" Kafka relates the epitaph of all Corneille's heroes: "While he plunged into this unfathomable abyss with his head still raised, his name was quickly engraved with great flourishes upon the stones of Heaven." Neither Kafka nor Corneille concern themselves with the possibility that in Heaven even the stones may crumble. When Medea is asked:

> *Dans un si grand revers que vous reste-i-il?*

she answers in words which echo Seneca's *Superest:*

> *Moi.*
> *Moi, dis-je, et c'est assez!*
>
> (MEDÉE, I, V)

She is indicating her belief that the stones in Heaven do not crumble, that honour is eternal and the self equally eternal. It is doubtful whether Corneille, though he suffered from a grotesque sense of his own worth, possessed the same belief. He delighted in exuberant statements of power, but when Augustus Caesar cries:

> *Je suis maître de moi comme de l'univers;*
> *Je le suis, je veux l'être. . . .*
>
> (CINNA, V, III)

we are oppressed by the thought that the desire and the reality are separated by an abyss. He desires to be master of himself, but he is not, and the famous invocations to the universe nearly always have a conditional clause. Not Corneille, but Rotrou was the first author of the "heaven-defying line":

> *Sans rendre ni raison, ni compte de mes voeux,*
> *Je veux ce que je veux, parce que je le veux.*
>
> (LAURE PERSECUTÉE, I, X)

But once again we are in the presence of an expression of desire rather than of any reality of power. But what is the reality of power? Descartes had enunciated the theorem that "the will may, in a certain sense, be said to be infinite." Unfortunately for Germany, the phrase "in a certain sense" was never clarified, and fortunately for England, and very characteristically, Locke replied intelligently that the doctrine was completely absurd for "the question is not proper, whether the will be free, but whether a man be free." Corneille was not in the least concerned whether man should be free. In terms of modern psychology, he lived under the compulsions of a father-image. It is here once again that Corneille touches Kafka, who wrote an essay entitled "The Anxieties of the Heavenly Father", in which he describes a hero called Odradek, of whom it is said: "Everything that dies has had before some kind of activity, and has consumed himself in it, but this does not apply to Odradek." This peculiar mythological creature Odradek, living everywhere and nowhere, having no reason for existence, obeying laws he never understands, compelled to inexplicable action and in desperate search of his own eternal triumph, is the Cid, Medea, Horace, Polyeucte and the rest of the Corneillian heroes who wear Spanish masks, talk in resounding French and attempt in their world-shaking gestures to imitate the Italian *terribiltà*. For them even the will is not enough: much more than the will is required—what is required is the sharp cutting edge and a desperate occasion for its employment. "There is no need for hope in order to begin an enterprise," said William the Silent, "no need for success in order to achieve it." It is a statement that both Corneille and Kafka would have approved of.

As he grew older, Corneille grew less proud. He had written once:

> *Je satisfais ensemble et peuple et courtisans,*
> *Et mes verse en tous lieux sont mes seuls partisans.*
> *Par leur seule beauté ma plume est estimée:*
> *Je ne dois qu'à moi seul toute ma renommée.*

Towards the end the flavour of this pride palled, humility intervened and he even set about translating the *Imitation* of Thomas à Kempis, making more money from the translation than he made from any of his plays. He continued to write, but there were long silences, while he grappled with the problem of the will. He began to write devotional verses full of a throbbing spiritual energy, but often the will remained triumphant. Like Cowper, who also suffered from spiritual pride, and for the same causes, Corneille came to see himself as the worst, the most terrified, the most abject of sinners:

> Je demeure immobile en ce mortel effroi,
> Et partout sous mes pas je trouve un précipice,
> Je vois quel est mon crime et quelle est ta justice,
> Et je sais que le Ciel n'est pas pur devant toi.

A fierce pride is concealed in the gnawing humility: never were pride and humility so fiercely combined. And yet this humility is not far from the cry of Titus:

> Maître de l'univers sans l'être de moi-même,
> Je suis le seul rebelle à ce pouvoir suprême:
> D'un feu que je combats je me laisse charmer,
> Et n'aime qu'à regret ce que je veux aimer.
> En vain de mon hymen Rome presse la pompe,
> Je veux de la lenteur, j'aime qu'on l'interrompe,
> Et n'ose resister aux dangereux souhaits
> De préparer toujours et n'achever jamais.

(TITE ET BÉRÉNICE, II, I)

The "*dangereux souhaits*" remained; they were part of the atmosphere of the Court—grandiloquence and conquest go together, and Corneille belonged to that small group which helped to sustain the King in his desire for military glory. Such pride is dangerous. Sooner or later Corneille was to find himself stumbling near the abyss which perplexed and terrified Pascal, but to the very end he waged his desperate battle with his singularly brutal poetry. The end was disaster either way; but Corneille almost retrieved himself from the disaster he saw so clearly by making a truce between the imperious demands of pride and humility. Hungry for glory and also for the peace which glory rarely permits, he wrote in his last years a strangely moving and rarely-quoted song which shows the last stage of his progress away from pride. The song comes in his admirable play *Oedipe*, sung by Dikte Dirce, who seems to be Hubris himself:

Impitoyable soif de gloire
Dont l'aveugle et noble transport
Me fait précipiter ma mort
Pour faire vivre ma memoire,
Arrête pour quelques moments
Les impétueux sentiments
De cette inexorable envie,
Et souffre qu'en ce triste et favorable jour
Avant que te donner ma vie,
Je donne un soupir à l'amour.

Ne crains pas qu'une ardeur si belle
Ose te disputer un coeur
Qui de ton illustre rigueur
Est l'esclave le plus fidèle.
Ce regard tremblant et confus
Qu'attire un bien qu'il n'attend plus,
N'empêche pas qu'il ne se dompte.
Il est vrai qu'il murmure, et se dompte à regret;
Mais s'il m'en faut rougir de honte,
Je n'en rougirai qu'en secret.

. . . .

J'en fais gloire, mais je me cache
Un comble affreux de déplaisirs;
Je fais taire tous mes désirs,
Mon coeur à soi-même s'arrache.
Cher prince, dans un tel aveu
Si tu peux voir quel est mon feu,
Vois combien il se violente.
Je meurs l'esprit content, l'honneur m'en fait la loi,
Mais j'aurais vécu plus contente,
Si j'avais pu vivre pour toi.

The astonishing conclusion, the complete surrender of pride, the quite extraordinary effect produced by the elongation of the line towards the end of the verse, so that the rigidity of the phrasing is destroyed, the sense of "all passion spent", even though the metrics of a proud passion of humility remain, all these give the poem a place in the litanies of the humble who have once been proud, and who are therefore all the more humble because a shadow of their former pride remains to remind them of the heights they have ascended. Nor is it enough to explain the peculiar effect of these verses by evoking the ancient French contraries of love and pride: it is not love, or old age, or weariness after the struggle which has produced the deeply religious feeling of these lines. Some new element has been introduced: the humility is rigid still, and it devours as pride devours, and retains nearly all the elements of pride, yet it is recognisably humility. Nothing like these verses was ever to be produced again in France: they stand alone, proud emblems of his own defeat, a humility such as a dying King might have, a humility of power.

This note of complex and powerful humility was not to be heard again, except from the lips of Pascal, until the time of Baudelaire. Compared to those who follow, with one exception, Corneille remains supreme. When Boussuet speaks of pride, all is gentleness again:

> The pride of which we speak consists of a certain false power, which renders the soul proud and disobedient, enemy to all fears; and so by an excessive love of freedom, it aspires to a kind of independence, which is the reason for its especial pleasure in refusing to obey, and why it is angered by prohibitions.
> (TRAITÉ DE LA CONCUPISCENCE, XIV)

He is more precise when he speaks later of the pride which "glorifies itself in everything, even glorying in the consciousness that one has of one's own nothingness, and as pride turns upon itself it multiplies itself infinitely." Yet this has been said before, and far more competently, by the fathers of the Church. Voltaire adds little. He says simply that "self-love is the instrument of our preservation; it is necessary and dear to us, it gives us pleasure and we must conceal it." But the desperate reasons for the concealment are never explained. When Stendhal comes to define pride, it eludes him, though he watches it closely and with a delighted clairvoyance; it is the centre of nearly all his writings, yet in comparison with the last song of Corneille, even the chapter called *Le Chant du Coq* in *Le Rouge et Le Noir* seems to be lacking in precision and strength, or even in understanding. Julien Sorel gazes into the mirror of his own mind, sees his conquests all round him, determines upon greater conquests, and then hesitates—there is a temporary failure of nerve:

> But in the most delicious moments, victim of a strange pride, he still attempted to play the role of a man accustomed to captivating women: he made incredible efforts to destroy his natural kindness of soul. Instead of paying attention to the transports he excited and the remorse which only made them more lively, he was obsessed with the concept of duty. He feared the horrors of remorse and undying ridicule if he abandoned the master plan he had set himself to follow. In a word, what made Julien a superior being was precisely what prevented him from enjoying the happiness offered to him on all sides. He was like a well-complexioned sixteen-year-old girl who goes to a ball and is silly enough to put on rouge. . . .

The constant fear of ridicule keeps the Stendhalian heroes awake at nights; it is their enemy; the laugh of a young girl can shatter their most sacred impulses. The world has grown more courtly; in a previous age it was the laughter of the gods which made men shiver with a sacred fear.

In the nineteenth century all the conditions under which pride could grow are absent, or nearly absent. Industrialisation destroys the gods, and though there are titanic struggles in the first years of the nineteenth century, by the 1850s pride has been tamed in Europe, to revive only in Dostoievsky's Russia. Baudelaire at least will turn industrialisation to his own uses, inventing the mechanical dandy as a final response to the overwhelming powers of an increasingly mechanical universe; but the theme is beginning to wear thin; in the world of frock-coats and Louis XVIII furniture the relentless struggle for power, even spiritual power, must seem in vain. We are accustomed to regard Flaubert's *Tentation de St. Antoine* as one of the last vestiges of romantic pride, but when St. Anthony is overwhelmed by the demon of pride, he can only drool that he would like to be some kind of animal which flows like water, vibrates like sound, penetrates all nature:

I long to fly, to swim, to bark, to bellow, to howl! I would divide myself among all things, be in everything, be diffused into odors, grow like the plants, flow like water, vibrate like sound, shine like light, vanish into all shapes, penetrate the very atoms, plunge into the depths of nature, become matter itself.   (TENTATION DE S. ANTOINE, VII)

This is not what Leon Bloy had called "*la montée furibonde vers l'Absolu*", though this is what it is intended to be. The weariness, the absence of the appropriate desire are only too evident. There will come later the three great poets Rimbaud, Mallarmé and Valéry, who know the extent of the Kingdoms to be overthrown; the Kingdom which St. Anthony assails is not worth the victory.

There occurs in the history of pride in France a curious decline. We believe in the victories of the heroes of Corneille, for they are real victories, corresponding to the victories perhaps of the French armies in Spain and Flanders, and to an expanding national consciousness. André Gide, searching for a crime he can exalt, discoveries pederasty and later the *acte gratuit*, by which the hero will demonstrate his own splendour and will-power. "A motiveless crime," says Lafcadio in *Les Caves du Vatican*, deciding to prove his will-power by throwing a stranger out of a railway carriage. "What a nuisance it will be for the police!"

It is hardly credible. One reads the words with amazement, wondering why Lafcadio should trouble himself by embarrassing the police. Have the police become the symbols of the gods? Must their embarrassment be taken seriously? It was not the embarrassment of the police which frightened Raskolnikov; he was far more afraid of the consequent turmoil in his own soul. When the hero of Gide's novel discovers that he is suffering from pride, he punishes himself by jabbing his thigh with a pen-knife; so, on a higher plane and with a greater aim, Pascal had worn a spiked ring round his wrist as delicately as the Chinese scholar will wear a ring of jade to remind him of an essential purity.

The *acte gratuit* debases morality and debases equally the performer of it, for every child performs such acts and every adolescent surrenders to them. Such immaturity is sometimes charming, but it is incomprehensible that a philosopher should erect upon the conception of senseless crime a whole interpretation of the world as he sees it. The astonishing crimes committed by the guards of German prison-camps suggest, however, that a national neurosis may acquire the form of a perpetual *acte gratuit*. Men committed crimes not only for no reason, but against all reason, and especially against any conception of honour; the sleep-walking murderer was a Lafcadio with power to hurl a whole nation out of a railway carriage.

The same dangerous and meaningless theorem that the will is most decisive when it has no power over itself was repeated by Bergson, who wrote that "it is only at the great and solemn crises, decisive of our reputation with others, and yet more with ourselves, that we choose in defiance of what is conventionally called a motive, and this absence of any tangible reason is all the more striking the deeper our freedom goes." Nothing is stranger in the works of Bergson than the discovery that in a mind so keen for truths, so capable of exploring the subtleties of the human soul, there should be a reliance upon the *acte gratuit*, a determination to give perpetual credence to the unconscious workings of the mind. But on the last page of his last book Bergson makes amends. At that moment, already dying, he threw out his defiant challenge at the universe, saying that the universe is a machine for the making of gods; and every man is an accomplice in the workings of the machine.

The pride of France remains almost an unchanging thing. There arise at intervals the strange giants of pride, Corneille, Pascal, Rimbaud, great ships ploughing huge furrows over the ocean; then the ships pass, and the waves settle again. Sometimes mirages appear: the ships seem to be about to appear, and in the silence we hear the voice of a Gobineau, declaiming in accents derived from Corneille: "*Tant que j'éxiste, le monde est à moi. J'ai le pieds dessus.*" "As long as I live, the world is mine. I have it underfoot." Unfortunately for the secretary of De Tocqueville, we have heard already the voice spoken in its authentic primitive tones; and Rimbaud has only to say: "*Je suis mille fois le plus riche,*" for us to believe him, while Gobineau may repeat his threats forever without anyone paying attention to him. Pride is not shown by a statement; it is a tone of voice, a gesture, a desire to wrestle with the gods, a solemn assertion of man's powers when confronted with the mysterious silence of the universe. So Pascal, who had heard the shrill voice of Corneille in his own home, listening to the poet helping his sister Jacqueline to compose her interminable verses, wrestled and gestured and asserted himself gravely against his God.

But the main current of French pride does not pass through the giants. "Be on your guard against the pride of humility," said Gauguin, and no other nation has been so sensitive to the humblest pride. It was in France, in the cloisters of the Victorines, that French pride had its birth, remaining for the most part an extraordinarily gentle thing. One of the fragments of Pindar records a desire "to stretch in haste a ladder to the steep sky". The French were so much in love with their earth that they rarely erected ladders; it was enough to walk casually and gracefully over their flowering earth, remembering like Rimbaud that *"le combat spirituel est aussi brutal que la bataille d'hommes; mais la vision de la justice est le plaisir de Dieu seul."* "The spiritual combat is as brutal as the war between men; but the vision of justice is the pleasure of God alone." From this conviction they derived their human strength.

Pascal's Abyss

THERE come occasionally into the history of the human soul men so determined upon uncovering its secrets that they seem to have spent their whole lives on a single errand. Where St. Augustine is diffuse, contemplating in turn all the problems of the universe, thinking deeply upon some and dismissing others with irrelevant but intelligent comments, there are others who throw their whole weight against a single problem, and worry it as a dog worries a bone, refusing to part with it, so that the problem becomes a part of themselves, so intimate a part that it is impossible afterwards to dissociate the fortress and the assault. Where am I? Who am I? Where shall I go? The terrible questions demand an answer, and none are wholly independent of each other. For Pascal one question superceded all others: How shall I be saved? It was a common question in his time, but no one else attempted to solve it precisely as Pascal did, for he measured his distance from salvation, calculated the risks and commented at length and with grave humility upon the gambler's throw of the dice. There are moments when one wonders whether he could ever have heard of the fantastic utterances of Krishna in the *Bhagavad Gita*, who announced himself as "the gambling of the cheat and the splendour of splendid things." What is clear is that Pascal recognised, as Kafka recognised later, that cheating might be necessary in order to enter the Kingdom of Heaven.

In one of those *pensées* which begin in the middle of a thought, Pascal wrote: "*Vanité: jeux, chasse, visite, comédies, fausse perpétuation de nom.*" "Vanity: the hunt, games, visits, comedies, the false perpetuation of a name." It would be a singular injustice to Pascal to believe that by the game, the hunt, the visit, the comedies and the false perpetuation of a name he was referring to the life of a young aristocrat in Paris. The game was the game of grace abounding confronting implicit evil, the hunt was surely the spiritual combat, the visits were to the salons of the soul and the comedy was of the same kind as induced Dante to call a poem which embraces the whole universe, from Hell to Christ, by the same title. For Pascal the false perpetuation of a name was an unthinkable horror, and indeed the perpetuation of any name except the name of God was an irrelevance and a defiance of the first commandment. His own fame tormented him. "*Nous brulons du désir d'approfondir tout, et d'édifier une tour qui s'élève jusqu'à l'infini. Mais tout notre édifice craque, et la terre s'ouvre jusqu'aux abîmes.*" "We burn with desire to delve into all things, and build a tower which will reach to infinity. But the building cracks and the earth opens into bottomless chasms." The earth opens. What then? An eternity of locked doors, endless silence, numbing loneliness? Think as he could, with the sharpest and most penetrating brain that France has ever produced, he could see no other end in sight. All was vanity. The man who raised the towers was more cursed than he who lived in humble faith; those who attempted to wrest the secrets of nature were doing no more than attempting a false perpetuation of name. All things lay in God, and God was unapproachable except by prayer and fasting, and by chastising the flesh.

One watches Pascal's approach towards the Godhead with the fascination which must come from horror, the same fascination with which we listen to Job. Here at last, divested of all the impediments of learning, we see the naked human soul stumbling frantically in search of salvation. Nothing in French drama, not even the cry of Corneille's *Médée*, is as exciting as the sudden moment of recoiling horror which occurs when Pascal realises that his mathematics are faulty. He has measured his distance from God; the measurement of the distance has been the singular preoccupation of his intelligence, but quite suddenly he realises that there was never any standard of measurement, and in the world of devotion there are no precise instruments of calculation. Hence-

forward neither God nor man can have validity: validity belongs
only to the wavering and uncertain line which stretches between
him and God, the prisoners' walk he measures eternally. Hence-
forward, too, the very intensity of his inward life paralyses his
power of action. In terrible fear he walks the prisoners' walk,
afraid of everything, even of God, recalling the calculations he
made in moments of leisure, summoning his strength in order to
break through the bastions of the heavenly fortress; and then,
having failed, he returns disconsolately to the waste-land which
stretches in every direction, only to summon his strength again
and make a further assault. Once, on a winter night, he seems to
have entered and seen the fortress in the flame-light. The amazing
poem written to celebrate the occasion has the same authenticity
as Hölderlin's *Patmos*. One does not write such things without
having been there.

To surrender mathematics for the hair-shirt, to follow the
knife-edge line beyond all reason and to worship God ardently
in the face of entire annihilation, this was a spiritual exercise of the
first magnitude. For Pascal it was not enough to imitate Christ.
What was necessary was to imitate the Last Judgment, to be
judge and accuser, the slayer and the slain. In spite of the desperate
pleas for grace, nowhere is there to be found among the papers
of Pascal an expression of simple humility comparable with Baudelaire's prayer to his nurse. The battle was fought sternly, implacably, and on a level where there were no simplicities of faith.
Pascal confessed as much to his confessor. "I am ready to abase
myself in all the rest, but in essential matters I am well resolved
to be inflexible, and obstinate, if you will, and singular, and superb."
The complete stripping of the athlete before the combat, the sense
of desolation, the certain knowledge that there is no progress
without grace, all these are the familiar toils through which the
proud man goes. It is this which is so convincing in the disjointed
notes which Pascal left behind him: the mind so tense and so
determined upon salvation that inevitably it turned in upon itself,
sought refuge in itself, contemplated its own powers, and by remaining inflexible, singular and superb, defeated itself; and what
is so compelling in Pascal's notes is that he seems to be perfectly
aware of these dangers, but must yet go on, secure in the knowl-

edge of defeat, without any hope except a still greater grace of God.

Though the medieval commentators exercised themselves to invent a terminology appropriate to the history of pride, it is very rarely that they show acquaintance with the authentic accents of the passion of pride. We have seen that the early Christian homilies content themselves with disquisitions on pride no more complex than the similar disquisitions on gluttony. There are exceptions, of course. St. Jerome and St. Augustine both speak of a pride which is communicable in the accents of today. But it is Pascal above all who speaks with authority, and for the first time, of the battle which men wage against God when they must love God—of the schizophrenia of the soul. The man who said, even though possessed of the most intense religious feeling: "I am ready to abase myself in all the rest, but in essential matters I am well resolved to be inflexible, and obstinate, if you will, and singular, and superb," goes beyond Leonardo da Vinci's *ostinato rigor* and makes a virtue of singularity. In Pascal we hear for the first time in words we understand because they belong almost to our own generation the voice of pride in anguished rebellion with itself, tormenting itself, attempting by every means possible to escape from the coils, like Hercules in the poisoned shirt, and simply by the violence of his endeavour to escape he makes his own fall more certain.

It is precisely here that we measure the greatness of Pascal's soul. There are ambivalences in the spiritual world which have not yet been, and may never be, fully explored. That the abyss may itself be the spiritual fortress, that the greatest evil may contain the greatest good, that God may appear on occasions in the disguise of the Devil, all these things had been dimly suspected before, but it is Pascal who has given these ambivalences their modern outline, and it is Pascal who first stated, in words that appear at first to have been drawn from a black Mass, that "Jesus Christ is more abominable than I, and far from abhorring me, he holds himself honoured that I should go to him and succour him." Nor is it difficult to understand why he should have been compelled to cry out in this strange way. Read in its proper context, the words are not those of a proud man, though they are the words of an unbelievably unhappy man. Towards the end of *Le Mystère de Jésus* he gathers up the threads of the long discourse with Christ on the night of Gethsemane, and confesses the final conclusions:

> I see my abyss of pride, of curiosity, of concupiscence. There is no link between me and God, nor to Jesus Christ the just. But he was made sin by me; all your chastisements have fallen upon him. He is more abominable than I, and far from abhorring me, he holds himself honoured that I should go to him and succour him.
>
> But he has healed himself, and all the more will he heal me.
>
> I must add my wounds to his, and join myself to him, and he will save me in saving myself.
>
> But no more may be added in the time to come.
>
> *Eritis sicut dii, scientes bonum et malum.* The whole world makes itself god by passing judgment: "This is good or bad"; and so rejoicing too much or sighing over whatever happens.
>
> (PENSÉES, 553)

Flaubert recorded once that the sight of a judge passing judgment over a prisoner filled him with almost insane laughter at the thought of so much presumption. Pascal at the end of his life found himself aghast that anyone at any time should pass judgment on anything whatsoever, for judgment lay entirely with God; and it is no accident that almost the concluding words of *Le Mystère de Jésus* should contain a reference to the classic statement of the pride of the Titans in *Genesis*. Nothing had changed; the problem was exactly what it was in the beginning, and there was only one response to the law of God—enduring faith, complete abandonment to God's purposes. All reason must be abandoned, Descartes must be abandoned, the only true earthly wisdom is natural ignorance, reason may speak as it will, but it cannot fix the values of things, and the greatest delight of the man who had pushed reason to the uttermost when attempting to unravel the mysteries of nature was to see proud reason humiliated and begging for mercy. *Que j'aime à voir cette superbe raison humiliée et suppliante!*

It is a strangely disturbing spectacle. As though we were by his side, we watch the most intelligent and clear-sighted mind of France floundering in despair, inventing paradoxes, deliberately employing all the resources of his imagination in accurately defining the whole area of man's crisis in relation to God. There come from him, not poems or sermons, but sparks of fire which have been ignited in the naked combat. He defines his fears with a precision which is even more terrible than fear itself; and not until Kierkegaard wrote *Fear and Trembling* has so acute a mind struggled with the mathematics of separation. It is not only the cry: *Je m'en suis separé . . . Que je n'en suis pas separé éternellement*, that haunts us. We are haunted by the spectacle of the genius of mathematics in love with the mathematics of God.

But there comes a time when Pascal must be examined according to his own premises. There comes a time when his desire for salvation is seen to be only another form of his superb singularity; he desires above all to become a saint, but this desire is hardly to be distinguished from the desire to excel, the *libido excellendi*. Reason is anathematised, but not always convincingly. He can say succinctly, as though announcing a truism, that there is nothing so conformable to reason as this disavowel of reason, but he is no more convincing than when he says that "Nothing is good but mediocrity. To leave the mean is to abandon humanity." There are too many repetitions, too many evasions to allow us to believe completely in the motives he suggests, and it is not unreasonable to demand why he should invoke humanity at this stage in his progress. He had never loved humanity with any particular love. He was self-centred to a degree. The whole power of his intellect was concentrated away from man and in the direction of God. *Humiliez-vous, raison impuissante!* And when Gilberte speaks of the iron belt with sharp points which he dug into his skin whenever a visitor was announced, saying that he did this because "the spirit of mortification is the very spirit of charity", we seem to hear once more the authentic words of Pascal at war with himself, as well as at war with God. St. Catherine of Siena once spoke of uprooting self-love with the knife of self-hatred, but what happens, Pascal might well ask, if self-hatred is only another form of self-love? Can one uproot pride with pride? Pascal might answer that even this was possible, and in an extraordinary passage he compares the great scientists, the men of genius, with the saints of God:

> Great geniuses have their empire, their glory, their grandeur, their victory, their lustre, and they have no need of carnal powers, with which they are incommensurable. They are seen, not with the eyes, but with the mind, and that is enough.
>
> The saints have their empire, their glory, their victory, their lustre, and they have no need of carnal and mental powers, with which they are incommensurable, for they neither add to them nor subtract from them. They are seen by God and the angels, and not by the bodies, nor by curious minds. God is sufficient for them.   (PENSÉES, 793)

What is significant here is that Pascal suggests that the great geniuses are not only comparable with the saints, but they are comparable with God, for it cannot be an accident that each paragraph ends with a statement of the parallel sufficiency. Here, too, he invokes the pure mind in contemplation of its own powers, and he is careful to divorce the pure mind of all its earthly panoply. *They have no need of carnal powers, with which they are incommensurable.* The conquests of the emperors—those conquests which he had gazed upon at various times with amused tolerance, suggesting that Cæsar was too old to go in conquest of the world and that the power of Cleopatra lay in the length of her nose—such conquests were insignificant in comparison with the achievements of the pure mind confronting itself, and achieving empire, glory and grandeur by the measure of its understanding of itself. There can be no ambiguity here. For the first time there enters upon the stage the figure which was to be characterised three hundred years later by Paul Valéry under the name of M. Teste, the pure geometer, who lives for thought alone and is immeasurably excited by the discoveries of the mind, and most particularly by those which cannot be put to any use among men; and when, in the famous *Introduction to the Method of Leonardo da Vinci*, Paul Valéry attempts to isolate the essential quality of Leonardo's mind, he is more properly isolating the essential quality in Pascal's, and indeed the essay includes an apparent confusion between the two scientists of genius. Again and again in the essay Valéry finds himself confronted with the permanence of the self, which can never lose itself, or shake itself from itself, but must continually hide from itself only to see itself more clearly, and without batting an eyelid Valéry says that the only definition of the self is "that every roads leads back to oneself," as though he was barely conscious of sentencing the self to perpetual imprisonment. And indeed for Valéry's Leonardo, as for M. Teste and for Pascal, the self is the perpetual and dissonant accomplice of a man's existence:

> At every moment of life the private soul possesses, deep down within itself, like a concealed treasure, a fundamental permanence of consciousness, which depends on nothing. As the ear will often hear and then lose and then hear again through all the varying movements of a symphony some grave and persistent *motif*, which never ceases to be there, though often it will seem to have disappeared, so the pure self, the unique and continuous element in each being in the world, has its home within our intelligence eternally, and loses itself and finds itself again; and this deep note of music dominates all the entangling circumstances of our existence from the moment it is heard.

This note we have heard before: it comes for a brief moment in the dialogue between *Homo* and *Anima* of Hugo of St. Victor, where it emerges for the first time, fresh as a young flower; but already there were hints of the disasters to come. It is inconceivable that all the worshippers in the medieval cathedrals were conscious of this deep organ-note; their music was simpler, as the Gregorian chant was simpler than the orchestrated symphonies of our time; nor is it possible to believe that in the medieval Church anyone could be found to believe in a fundamental permanence of consciousness "which depends on nothing", for they would have said that it depended entirely on God, and was given by God for a little while for a definite purpose, and this purpose was to assist the greater glory of God. The precise measurement of the distance between Valéry's understanding of consciousness and the medieval understanding of consciousness lies in the definition of consciousness itself, for in the Middle Ages "every road leads back to God", and it would have seemed intolerable to live in a world where "where every road leads back to oneself".

But Valéry was perfectly aware that the "great genius" lived in an intolerable world of his own creation, and speaking more precisely of Pascal than of Leonardo he invented a mythology of pride which has nothing whatsoever in common with the familiar mythology of the Titans. In this new mythology pride may be redeemed on the heights and change, as though by magic, into the utmost simplicity after passing through the fires of itself. In a passage which is made moving by his determination to speak only in terms of what is known, but deriving from the mythologies of the Middle Ages, Valéry maps the course of the rocket until the moment it explodes:

> Overwhelmed by the restless desire for uniqueness and led on by a rage for omnipotence, this same being passes beyond all creation and all he has accomplished and all his greatest designs at the same moment that he puts away all tenderness for himself and all his preference in his own desires. In one instant he immolates his own self. He feels himself pure consciousness; and two of these cannot exist. He is the I, the pronoun of universality, the name of that which has no relation to appearance. O, to what a point has pride been transformed! How it has arrived at a position it did not even know it was seeking! How temperate the reward of its triumph! A life so firmly guided, one which has regarded as obstacles to be avoided or to be mastered all the objects it could propose to itself, must after all have attained an unassailable conclusion, not in time but within itself. Its pride has brought it to this distant place, and here its pride is consumed. Pride, which led it here, leaves it astonished, naked, infinitely simple, in the centre of the treasure-house.

Nothing could be more dissimilar to the funeral elegies of Bossuet than Valéry's attempt to describe the rewards of pride—the naked and infinitely simple soul confronting the treasure-house it has created at the moment of its greatest triumph—yet consciously or unconsciously Valéry has here imitated the tones of Bossuet lamenting over the death of a young Queen of France. We read, and wonder where we have heard these overtones before. "O, to what a point has pride been transformed! How it has arrived at a position it did not even know it was seeking! How temperate the reward of triumph!" The Queen lies within the catafalque, the choirs are singing, the censers fill the air with overpowering scents, and the grave bishop advances to remind the princes and all the generations of France that the Queen is now no more than a naked and infinitely simple soul standing astonished in the centre of the treasure-house of Heaven. It is a strangely evocative moment. The elegies of Bossuet, the over-reaching mind of Leonardo, the progress of the mortal soul towards death and the rewards of pride come together in a single litany. We have heard before that the over-reaching mind enters the world of death, but never before had there been so curious a reversal of values. And so, to the very end, the *Introduction to the Method of Leonardo da Vinci* continues to celebrate a purely pagan pride with overtones of medieval humility.

For Pascal, the complexities of pride were endless, and were never so easily solved: the astonished, naked and infinitely complex soul of Pascal saw the treasure-house only once, and then in such anguish that he saw it shining in fierce flames, and he could describe it in no other way than by repeating the word for flame. It is significant that even in the moment of beatitude, when the flames of Heaven tremble before him, he invokes the God of Abraham and Isaac, and deliberately eschews the philosophers, though he is compelled to mention them. For him the terror was a real terror. The desire for grace is overwhelming, and at the same time it is hardly more than desire—a paroxysm of desire. There is no grace that he can be sure of. "We run heedlessly towards the abyss," he wrote, "having put something before us to prevent us seeing it." Then how to avoid the abyss? How to avoid the monstrous confusion of aims? He hardly knows. He knows that "grace and sin humble infinitely more than reason can do, but without despair, and exalt infinitely more than natural pride, but without inflating it". But the temptation of pride is always there—it is not only Epictetus who is the *superbe diabolique*. There are hints of it in himself. In one of the most amazingly poetic of the *pensées* he finds peace in the contemplation of the dilemma of pride faced with the human misery:

Who then can refuse to believe and adore the heavenly light? For is it not clearer than day that we perceive within ourselves ineffaceable marks of excellence? And is it not equally true that we experience every hour the results of our deplorable condition? What does this chaos and monstrous confusion proclaim to us but the truth of these two states, with a voice so powerful that it is impossible to resist it?

(PENSÉES, 435)

So at last the mathematics of men are seen to be in vain. One would have thought it enough to admit defeat, but no, he must discover new subterfuges and wage continual war almost with his last breath. *Le combat spirituel est aussi brutal que la bataille d'hommes.*

With Pascal, the epic strength of theology turned left, and became revolutionary. There was a need—perhaps there had never been a greater need—for someone to speak of God with the bitterness of a confidant who has lost faith, yet knows that faith is supremely necessary. With him, it becomes possible to believe that love of God and hate of God are compatible in the same person, in the same worshipper. There is a sense of intimacy in the conflict Pascal wages against the heavenly fortress which is equalled only by the conflict waged by Job; and this is something wholly absent in the long curricula of the schools. He speaks directly, from the heart inward, as later Hölderlin was to speak, and if occasionally, as when he talks of Christ as "more abominable than I", we seem to find ourselves in the same territory as Luther when he cried: "Blasphemy sometimes sounds in God's ears more agreeable than Allelujahs or solemn hymns of praise; and the more frightful and repulsive the blasphemy, the more agreeable it is to God," yet there are at least important differences. The battle waged by Pascal was more naked than Luther's, and all the weapons of science are employed to prove God's love. There is a sense in which Pascal wears the robes of the tragic hero; his pride is not a play on the letter "I", but a bitter and remorseless offering to the Creator who must spurn it, humble it and throw it to the dust, and nothing is so fascinating as to watch Pascal continually making the effort of surrender.

Pascal possessed a monstrous pride, for he was gifted with a vivid and terrible self-awareness. Nearly a quarter of the *Pensées* is in some way connected with the problem of pride. Though we are often oppressed by the sense of some *arrière-pensée*, some hidden motive for the continuous distortion, we are impelled to recognise the urgency of his theme and to applaud his progress as he storms the heights. There are moments when the nerve breaks, bends, twists in upon itself, when the weariness and hopelessness of the combat are only too evident, and we could wish the act of surrender had been less tormenting—but that cannot be: the mathematics of his time and age demanded just such a struggle between faith and reason. What is so singular is the extraordinary accuracy with which he measures the distance between himself and God, and the extraordinary ease with which he countered so many of the obstacles placed before him. We read breathlessly—it is part of the charm of the *Pensées* that their very disjointedness gives the impression that they are fresh on the page, the ink still wet and the breath of the philosopher still in the air we breathe. He does not work deep in his tunnel, burrowing in darkness like a mole. It is all in plain daylight. The reader is never given a rest, never a chance of sinking back on his five senses: all the ordinary levels of the mind and character are utterly ignored, left far below, "outsoared" as Shelley would say. Very few dare climb to these heights, and perhaps there is a grave significance in the fact that the heroic combat between faith and reason which Pascal fought in himself should have come about at a time when reason, following Descartes, was about to emerge as the instrument of man's most incalculable powers. Yet the dissonances remain. Like the defeated knight in the legendary tourney who goes from land to land seeking the identity of the Red Dwarf who has unhorsed him, Pascal goes in quest of his God, hardly realising that the Red Dwarf is forever concealed within himself.

Yet if Pascal failed, as he seems to have failed, almost completely in diminishing the inviolate distance which separated him from God, there were moments when the lightning struck, when everything suddenly and instantaneously became clear to him, when the Red Dwarf appeared in all his awful majesty to sustain and comfort him. Suddenly, and for no reason at all, with one of those amazing leaps which occur only at the rarest intervals in the history of religion, Pascal leapt into the heart of the hidden fastness, and afterwards he wrote an account of the leap which is more convincing than anything written by the mystics. Nowhere else, not even in the celebrated invocation which he inscribed as an amulet and placed next to his heart, are we confronted with a leap of such evident authenticity. With a single bound he found himself at Gethsemane.

It is astonishing enough that he should have been able to do this, even though he had weakened his body and driven himself into a spiritual state where the visionary consciousness was sharpened unmercifully. One might have hoped for a brief annotation, an illegible scribble, a hint of the splendours he had seen, but no— he returns with a long document, which must always remain one of the most important documents of the European consciousness.

In form the *Mystère de Jésus* is precisely what it says it is: a mystery play, but it was not unlike those exercises, similar to those the Jesuits demanded of their novices at retreats, in understanding the passion of Christ. It is clearly written under the stress of great emotion, and would appear to have been composed after having thrown himself down before the altar; in that position, and overwhelmed with his own responsibility and desperate need of grace, in penitence and despair, he assumed in himself the agony of Gethsemane, and what is so striking is that when he came to write down the drama he had seen, we are aware that he has overheard the whole colloquy between Christ and God, which is also the whole colloquy between man and God. No one else had ever penetrated into that garden. On the night when the fate of the whole world seems to hang in the balance, Pascal is present. He even speaks to Christ and admonishes him, and there are moments when a strange identification between Christ and Pascal takes place.

It is necessary to refer to the *Mystère de Jésus* at some length, because we are here confronted with a vast Etna-flare of consciousness and of spiritual pride. Poets and some mystics had already recorded or invented the words of Christ, kings and emperors had rivalled Christ, saints had received the *stigmata* of Christ, but no one else had overheard the colloquy between God and Christ at the moment of the agony, and taken so intimate a part in the passion of Christ. The mystery is divided into three parts. In the first part Christ is seen suffering the passion alone, uttering the cry which Pascal had cried in the loneliness of his heart: *Que je n'en suis pas séparé* . . . Christ in the loneliness and torment of separation searches for friends, but his friends are asleep. They have left him with complete indifference, "having so little pity that it could not prevent their sleeping even for a moment". So Jesus is left alone to the wrath of God, and the stage is set for the two great contestants:

> Jesus is alone on the earth, without anyone not only to feel and share his suffering, but even to know it; he and Heaven were alone in that knowledge.
>
> Jesus is in a garden, not of delight as the first Adam, where he lost himself and the whole human race, but in one of agony, where he saved himself and the whole human race.
>
> He suffers this affliction and this desertion in the horror of night.
>
> I believe that Jesus never complained but on this single night; but then he complained as if he could no longer bear his extreme suffering. "My soul is sorrowful, even unto death."
>
> Jesus seeks companionship and comfort from men. This is the sole occasion in all his life, so it seems to me. But he receives it not, for his disciples are asleep.
>
> Jesus will be in agony even to the end of the world. We must not sleep during that time.
>
> Jesus in the midst of this universal desertion, including that of his own friends chosen to watch for him, finding them asleep, is vexed because of the danger to which they expose, not him, but themselves; he cautions them for their own safety and their own good, with a sincere tenderness for them during their ingratitude and warns them that the spirit is willing and the flesh is weak.
>
> Jesus, finding them still asleep, without being constrained by any consideration for themselves or for him, has the kindness not to waken them, and leaves them in repose.

Jesus prays, uncertain of the will of the Father, and fears death; but when he knows it, he goes forward and offers himself to death. *Eamus. Processit.*

The scene ends with the words "Let us go. He goes forth." What is extraordinary is that in the world *Eamus*, Pascal has announced his own presence in the agony, for it does not occur in the scriptures.

The second act of the drama takes place at the same time as the first, but the action is seen under an entirely different light. Previously the dark landscape of Gethsemane had been brilliantly lit; there were intimations of terror; even the ghostly journey of Christ to the sleeping disciples had been accomplished with the quality of terror, for he had spoken to them and they had not answered, and indeed it was unnecessary for them to answer, for his words had penetrated into their sleep. Now Christ offers salvation to the sleeping disciples, and afterwards performs the act of magnificent grace by which all the righteous have their salvation wrought for them, "both in the nothingness before their birth, and in their sins after their birth," and he does this while they sleep. Thereupon:

He prays only once that the cup pass away, and then with submission; and twice that it come if necessary.

Jesus is weary.

Jesus, seeing all his friends asleep and his enemies wakeful, commits himself entirely to the Father.

Jesus does not regard in Judas his enmity, but the order of God, which he loves and avows, since he calls Judas friend.

Jesus tears himself away from his disciples to enter into his agony; we must tear ourselves away from our nearest and dearest to imitate him.

Jesus being in agony and in the greatest affliction, let us pray longer.

There follows a prayer which can only be spoken by Pascal or by the unseen chorus. It is a prayer of no particular relevance to the drama which has unfolded, but a simple prayer which Pascal may have overheard at church:

We implore the mercy of God, not that He may leave us at peace in our vices, but that He may deliver us from them.

If God gave us masters by his own hand, oh! how necessary for us to obey them with a good heart!

With these echoes of the Lord's Prayer and the text "Render unto Cæsar", the scene ends; and as though to mark the beginning of the final act, Pascal inscribes a notation from a chorus of Æschylus: "Necessity and events infallibly follow," and so emphasises the quality of the heroic action which is now announced.

With the third act we are present in still another landscape. Previously there had been some kind of dialogue between Jesus and himself, a desperate pacing between the frontiers of the prisoners' walk, a waiting and an offering, and a last turning away from humanity towards the mercy of God. And then suddenly God speaks, and what follows is the dialogue between God and Christ:

God speaks

Console thyself, thou wouldst not seek me, if thou hadst found me.

Christ speaks

I have sought for thee in my agony, I have sweated such drops of blood for thee.

God speaks

It is tempting me rather than placing thyself on trial, to think that thou hast performed some absent thing: should it happen, then I shall perform it in thee.

Let thyself be guided by my rules; see how well I have led the Virgin and the saints, who have let me act within them.

Christ speaks

The Father loves all that I do.

Here Christ pauses, and the measure of the pause, the peculiar ambivalence of the speech of Christ appears in the manuscript, where Pascal, still obsessed with his own identity as an observer of the agony, carefully rings round the word "I", as though a guilt lay on it—*Le père ayme tout ce que* (*Je*) *fais*. When the colloquy is resumed, Pascal becomes the third character in the drama, and Christ directly challenges him:

Christ speaks

Dost thou wish that it always cost me the blood of my humanity, without thy shedding tears?

The conversion is my affair; fear not, and pray with confidence in me.

I am present with thee by my Word in Scripture, by my Spirit in the Church and by inspiration, by my power in the priests, by my prayer in the faithful.

Physicians will not heal thee, for thou wilt die at last. But it is I who heal thee, and make the body immortal.

Suffer bodily chains and servitude, I deliver thee at present only from spiritual servitude.

I am more a friend to thee than such and such a person, for I have done for thee more than they; they would not have suffered what I have suffered for thee, and they would not have died for thee as I have done in the time of thine infidelities and cruelties, and as I am ready to do, and do, among my elect and at the Holy Sacrament.

If thou knewest thy sins, thou wouldst lose heart.

Pascal speaks

I shall lose it then, Lord, for on Thy assurance I believe their malice.

It should already have been observed that something very extraordinary is happening. Christ's agony in the garden has become Pascal's agony, and Christ in relation to the Father is in the same position as Pascal in relation to Christ. The identification becomes all the more certain when we look at the original manuscript, where Pascal's text reads: *Je le perdrai donc, Seigneur, car* ~~vous~~ *je crois leur malice sur votre assurance*, where the confusion between "I" and "You" seems almost deliberate. There are mysteries everywhere in this mystery. When God says: "It is tempting me rather than placing thyself on trial, to think that thou hast performed some absent thing," there is a reference to the *Deus absconditus* "who has willed himself to hide himself." And when Pascal speaks of malice, he is once again referring to pride, for "when malice has reason on its side, it becomes proud, and parades reason in all its splendour", as he says in another fragment. The war in the garden is a war against reason and an apotheosis of faith, but it is fought on so many levels, with the actors possessing so many disguises, and the battle itself is summoned with so much deliberate confusion that we are appalled by the ferocity of the temptations which are offered to the tempted and agonising soul prostrate in this hour of divine reckoning. But the trial is not yet over. There is still the final act of worship to be made, the final confession of sins. Christ tells Pascal that the heart is not altogether lost, and the forgiveness of sins is offered by the grace of God in the agony:

Christ speaks

No, for I, by whom thou learnest, can heal thee of them, and what I say to thee is a sign that I will heal thee. In proportion to thy expiation of them, thou wilt know them, and it will be said to thee: "Behold, thy sins are forgiven thee". Repent, then, for thy hidden sins, and for the secret malice of those which thou knowest.

Pascal speaks

Lord, I give thee all.

Christ speaks

I love thee more ardently than thou hast loved thy abominations, *ut immundus pro luto*.

To me is the glory, not to thee, worm of earth.

Ask they confessor, when my own words are to thee occasion of evil, vanity, or curiosity.

Here the fragment ends. Pascal has come to the end of the page, and the self-examination which follows, and the desperate cry that "He is more abominable than I, and far from abhorring me, he holds himself honoured that I should go to him and succour him," is the furious coda. The stage, once occupied by God and Christ alone, is occupied only by Pascal; and Pascal sees himself, by the act of faith, the mediator between Christ and God.

So strange and uncompromising a verdict could hardly have been avoided; his own singularity had flowered until it encompassed the heavens and the garden. "I see only darkness everywhere," he once wrote. "Shall I believe I am nothing? Shall I believe I am God?" In another place he wrote: "The imagination enlarges little objects so as to fill our souls with a fantastic estimate; and with rash insolence it belittles the great to its own measure, as when talking to God." The *Mystère de Jésus* is the mystery of Pascal identifying himself with Jesus, in utter misery and the most astounding pride. He is like Baudelaire, in *Les Paradis Artificiels*, "admiring his remorse and glorifying himself, while he is losing his liberty." But the extraordinary brilliance of the poetic drama, the relentless pursuit of God at the moment of His greatest agony, remains one of the greatest dialogues of the human soul with itself, and perhaps the most frightening example of that dialogue when it takes place at the extremities of thought. Beyond this no one except Rimbaud was ever to go, and Rimbaud proceeded by a magical process of hallucination which possesses none of Pascal's subtlety, even though it arrives at the same conclusions. Where Rimbaud approaches to God by the "unreasoned derangement of the senses", Pascal proceeds by the "unreasoned arrangement of faith", stealthily, at night, seeing the *Deus absconditus* plainly before him, standing by Christ's side when Christ whispers over the sleeping apostles, praying beside Christ and sometimes looking up and seeing, on the tortured face of God, his own face magnified. So had Blake, in his illustrations for the Book of Job, given the same face to Job and to God, and both faces were the face of Blake.

Baudelaire provided a valid commentary to the *Mystère de Jésus* when he said: "We have seen men counterfeiting in a sacrilegious manner the sacrament of penitence, at once penitent and confessor, giving themselves an easy absolution, or worse still, they have derived from their condemnation a new field of pride."

For Pascal the abyss remains; it was to remain to the very end of his life. He hangs suspended above it, a point in space, with an uncomprehending look on his face, measuring the infinite distance which separates him from God with an accusing stare. He does not wholly convince us, and he is most convincing always when he speaks of his despair, as when he says: "Seeing too much for denial and too little for assurance, I am in a piteous plight."

He was not alone in his despair, for it is one which attacks the most religious natures and is at the mercy of paradox. When St. Teresa said: "*Pati, Domine, aut mori*,"—"Suffer, Lord, or die," we recognise the authentic accents of Pascal. There is in St. Teresa an outraged sense of individuality which only increases in the presence of God's agony, for the same reason that, by one of the most unhappy tricks of the nervous system, men are most conscious of themselves when they are in greatest pain. With the sharpest physical or mental pain comes the sharpest identification with God. Nor is it Pascal only who finds himself possessed of the extraordinary belief that "God is more abominable than I." It is a theme which can be traced through many of the mystics. St. Teresa when she enters the dark night of the soul wonders at God's incessant and ferocious cruelty, and in one of the most extraordinary and illuminating passages of modern times Marcel Jouhandeau speaks of "the terrible melancholy which I can give to God, for all the angels cannot console me of him. Hell is nowhere else but in the burning heart of God."

Pascal was to return to the theme of the hateful God in a passage which looks like a later addition to the *Mystère de Jésus*. It is written in a more crabbed handwriting, and would seem to have been composed some days later as a final act to the drama:

Christ speaks

Compare not thyself with others, but with Me. If thou dost not find Me in those with whom thou comparest thyself, thou comparest thyself to one who is abominable. If thou findest Me in them, compare thyself to Me. But whom wilt thou compare? Thyself, or Me in thee? If it is thyself, it is one who is abominable. If it is I, thou comparest Me to Myself. Now I am God in all.

I speak to thee, and often counsel thee, because thy director cannot speak to thee, for I do not want thee to lack a guide. And perhaps I do so at his prayers, and thus he leads thee without seeing. Thou wouldst not seek Me, if thou didst not possess me.   (PENSÉES, 555)

The wheel has turned full circle; he is back again where he started, in the world of the paradox, in the world where seeking is finding. Once Pascal had written: "The Stoics say: 'Enter into your own selves; there you will find your rest.' And this is not true." It was not true for Pascal for two reasons, for when he entered himself he found God, and there was no rest.

But Pascal is not alone in this restlessness, in the desire to plumb to its uttermost depths the dangerous mirror. There are times when La Rochefoucauld, his contemporary, can write of the soul's engagement with itself with the same fascinated horror, the same ambiguous reasoning and the same poignancy; behind the cultivated and unpitying mask there are eyes lit with terror. La Rochefoucauld accepts the world as it is; he does not cry out for super-human certainties. It is an evil world, where all emotions are reduced to permutations and combinations of *amour-propre*; all gentlenesses are self-seeking. It is the world of Pascal without the infinite spaces and without the garden, a world where God is indeed the *Deus absconditus*, and "neither death nor the sun can regard themselves fixedly". Like Pascal, he believes that men could hardly endure the society of one another if they were not dupes of one another. He knows that we love those who admire us, and do not always love those we admire. He knows that in the most outrageous self-seeking there may be an element of charity, and in the most humble act of charity there may be an element of self-seeking, yet once or twice we come upon him at the moment when the mask has cracked wide open, and what we see is the terrified glance of the nobleman as he catches himself in the mirror. Even then he speaks slowly and with grace, with a kind of deadly delight in the image he had hoped to conceal from himself. In this portrait of the man walking into the abyss, a portrait which he printed once in his *Maximes* and then mysteriously withdrew, perhaps because it was unbearable for him to see it in print, he describes the proud man in words that are like those of Gregory the Great, but with a psychological delicacy foreign to the Pope:

> Nothing is so impetuous as the desires (of the proud man), nothing so concealed as his intentions, nor so cunning as his conduct. His subtlety goes beyond description, his transformations go beyond metamorphoses, and he is more refined than any chemistry. No one can plumb his depths or pierce through the darkness of his abyss. Where the most penetrating eyes gaze upon him, he makes a thousand imperceptible journeys backwards and forwards; where he is often invisible, even to himself, he conceives, nourishes and raises innumerable affections and hates; and some of them are so monstrous that when they are held to the light, he fails to recognise them, or he dare not confess them. Out of the night that covers him there descends the ridiculous conviction he has of himself; thence come his errors, his churlishness, his ignorance and stupidity concerning himself; thence comes his belief that his sentiments are dead when they are only sleeping, and he imagines he has no desire for action once he is rested, and no taste for things, since he believes he is surfeited. But the dark shadows which enclose him and hide him from himself do not prevent him from seeing perfectly what is outside himself, and in this he bears a resemblance to our own eyes, which reveal everything, and are only blind to being unable to see themselves.

No one else, not even Pascal, has so perfectly expressed the awareness of "the dark shadows which enclose him and hide him from himself". It is not only that the dimensions of the abyss are stated with superb force, but we are made immediately aware that La Rochefoucauld is writing about something he has studied at long intervals, with penetration and deep understanding; and it is impossible to escape the suspicion that he, like Augustine, Jerome, Gregory, and indeed all those who have written well and abundantly about pride in the past, suffered from the disease *in extremis*. He knows all the strange tricks which pride plays on men:

The proud man is so strange that he will often employ the whole of his strength in the most frivolous fashion; he finds his pleasure in the most outworn employments and retains his pride for those which are least worthy. He lives everywhere, he lives of everything, and he lives of nothing; he accepts things and the privations that go with them; he even goes over to those who will make war on him, he will take part in whatever plans they make—and this is the most admirable of all—he hates himself with them, he plots his own destruction and works toward his own ruin. He has no care for anything except his own existence, and as long as he exists, he desires to be his own enemy.

Only once is the Count de la Rochefoucauld guilty of humility, and that is when he comes to the conclusion that "whatever discoveries are made in the country of pride, there still remain unknown territories." There is a sense in which the whole of the *Maximes* is an exploration of the country of pride, and it is hardly conceivable that any part of this country was left unexplored by him. He said of himself: "I have little understanding of pity, and would that I had none at all." And in words that echo down from a famous statement of Duns Scotus, he said that "our virtues are for the most part our vices disguised." There is something almost exhilarating in the eagerness of his pursuit of pride; at last he has trapped it in a corner, where, weakened by the chase, it can do nothing but reveal itself. He denies God, but he faces the same problem that faced St. Augustine, and he has the merit of seeing more clearly than the Christian fathers the peculiar dissonances of the human spirit. All that Corneille prized in his characters is ruthlessly examined: *l'énergie, la fermeté, l'honneur, la constance,* all are seen to be delusions, and all the more vicious because man's habits of self-delusion are seen to be curable, for "hypocrisy is only the homage which vice renders to virtue," and though "the virtues lose themselves in self-interest, as rivers lose themselves in the sea," yet somewhere, in these abandoned regions, he hints at the presence of the virgin fountainheads. It is not his fault if he has not been there; he too loses himself in the sea.

It is the peculiar virtue of La Rochefoucauld that he sees the world as it is, knowing that ridicule dishonours more than dishonour, and that there are heroes of evil as there are heroes of good. He does not attempt to ape God. To him suffering is something vile and beyond all things uncalled-for, and the least suffering is undeserved. "Know, proud man, what a paradox thou art in thyself," said Pascal, adding like a whispered prayer: "And let this foolish nature keep silent." La Rochefoucauld does not keep silent. He knows the paradox of pride—the paradox which resolves itself into the sight of the most gifted of men chasing their own tails and determined upon their own destruction.

In the end it is Pascal who wins, because he goes further. Nearly all of the *Maximes* are contained in the *Pensées*, but Pascal possesses an urgency that drives him further. Men are stripped of their pretensions by the Count; the mathematician strips them of everything except their position on the Cartesian co-ordinates: "For what is man before Nature? A nothing with regard to the infinite, an everything in regard to nothingness, a point between nothing and all." And God is all.

It is not quite so simple, of course: pride remains. There is always Melville's "venomous small thing which tickled with the poisoned straw." La Rochefoucauld approved of pride—the ordinary pride of *l'homme moyen sensuel*, for this alone gave a man a desire to live: "Nature, which has so wisely arranged the organs of the human body in order to give us happiness, has given us pride to spare the sorrow of realising our imperfections." It was the middle way. Beyond that, pride became the thing which stares desperately out of a corner, as blind as the inner recesses of the eyes, a thing so terrible that he almost quails before his own description of it, and in his lifetime never allowed it to be published again, as though he knew he had revealed too many secrets about himself.

Beyond everything the abyss remains for Pascal, as it remains, discreetly hidden in the background, for La Rochefoucauld. Almost it is as though the abyss of God were the only certain things. It is by chance that men are born, a tiny grain in the ureter of Cromwell alters the destiny of England, the least movement affects all nature, and even knowledge is no guarantee of justice, for "he who knows the will of the master will be beaten

with more blows, because of the power he has by his knowledge."
In this desperate plight only grace seems of any avail; grace, and
that desperate little prayer for mankind which is heard, under
various disguises, through Pascal's whole work: "People would
never get into trouble if they could learn how to dwell in peace,
in a room. . . ."

The Titans

MICHELANGELO sketched the Christian Prometheus in two designs: one representing the Titan gnawed by the eagle, the other crucified vertically on the branches of an enormous oak. Somehow, and very gradually over the centuries, there had come about an identification between Christ and the Titan princes. Christ was the tragic hero, who harrowed hell after suffering as Prometheus had suffered; and in the high Renaissance Christianity and paganism found common ground.

It is easy enough to understand why the Titans should have appealed to the Renaissance: it is less easy to understand why six great poets at the turn of the eighteenth century—Goethe, Hölderlin, Blake, Shelley, Keats and Wordsworth—should have been tormented by the legend of the Titans to such an extent that each felt himself compelled to write about them at length. Only one succeeded in writing about them with any peace of mind. With the others the process is fragmentary; they return repeatedly to the contest; they wrestle with the Titans, and find themselves defeated. It was a time of decaying traditions. There had been (in the words of Coleridge) "in some sense, a Fall". The steam engine was coming in. The American revolution had shattered autocracy, but though a new power and a new pride were coming to men, and men believed more than ever that they could control natural forces, there was also a feeling of loss and despair, for they were surrendering the safeguards of religion. So there comes gradually into the world of the late eighteenth century a sense of guilt and a hopeless desire to return to Eden. This loneliness, this pride, the sudden desire to imitate the Titans and to wrestle with them and finally to pity them and abandon them, and then return to them again, forever being tortured by them, desiring to make men in their image, is clearly confessed by Goethe in *Dichtung and Wahrheit*:

The common faith of man must fall most heavily on those whose intellectual powers develop early and widely. We may rise in the world under the protection of our parents and relations, we may lean upon our brothers and sisters and friends, and be supported by our acquaintances and made happy by those we love, but in the end a man is always thrown back upon himself. It seems as though God has so placed himself in relation to men as not always to be able to respond to their reverence, trust and love; at least not at critical moments. Young enough, I learned that in the moments of greatest need, the call came to me: "Physician, heal thyself," and how frequently have I been compelled to sigh out in agony: "I tread the wine-press alone. . . ."

As I reflected upon my natural gift, and found that it belonged to me alone, and that it could neither be hindered nor favoured by anything foreign to me, I found I could base my intellectual life wholly upon it. This idea thereupon confronted me in a new form: the old mythological figure of Prometheus occurred to me, who, separated from the gods, peopled the world with his own workshop. I felt quite clearly that one can only create something of importance when one is completely isolated. . . . So, in the fashion of Prometheus, I separated myself from the gods also, and so much the more naturally, as with my character and way of thinking one sentiment always swallowed up and repelled another.

The fable of Prometheus became alive in me. The old Titan garment I cut up in my own shape. . . . Nevertheless, the spirit of the Titans and Giants storming heaven afforded me no material for my poetic art. Rather did it seem fitting for me to represent the peaceful, sculptural and always patient opposition, which recognises the superior power, but wishes to take an equal position. Also the bolder persons of that breed, Tantalus, Ixion, Sisyphus, were my saints. Received into the society of the gods, they would not behave submissively enough and like supercilious guests they deserved the wrath of their patronising host, and drew upon themselves a melancholy banishment.   (DICHTUNG UND WAHRHEIT, XV)

The loneliness, the sense of banishment, the desire to cut the Titan garment into his own shape, all these were to remain and to become transmuted into the figure of Faust—the fist shaken at the heavens. In an oration delivered at Strasbourg when Goethe was twenty-one, he spoke of Shakespeare rivalling Prometheus, possessing *colossal* size. But when Goethe wrote poetry concerning Prometheus, there was no effort to fashion the Titan on a colossal scale; instead, he depicted a young and generous god who, out of his innate generosity and courage of soul, defies the evil powers of heaven. The poem should be quoted at length. It is the first of the Prometheus-poems which were to fill the anthologies of the early nineteenth century. Goethe draws the picture of an adorable youth, not unlike the archaic Apollos of the early Greek sculptors, a youth made suddenly conscious of his powers. The portrait of Prometheus will change till at last, in the hands of Blake, Prometheus-Urizen grows old and withered and burnt in the sun. Meanwhile, in Goethe's poem *Prometheus* we see the young god, naked and handsome, shouting his proud defiance at the King of Heaven:

> O curtain thy Heavens, Zeus,
> With misty vapours,
> And rage as thou wilt on the heights
> And upon the oak-trees,
> Like a boy lopping thistles,
> Yet must thou leave me my earth
> And my hut thou never built
> And my hearth also,
> Whose bright flame
> Thou enviest.
> I know nothing so pitiful
> Under the sun,
> As the gods miserably feeding
> Upon the savour of prayers

And proffered sacrifices,
So rejoicing their majesty.
O, they would suffer want
Were it not for children and beggars
And the fools without hope.

Once in my childhood I
Was innocent of all things,
And lifted my erring eyes
Towards the sun above me,
Believing the sun was an ear
To hear my lament, or a heart
Like mine to comfort the oppressed.

Who then was it helped me
Against the pride of the Titans?
Who saved me from death,
Who saved me from slavery?
Hast thou not accomplished all thyself,
O sacred burning heart?
In thy innocent youth, though deceived,
Didst thou not render grace for thy salvation
To him who sleeps above?

I reverence thee? Wherefore?
Hast thou softened the pains
Of those who are heavy-laden?
Hast thou stilled the tears
Of those in anguish?
Who fashioned me man?——
Was it not Almighty Time
And Fate eternal,
My lords and thine?
If the choice were thine,
I would hate my life,
I would flee to the wilds,——
For then not one
Of our flowering dreams would ripen.

Here I sit and shape
Man in my image,
A race like myself
That will suffer and weep,
And rejoice and enjoy,
And scorn thee
As I do!

It was almost his first poem, and never again except in *Iphigenie auf Tauris*, and then only at odd moments, was he to recapture the tone of innocent effrontery. It is hardly pride. A youth awakens on a summer's day and idly challenges the gods, and we do not entirely believe in the race that will suffer and weep and scorn the gods, for Goethe is only twenty-four. Disillusion will come later; the tone will grow harsher; the brightness will go out of his eyes. But for a brief moment Goethe had captured the exhilaration and powerful delight of those early days when the French Revolution still offered men the hope of realising their dreams. Fifteen years later something of the intoxication remained, and the poet Hölderlin could write: "Boldly forget what you have inherited and won—all laws and customs—and like new-born babes lift up your eyes to godlike nature." There is a sense in which Goethe's Prometheus is not even a youth, but a babe intoxicated by sunlight and the power to move his muscles. We shall recognise he is a Titan only when he is muscle-bound.

In 1779, the date of the first version of *Iphigenie auf Tauris*, Goethe entered his thirtieth year. The visionary dreams were over; never again was he to imagine himself larger than nature. He began to work slowly, deliberately, almost ponderously. The drama, which was to relate the story of a descendant of the Titans, refused to be written in a form acceptable to the poet. On a September morning seven years later, while he was idly watching the waves of Lago di Garda breaking against the shore, a line from Virgil's *Georgics* slipped into his mind—it was the tremendous *fluctibus et fremitu resonans, Benace, marino*. The line supplied the passionate music for describing the Titans, but he was still in need of a portrait of the Titan princess. Sometime later, wandering into a church in Bologna, he came face to face with a painting of St.

Agatha; in her he seemed to see the fierce health and assurance he demanded of his heroine, and he declared later that he would never allow Iphigenia to say anything that the saint might not have uttered. So extraordinary a mingling of Virgil, a Christian saint, a Titan princess and a youthful enthusiasm for the heaven-storming Giants could hardly be expected to be a complete success; what is surprising is that he succeeded so often in striking fire from the assorted flints. When Agatha-Iphigenia proclaims:

> I have delivered now into thy hands
> The remnants of the house of Tantalus.
> Destroy us—if thou darest,

we hear the authentic accents of the genius of pride, and when Agatha-Iphigenia offers herself to the executioner and bares her breasts, the accents of Christian hagiography have wholly disappeared in *Vernimm: ich bin von Tantalus Geschlecht*. See: I am of the race of Tantalus.

But there are many kinds of pride, many ways in which the over-weening soul declares itself. There is the pride which is direct, a fist smashing into the face of heaven, and there is the more contemplative pride of the Promethean who sees himself quietly in possession of the heavenly mansion; and this pride, too, Goethe possessed, or at least spoke of in his poetry. Scattered among the fragments of the unfinished Prometheus-drama there are intimations of the kind of immortality which the proud man desires, an immortality of power:

PROMETHEUS

> That which I have they cannot rob me of;
> That which they have, let them guard well.
> Here mine, here thine;
> And thus we are distinguished.

EPIMETHEUS

> What, then, is thine?

PROMETHEUS

> The circle that my activity doth fill.

Here pride has reached its term, and it is no longer necessary for Prometheus to shout against the gods—all is accomplished. In the beginning was the deed, and the deed has been taken over wholly by Prometheus, who can contemplate the immense circle of his accomplishment with a quiet assurance that it will never be taken from him. This fragmentary Prometheus describes "the spirit who affirms", while Mephistopheles is no more than a spirit who continually denies. What there is of affirmation in *Faust* is given over to the Wittenberg doctor. Mephistopheles tells him that no goal or measure has been set to him and every desire will be granted to him, but it is not the self-fulfilment of a Titan that Faust desires; he desires the extremes of excitement:

> Hearken, the thing I aim for is not joy:
> I thirst for tumult, agonising bliss,
> Hatred in love with hatred, quickening woes.
> Purged of a love of knowledge, my heart shall be
> Wide open to all men's sorrows,
> And all that men have suffered shall be mine,
> My mind shall seize the highest and the lowest,
> And I shall heap about my heart the good and evil,
> And so increase myself to reach those bounds
> They reach, even to entire destruction!

Prometheus was more convincing. A shadow has fallen somewhere: it is a shadow which is to pursue Faust to the very threshold of the Mothers. These are not the aims which a rebel demands of the King of Hell; there is nobility certainly, but it is the kind of nobility which Walter Pater demanded of his pupils. Offered the universe, Faust shouts at the top of his voice and asks for a *frisson!* It is a strange enough desire, and perhaps the explanation lies in Goethe's autobiography, where he explains that he turned away from the Titans in a kind of despair, having measured himself against them and found himself wanting, and something of that journey is expressed in the superb *Song of the Parcae* in *Iphigenie auf Aulis*, a song which seems to have been sung in old age by the same young Prometheus who once vaunted himself against the gods. Not the power of Prometheus but the power of the Immortals is celebrated:

They fear the Immortals,
The children of men!
The gods hold dominion
In hands everlasting,
And wield their powers
According to their will.
Let him fear them doubly
Who is exalted by them.
On cliffs and clouds
Their seats are ordered
Around golden tables.

When discord arises
The guests are thrown headlong
Down night-dark abysses,
Shamed and derided,
And vainly they wait there,
Fettered in darkness,
The judgment of justice.

And the gods remain
Eternally feasting
On golden tables.
They stride over mountains:
From throats of the abysses
Breath streams towards them
Like offerings of incense
On lightly-borne clouds—
Breath from the Titans
Who choke in abysses.

These Lords turn their eyes
Brimming with blessing
For whole generations:
Their gaze is averted
From features of grandchildren,
Still silently speaking
Of the loved ancestors.

So sang the Parcae.
The exile listens
In the night-dark cave,
The ancient, the songs,
Dreams of children and grandsons,
And shakes his head.

The vision of the Titans has faded; they have fallen to the uttermost pits of Hell, and there the exiles dream of the children they might have had, the race that will "suffer and weep and rejoice and enjoy and scorn the gods". It did not happen; the indifferent gods rule. From this point onward Goethe dismisses the Titans. Faust is not a Titan, nor is Mephistopheles; they are furious evangels of disaster, but they are not gods.

Almost at the same time that Goethe was writing *Iphigenia auf Aulis*, the poet Friedrich Hölderlin was coming to maturity. Handsome, supremely gifted, the most enviable in his youth of the children of time, he grew up to become the most tortured of men and to spend the last forty years of his life insane. Like Wordsworth he was born in 1770; like Wordsworth too he was to know a time when to be alive was very heaven. His early letters breathe a passionate love of the new age. He adored Schiller, whose *Hymn to Joy* would bring tears to his eyes; he played the flute with Hegel and Schelling; he roamed the countryside; he lived with an intensity which was unusual even in an age when the young in Germany were naturally intense. He wrote when he was twenty-three: "I love the race of the coming centuries. This is my most holy hope, the faith that keeps me strong and active—our descendants will be better than us. Freedom must come at last, and Virtue will thrive better in the warming light of Freedom than under the ice-cold sky of despotism. We live in an age when everything is working towards better things. Look, dear Karl, all my hopes are centred on this—this, that I may awaken in my own age the seeds that will ripen in the ages to come." One could expect that a mind so acutely in love with life would meet with reverses—he met so many that he broke under the strain. But when we recall him, we remember his physical beauty and the intransigence of his mind, which sparkled like frost on a sunny morning, and he seems to us the nearest thing that has ever occurred on the European mainland to a Greek god.

But if he was god-like—and all those who knew him in his youth speak of the radiance around him—he was also, in a singular way, a man whose whole life was devoted to his time, breathing the spirit of his time and having in a sense almost no identity of his own. His eye noted physical things, his body moved on a physical earth, he fell in love with another man's wife and knew the appalling sense of separation which occurred when he had to leave her and her children forever, he travelled to Switzerland and France, he broke off a friendship with Schiller, or it was broken off for him, he wrote letters and poems of amazing power, but most of all we are conscious that he was a nervous mirror reflecting without any refraction the circumstances of his time; and when he broke down, it was because something within the epoch had also broken: the crystal had splintered, there were to be no realised dreams of freedom and the great road followed by Europe until then turned abruptly at the point where he went straight on, to find himself in a nightmare world of exile. All through Hölderlin's poetry we are conscious of the sense of exile, the brooding desire to return home—but where was home? The gods were hidden from him—*dii absconditi*—and he hardly recognised the faces of the people he met on the streets; there was only one face, that of the girl whom he called Diotima, but she was taken from him. So he lived on in the precarious world of madness, loved by his friends, but abandoned by the stream of time, a pure nerve, writing during the days of breakdown the terrible broken elegies which are now his greatest claim to fame.

In *Patmos* Hölderlin wrote as one would write in a moment of apocalyptic time. All of Europe is spread out before him, all history, all mythology are summoned to be surveyed, and the poet travels in an instant of apocalyptic time to Jerusalem in order to share the hero's passion, to take part in the last supper and to hear the heroic words of warning from the ascending Christ. Nothing less than a complete mythology or history, as Hölderlin saw it, is presented to the reader, but it is a mythology differing from all other mythologies in that it attempts at one and the same time to present Christ present and Christ absent, to show a world inhabited and ruled by God, and at the same time deprived of God; and the great turning point of the drama (for if the poem is a long lyrical fragment it is also like Pascal's *Mystère de Jésus* a mystery play) is when Christ disappears and leaves the world to men. It was one of Hölderlin's profoundest convictions that there are times when the gods rule and times when they altogether vanish from the scene; and when they have vanished men are in the same case as the fallen Titans, for they have neither home nor law, nor any way of discovering the truth; they are exiled from the hands of God, hungry, shivering and alone. In one of those fragments which were not finally included in the finished poem, a fragment that exists in its own right although it was never completed and could never be completed, Hölderlin wrote:

> O island of Light!
> For when, no longer guarded by men,
> The shadowless roads grieve and the trees,
> And the empires, the young earth of love, crumbled,
> Athletic, in ruins,
> And the native innocence
> Was split asunder. . . .
> For God with indomitable hate hates those
> With omniscient minds. But John on the earth
> Free of all chains remains pure.

It is the landscape of the fallen Titan world.

This landscape returns to haunt the long poem *Patmos* which he wrote when his mind was already breaking for the loss of his beloved Diotima. In this poem of grave power and quite extraordinary penetration, Hölderlin sees himself as setting out towards the island of Patmos. With memories of an early journey to Switzerland, he pursues his way alone across the length of Europe and Asia Minor towards this island seen in the setting sun or in the dawn-light—the light that is shed over the poem is brilliant and flickering, but it is impossible to tell whether it is late evening or early morning. A strangeness surrounds the journey. Huge and beautiful images are conjured up—the eagles dwell among the sum- mits of Time, bridges and ladders join the inaccessible cliffs, all Greece is bathed in a mysterious divine radiance. At last the poet comes to Patmos in search of John, the beloved of Christ, he who alone "on the earth free of all chains remains pure". But Christ is also present in some mysterious way upon the island; here he walks after the Crucifixion, shedding his love among the apostles for a while, but afterwards he ascends to Heaven, leaving Hölderlin and the disciples baffled. In the first verse of all Hölderlin describes the world after the Fall and his desperate desire to journey to the East and discover there the springs of a new faith:

> Near is
> And hard to seize the God.
> But where danger is, there rises
> The saving one also.
> In darkness dwell the eagles
> And fearless go
> The sons of the Alps over the Abyss
> On lightly built bridges.
> Therefore, since all round are piled
> The summits of Time,
> And the dear beloved dwell near, languishing on
> Inaccessible hills,
> Give us innocent water,
> O wings give us, that with most faithful thoughts
> We may go hither and return again.

> Thus I spoke, then I was led
> More swiftly than I could tell
> And far, whither I never
> Thought to come, by a Genius
> From my own home. There dawned
> In twilight as I went,
> The shadowy forest
> And the yearning brooks
> Of my Fatherland: I knew the lands no more.
> Soon in new splendour
> Mysteriously
> In golden smoke there gleamed
> Swiftly awakened

With the steps of the sun,
Fragrant with a thousand peaks,

Asia appeared to me and blinded I sought
Something I knew, for the broad roads
Seemed strange to me
Where down from Tmolus goes
Gold-ornamented Pactolus,
And there is Taurus and Messogis,
And full of flowers the garden,
A still fire. But in the light
High flowers the silver snow;
And sign of eternal life
On inaccessible walls
Grows the ancient ivy, and borne on
Living pillars, cedars and laurels
The solemn,
The divinely-built palaces.

There, bathing in the light of the Orient, he sees Patmos, sacred to the memory of John, the lover of Christ, and immediately afterwards, by a sudden and entirely unexpected leap, we are brought into the presence of Christ and the apostles at the last supper, as though this event took place on the island, or was continually taking place in the recollection of the saint as he sits brooding on the rock. As in a Greek tragedy, the death of Christ takes place off-stage; it is hardly mentioned. We are left with the grief of the apostles, who are depicted for us like Greek heroes—"the heroes of death", assembled together to mourn, while "the thunder of God rolls rumbling far over their boding heads". There was despair in the beginning—"God is near and hard to seize"—but at the moment when God seemed almost tangible, He has departed; and a greater despair comes over the poet and the apostles. It is not only that there has been a Fall; there is a second Fall; God has shown himself and then gone away from men, leaving them to their dread, their insatiable loneliness, and the despair of grief. Hölderlin looks back towards the time before God appeared. There was darkness, but the darkness was endurable:

It was joy
To live in loving night, preserving
In simple eyes steadfast
Abysses of wisdom. And the living images
Grew green in the depths of the mountains.

But now the greater darkness is intolerable, for God in showing himself for a moment and then departing has made the loneliness greater, and men are more completely separated from one another than ever before:

But when He died,
He on whom beauty chiefly clung,
So that a miracle was wrought in His image,
And the Heavenly Ones pointed at Him,
And when, an eternal enigma for one another,
They could not reach one another,
Though they lived together in memory of Him,
And the sand was not taken away
Nor the pasture, but the temples
Were seized, when the glory
Of the demi-god and of his disciples
Faded and even the Highest
Averts his face,
So that nowhere again is there
Anything immortal to be seen in Heaven or
On the green earth—why this?

There is no answer, except that the Lord will burn up the chaff with unquenchable flames, for the purpose of Christ's coming was to burn out evil; but gradually the vindictive purpose is forgotten, and the apostles, accustoming themselves to his absence, remember the power of holy script and song; and *Patmos* ends, like *Kubla Khan*, with a kind of spell, a praise of song and holy writ and an acceptance of defeat; for Christ is no longer expected to come.

In the most literal sense *Patmos* is a description of the world after the Fall. The apostles are given the power and the lineaments of the Greek heroes, but their strength is unavailing. There is hope, but of a different kind; for the rest of time we live in an El Greco landscape of thundering clouds and lightning, while hidden in the heavens is the secret calm of Christ:

> Calm is His Sign
> In the thundering heavens. And One stands beneath
> His whole life long. For Christ lives still,
> And they, the heroes, His sons,
> And holy script have all come
> From Him. And the deeds of the world declare
> The lightning till now.
> A race unceasing. But He is near. For all
> His works are known to Him from everlasting.

And in another fragment of the same poem Hölderlin suggests the final grace which alone gives meaning to the world: "The Heavenly Ones and the Living are joined together for everlasting."

It is Hölderlin's virtue that he could depict the world of the Fall with extraordinary penetration, measuring the hopes that remained, the grace by which men were preserved, and stating them all in verses that shine with the splendour of Pindar, from whom he derived his metre. *Patmos* begins in despair, leaps out of despair during the journey to the Orient and finally breaks down under the weight of despair when Christ leaves the earth, and yet something remains—and what remains is the art of song, which is sacred to the Greek gods and to the risen Christ. In these untravelled roads Hölderlin walks as an equal with the apostles; and he is present among them like a fourteenth guest.

The Greek world obtrudes everywhere in Hölderlin. In *Der Einzige* the conflict between Olympus and the Christian Heaven is fought out nakedly; and like a constant echo of an unseen chorus, there are heard warnings of pride. He is so desperate to escape from the Fall that he assumes himself some of the strength of the Titans, wrestles with Christ and at last admits His superiority. The same theme is continued in the poem *Die Titanen*, where Hölderlin describes a war against Heaven, and how the Thunderer strikes down the revolt of Chaos, "the unconfined abyss":

And in the depths the Thunderer
Seizes it, so that it shall become
Living, meaning
That the Heavenly One
Descends to the dead, and powerfully does it dawn
On the all-perceiving one
In the unconfined abyss.
But I dare not say
That the Heavenly Ones would become weak
When revolt already ferments.
But if
    ——and it breaks out
Over the summits of the Father, then
——
——and the bird of Heaven
Gives him warning. Marvellously in His wrath
He understands.

It is all broken fragments, clauses which are never completed, perhaps because it is impossible to complete them; a sense of heavy responsibility and destiny hangs over the poet. He sees by the light of lightning flashes; when they are gone, he trembles and waits. In *Die Wildnis* he attempts to complete the picture of the war in Heaven. The war takes place in some timeless moment of time, when the earth is being created and "shapely are the astonished hills, their foreheads touched with a sign" of holiness, for "they were marked with the trembling rays of God". At this stage Hölderlin explains the reason for the Fall: "The daughter of the Thunder-bearer dared to seize him in an unfilial way." Immediately "the sweetly scented fire from above" is extinguished; and once more there is a Fall, a rebellion against God, which is only brought to an end when God sends forth His grace:

So inwardly here and there
The rebellion is quieted,
For the Thunder-bearer pours out
Joys, and yet He had almost forgotten
Heaven in His wrath,
Had not Wisdom warned Him;

> But now it gleams
> In the poor place,
> And marvellously great will it remain.
> Mountains hang   Lakes
> Warm depths   but the winds cool them

The "poor place" of earth retains its splendour; almost the rebellion has been quenched at the source, and in the next four lines, thrown hurriedly on the page, Hölderlin attempts to suggest the glory of this time by a magnificent evocation of islands, peninsulas and a shield gleaming like roses:

> Islands and peninsulas, and
> Grottos to pray in,
> And a gleaming shield, quick
> Like roses.

It is almost a vision of paradise, but the rebellious souls are immediately afterwards heard muttering. Flames rise, striking upwards, and the luxurious weeds of envy writhe like these flames, till at length they cover the whole wilderness like a fermenting cloud; but in the middle of the passage Hölderlin creates a note of terror by suggesting that the Creator is jesting —*es scherzet der Schöpferische*. There is an extraordinary virulence in the poet's description of the birth of the Titans:

> There is created still another race,
> So there flowers many a luxuriant weed,
> Which seems more than it is, rises quicker
> Out of the earth, awkwardly: for the Creator
> Jests, and men do not understand it.
> Too much in anger it climbs and grows.
> And like flames beginning to consume a house,
> It strikes upward, thoughtless, and
> Spares no space at all, covering
> The helpless wilderness
> With a fiercely fermenting steaming cloud,
> Desiring to appear divine.
> But fearfully inhospitable, the sightless labyrinth
> Winds through the garden

Where a man with pure hands
Can hardly find a way out.
He who is sent goes seeking like a wild beast
What is necessary. So with his (bare) arms,
Full of foreboding, a man may reach the goal.
Here even the Heavenly Ones need a wall or a sign
To show them the way, or to bathe,
And the heart of man burns like a fire.

The passionate description of the beginning of pride is followed by an invocation of the Thunder-bearer above the clouds, surrounded by his eagles and angels and by the gods of Greece, who attend upon him. It is one of the most majestic evocations in all literature, and it ends, as we might have expected, with the classic warning to man against exceeding his limitations. Hercules and the Dioscuri stand by the side of the Thunder-bearer, and it is from them rather than from any Christian source that the Titans receive their punishment:

But the Father
Still has others with Him.
Far, far above the Alps
Are the Eagles,
Or so we must consider them lest men wrathfully
Interpret the poets according to their own senses,
And they dwell above the flying of the birds,
Around the throne of the God of Joy,
And they cover the Abyss, with Him, in the time of splitting
    asunder:
They are above the foreheads of men
And above the Prophets, and it may be
That the godless shadows of Hell are envious of them,
For they are in love with fear.

But *they* were driven away, revealing
A pure destiny, from the sacred tables of earth
By cleansing Hercules,
Who remains eternally pure, even now,
Beside the Sovereign Lord; and drawing breath

The Dioscuri mount up and down
On inaccessible stairways, when from the heavenly castles
The mountains draw away
By night and the daughter of Heaven—

Hölderlin says no more about the mysterious "daughter of Heaven",
who may have been the daughter responsible for the incestuous
crime. The last lines break down under the weight of the significance they are made to bear. There is no final solution. The peace
of Heaven is shattered by the intransigence of earth. Men must
help the Father, go according to the ways of the Father, they
must never exceed the measure or "grow at the wrong time".

> They help the Father,
> So they may be at peace. But when
> The useless busybodies of the earth
> Provoke them, and the Heavenly Ones are crazed
> —— ———— the signs, burning do they come.
>
> For the Meditating God
> Hates
> Growth at the wrong time.

It is the theme of *hubris*, which has indeed been implicit throughout the revolt of the Titans; but we never know how the revolt
took place, or where, and why the incestuous relation ever existed,
or who was "the daughter of Heaven".

These fragmentary poems seem to belong to an uncompleted
cycle; we can only guess at the direction the poet intended to
pursue, before he was struck down by madness and loneliness, to
spend the rest of his life in a small house overlooking the waters
of the Neckar in the care of an old carpenter. But the theme seems
to have been the projection, on a universal scale, of the theme
which had haunted him all his life—of pride robed in majesty
riding for a fall. He had stated it in *Empedocles*, which he wrote
three times, each time giving it a different ending. But Empedocles
is not only proud; he attempts something even greater. When the
gods favoured him, he tried to make them serve his own purposes.
Empedocles announces his own crime:

> Ah, it is over!
> Do not conceal it even from yourself.
> Your guilt is certain, unhappy Tantalus.
> You have defiled the sanctuary and rent
> In two with arrant pride the lovely bond,
> Ignoble man! When the genii of the world
> With love forgot themselves in you, you thought
> Only of yourself, O barren fool; you believed
> The good ones sold to you, and they,
> The Heavenly Ones would work for you like idiot servants.

But in spite of the inevitable punishment, he continues to see himself as god-like:

> So the Gods
> Became my slaves, and I alone
> Was God in arrogance and pride.

In Hölderlin's theoretical writing the same problem is faced, with even more alarming insight. He was concerned to know the limits of the power of the poet, the *vates* who by his words acts as a kind of mediator between God and mankind. To explain the nature of poetry, he was compelled to form a theory of poetic consciousness. It seemed to him that the poet's consciousness working at the highest pressure developed a peculiar identity with the things it contemplated. "It is a great aid to the soul secretly at work" he once wrote, "that on the summit of consciousness it evades the conscious. In a high state of consciousness the soul always compares itself with objects which have no consciousness, but which, because of their fate, assume the form of our consciousness." At another time he wrote, with even more penetration: "The point at which soberness (*Nüchternheit*) deserts you is the point at which you reach the limit of your inspiration. A great poet is never deserted by his self, however much he may lift himself above himself. *It is possible to fall into the heights as well as into the depths.*"

When Hölderlin was mad, a strange sharp-faced figure enclosed in mystery, stumbling over his words, hitting out at the thistles on his path, staring for hours at the blue milky waters of the

Neckar below his window and sometimes composing strangely brilliant poems which possessed no meaning at all, Bettina von Arnim came to visit him. Somehow—for the sentences she wrote down afterwards have the authentic ring of Hölderlin's prose— she succeeded in writing down the strange theories he wove out of the air; and now at last the terrible poetic desire to be a god had left him, for Hölderlin acknowledged that the law of poetry, as of life was: "Not as I will, but as Thou wilt," and in one blinding sentence he illuminated the problem which had troubled Æschylus and all the tragic poets—the problem of why the gods demanded so implacably their vengeance on the heroes:

> He who recognises Poetry in the divine sense must acknowledge the mind of the All-High as beyond his intellectual law. "Not as I will, but as Thou wilt." Therefore he must himself construct no laws, because Poetry will never allow herself to be fettered, and versification will always be an empty house inhabited by goblins. Law in Poetry is the form of the idea in which the mind must move, but not retard its steps. The Law to which man would reduce the Idea deadens the form of the Idea, and therefore the divine cannot be received in the human mind. The body of Poetry is the form of the Idea, and when seized by Tragedy becomes fatally positive, *for murder flows from the divine.*
>
> (BETTINA VON ARNIM, GÜNDERODE, XXV)

If we can believe the evidence of those last scattered poems, written on the verge of madness, in grief for the loss of Diotima, Hölderlin found himself compelled to wage war with the Titan princes, and the mythology of the times demanded their presence in his soul, for the same reason that Blake found them in himself.

In the same year that Hölderlin was working over the final drafts of *Patmos*, Blake had completed a work entitled *Jerusalem.* The aims were similar: to describe a fall from grace, and to show how paradise could be regained. There had been a fall, an abandonment of the essential ritual of life. Blake, too, had seen "the covenant of Priam" broken. The imagination quails before the elementals Blake creates as projections of his own wrath; there are as many spirits wandering through Blake's Hells as there are in

Tantric Buddhism. What can we make of Ozoth and Manathu Varcyon and their eight million children? If Blake had desired to express the eternal torments of Hell, he has succeeded well enough in *Jerusalem*, yet far more often than we might expect the image comes clear—we recognise Urizen, who "smells of dry figs", the "cold leper" in whose sight the heavens are impure. He is painted majestically in *The First Book of Urizen*. His eyes are closed, white leprous rays flow from his head, and on the face of Urizen there is all the suffering and nobility of Job, and indeed he is not far removed from Job, who asked so many questions of the Deity that in a rage God showed him Behemoth and Leviathan, the instruments of His power. Blake almost trembles with rage when he describes Urizen, who is all that Los (the sunlit imagination) and Luvah (loving compassion) are not. He is the "creator of man, mistaken demon of Heaven", and as he wanders hither and thither in search of his prey, anointed with the selfhood, proclaiming himself "God from Eternity to Eternity," and bidding everyone know that "the spectre is the man; the rest is delusion and fancy," he acquires an almost physical presence, however monstrous and huge, and however often he changes his shape. He begins as a principle of light, for there was a time when he was joined to Los; then he is rent from Los' side, to become "prolific, self-enclosed, all repelling", shouting against his selfhood or proclaiming its majesty as the spirit wills him, but always enslaved in his own selfhood or "in his spectre's power". He is the continuing character of all Blake's work, brother of Nobodaddy, Creeping Jesus and "the strong man" in the *Descriptive Catalogue*, who acts from "conscious superiority, and marches on in fearless dependence of the divine decrees, raging with the inspirations of the prophetic mind." It is possible that he derives his name from Uriel, the archangel of the sun in *Paradise Lost*, but everything else about him is Blake's own, signed with Blake's characteristic sign-manual, as elemental as Caliban or Grendel, and more ferocious than either.

The theme of pride pursued Blake from the beginning. As early as *The Visions of the Daughters of Albion*, engraved and printed in 1793, he sees self-love as "a creeping skeleton with lamp-like eyes watching round the frozen marriage-bed". In *Songs of Experience*, produced a year later, he described the landscape of the fall in several poems, and never more concretely than in the lines where he speaks of "the Holy Word", walking among the ancient trees, calling upon the lapsed souls. There are, in Blake's work, a hundred portraits of the "lapsed souls". He is not always Urizen. He has many names, and once at least he is Christ. In *Jerusalem* the fallen Titan is portrayed in all his misery and glory:

> In a dark and unknown Night
> Outstretch'd his Giant beauty on the ground in pain and tears:
> His Children exil'd from his breast pass to and fro before him,
> His birds are silent on his hills, flocks die beneath his branches,
> His milk of Cows and honey of Bees and fruit of golden harvest
> Is gather'd in the scorching heat and in the driving rain.
> Where once he sat, he weary walks in misery and pain,
> His Giant beauty and perfection fallen into dust. . . .
>
> (JERUSALEM, I, 18, 19)

It is an extraordinary picture, with its overtones of Gethsemane and the silent traveller under the Hill, its lilting terror and planetary misery. "It is given us nowhere to rest," cried Hölderlin's Hyperion in his *Song of Fate*, and it is to the achievement of Blake that he has perfectly described the "nowhere" of the lost souls. It is a world of Titanic despair, such as Rousseau described:

> All that is outside myself is henceforth foreign to me. I have no neighbours in this world, none who are like me, no brothers. I feel as though I had fallen on to this earth from a foreign planet where I lived before. Whatever I notice in the external world brings to my heart only pain and affliction; whenever I cast my eye upon things that surround me and are connected with me I always find in them some aspect or other which arouses my spite and indignation, or else gives me pain. Alone for the rest of my life—since I find the only solace, hope and peace within myself, I must not, and no longer want to occupy myself with anything else except my own self.
>
> (LES RÊVERIES DU PROMENEUR SOLITAIRE, I)

For Blake it was precisely the same problem; he rages against the self, vows it to perdition, destroys it, tramples it into a thousand fragments, and when he has destroyed it utterly it rises anew to confront him. "The eternal man weeps in the holy tent." "The eternal man is seal'd, never to be delivered." In spite of the lyrical fragments which arise at intervals in the prophetical books, the darkest melancholy broods over the scene. Selfhood is the perpetual enemy:

> . . . however loving
> And merciful the Individuality, however high
> Our palaces and cities, and however fruitful are our fields,
> In Self-hood we are nothing; but fade away in morning's breath.

The cry comes from the heart, lost like the footprints of Adam in the garden, the cry against the ultimate dissolution of the Self. So Hölderlin, in one of his many recensions of *Patmos*, spoke of the same terror:

> Like morning mist are the names
> Since Christ. Becomes dreams. Fall like error
> On the heart, and deadly if no one
> Wonder what they are and understand.

For Hölderlin, only the "heedful man" among the vineyards, the man who is present at the last supper, is safe from annihilation. God demands his forfeit: the forfeit of the name, the deepest identity, the self in its remote cave, and there can be no love until the self is dedicated to its own annihilation. It was the continual complaint of the mystics, and for Blake the self lies always in wait for man; and whether it wears the disguise of Urizen or one of his many emanations, for here as elsewhere he follows the mystic tradition, it is still the greatest terror:

> And I will go down to Self-annihilation and to eternal death
> Lest the Last Judgment come and find me unannihilate,
> And I be seiz'd and given into the hands of my own Selfhood.
>
> (MILTON, 15)

The cry comes from the heart, and it was at all times close to Blake's lips. He said once to Crabb Robinson that "he denied God had any power" and the language of the Bible as to God's omnipotence was "poetical and allegorical", but at another time he said, as though the idea had occurred to no one before: "God is within and without; he is even in the depths of Hell," and in his *Vision of the Last Judgment*, he wrote: "In Hell is all Self-righteousness."

Blake was plagued with his own pride. The self was the *roi fainéant*, the perpetual accomplice of his visions. He would drive the self away, only to find it waiting for him on his own door-step. "Every man has a devil in himself," he said, "and the conflict between the self and God is perpetually carrying on." It could hardly be otherwise in a man who attempted singlehanded, with immense genius, to reveal the secrets of the creation, for the prophetical books attempted nothing less. But it puzzled him that the self should have so many disguises; there were masks upon masks; underneath the last of the masks there were still others, and if you peeled off the masks until there was nothing left except a thing the size of a small pea, lo! a whole world was contained in the pea. For him even those who perform acts of mercy might be guilty of pride. "He who performs works of mercy, in any shape whatsoever, is punished, and, if possible, destroyed—not through envy or hatred or malice, but through self-righteousness, that thinks it does God's service, which God is Satan."

It is not an ignoble philosophy. Blake deliberately pits himself against the Godhead, and he is prepared to suffer the consequences; and among those consequences is that he should find God in Hell and discover that mercy is a pretence to divinity. He wrote on the fly-leaf to Swedenborg's *Angelic Wisdom*: "There can be no good Will. Will is always evil." And so it remained. He could not think of it otherwise, even though it led him into strange and intolerable heresies, as when, shortly before his death, he said: "Jesus is the only God, but so am I, and so are you." The gentle simplicity of the statement should not blind us to the fact that Blake, like Hölderlin's Empedocles, and like Hölderlin himself, was attempting to seize heaven by violence.

There is, however, a curious ambivalence in Blake's pride. "Shame is pride's cloke," he wrote in the *Proverbs from Hell*, but in almost the next line he wrote: "The Pride of the Peacock is the glory of God." He is certain that he has no love for pride, and cannot escape from it, and shouts too often to allow us to believe the struggle has been disengaged. So he wanders, followed by a shadow "like a spider's web, moist, cold and dim", in search of the peace where neither pride nor the shadow of turning can ever enter. Like his Urizen he has committed the fatal sin of enquiry, and must suffer the punishment. When he painted the fallen Urizen like a black charred skeleton in the rays of the burning and un-comprehending sun, he was painting himself.

The young Prometheus of Goethe, rising magnificent in his youthful arrogance, has become at last a hideous scorched skeleton. Though Blake hated the black skeleton with all the hatred of which he was capable, Urizen exerted upon him an extraordinary fascination. It is not only that he is continually referring to it, but in the prophetical books, whenever there is a moment when inspiration is lacking in him, when the words begin to crawl over one another, and almost no sense can be made from them, then Urizen is sum-moned out of the depths where he has been hidden, and immedi-ately the verse takes on colour and definition, and almost to the very end he remains "Urizen the King, King of the Heavenly Hosts".

If Blake takes heaven by storm, he takes it from the very heart, from inside sapping at the foundations. Keats pursued an equally dangerous task, but he came slowly, from without, thinking upon each step of the journey, never until the end entirely sure of him-self. Blake uttered his anathema against the self; Keats wondered why it was that he possessed no self at all, assumed the colour of his surroundings and instead of committing himself to self-annihila-tion, was annihilated even by the presence of children:

> When I am in a room with People if I ever am free from speculating on creations of my own brain, then not myself goes home to myself: but the identity of every one in the room begins to press upon me that I am in a very little time annihi-lated—not only among Men; it would be the same in a Nursery of children.   (LETTER TO WOODHOUSE, OCTOBER 27, 1818)

A year earlier, in a famous letter to Bailey, he had made a distinc-tion between men of genius and men of power, a distinction which had destroyed in him for a while any effort to become "a superior man". He would take the fortress by humility, he would open his own gates wide and the fortress would come running in. He was concerned with his own genius only in as far as it produced poetry; the rest was immaterial, and there was no great certainty that the genius would endure. The humility of the letters is captivating; greatness shines from them; we are aware that it is the most complicated humility, a humility that does not admire itself, but seeks to run away from itself, as fluid as his own epitaph. Of his own humility he was in no doubt:

> In passing however I must say of one thing that has pressed upon me lately and encreased my Humility and capability of submission and that is this truth—Men of Genius are great as certain ethereal Chemicals operating on the Mass of neutral intellect—but they have not any individuality, any determined Character—I would call the top and head of those who have a proper self Men of Power——
>
> (LETTER TO BAILEY, NOVEMBER 22, 1817)

There he abruptly breaks off, saying that he could not do the subject justice "under five years Study and 3 vols octavo," but though he tries to avoid the subject, he returns to it later, as though impelled by a force greater than himself. The mirror hovers. He must look into it, search for the springs of his own poetic activity, and when he finds it, the banners are waving and the trumpets blowing over the captured city; but what he finds is something extraordinarily like the Oriental experience of *samadhi*, a relentless "keeping open of all the gates of the mind", a quietism, a waiting for the moment of divine inspiration, the "old wine of Heaven". "The setting Sun will always set me to rights—or if a Sparrow come before my Window I take part in its existence and pick about the Gravel." He will identify himself with all he sees, and so escape from himself, but the very identification of oneself with transient things produces darkness and misery: it is the complaint of the poet as he watches the nightingale. In this world nothing is as it seems to be; the music rises, as in the posthumous quartets of Beethoven, into a world filled with rumors of astonishing revelations, and the most astonishing of them all is death, the note of music dying and taking the world with it, the poet remaining in his death-in-life. It is at this moment that the Titans enter the scene. Keats announces their presence casually in his dissertation on the Chambers:

> We no sooner get into the second Chamber, which I shall call the Chamber of Maiden-Thought, than we become intoxicated with the light and the atmosphere, we see nothing but pleasant wonders, and think of delaying there for ever in delight. However among the effects this breathing is father of is that tremendous one of sharpening one's vision into the heart and nature of Man—of convincing one's nerves that the world is full of Misery and Heartbreak, Pain, Sickness and Oppression—whereby this Chamber of Maiden-Thought becomes gradually darken'd and at the same time on all sides of it many doors are set open—but all dark—all leading to dark passages—— We see not the balance of good and evil. We are in a Mist. *We* are now in that state—— We feel the "burden of the Mystery".   (LETTER TO REYNOLDS, MAY 3, 1818)

It is almost the landscape of Urizen's wanderings. The sun has set; Adam has left the angels of the flaming swords behind him, and in front of him he sees, dark against the twilight, the huge shapes of the fallen Titans. He climbs towards them, and calls out. "Grey-haired Saturn, quiet as a stone" is lying in the dark:

> Along the margin-sand large footmarks went,
> No further than to where his feet had strayed,
> And slept there since. Upon the sodden ground
> His old right hand lay nerveless, listless, dead,
> Unsceptred; and his realmless eyes were closed;
> While his bowed head seemed list'ning to the Earth,
> His ancient mother, for some comfort yet.
>
> (HYPERION, I, 15)

The wastes of the sandy shores were the natural place to find the Titans. Keats might have found Theotormon there, "upon the margin'd ocean, conversing with shadows dire." There, too, were some of the fallen creatures of Shakespeare's imagination.

He goes on; there is a confused roar as huge Enceladus summons them to awaken and to be led by Hyperion. It is a moment like the moment in Hölderlin's *Die Wildnis* when rebellion sprouts from the bottom of Hell. Hyperion appears, robed in majesty:

> . . . a granite peak
> His bright feet touched, and there he stayed to view
> The misery his brilliance had betrayed
> To the most hateful seeing of itself.
> Golden his hair of short Numidian curl,
> Regal his shape majestic, a vast shade
> In midst of his own brightness.
>
> (HYPERION, II, 367)

It is a moment of almost intolerable poignancy, for Keats has created an image of himself and the word "brilliance" must be taken in two senses; beyond this it is hardly possible to go. There are overtones which make the figure of Hyperion even more impressive than it is. Why the hair of "short Numidian curl", if there was not somewhere in his mind the reflected glow of the "oil'd and curl'd . . . Assyrian bull, smelling of musk and of insolence"? Hyperion stands there poised for vast action, silent, his hands pressed together in contemplation, and the fallen Titans, all except Saturn, come towards him where he towers on his eminence. Then the scenery of the poem changes abruptly and inexplicably to a meadowland, and here there comes a goddess who speaks of the poet's great gifts. She is Mnemosyne, the Titan goddess. The poet answers her, disguised as Apollo, and begs that she should point out his star, and then suddenly he is compelled to make his urgent demand for power:

> I have heard the cloudy thunder: Where is power?
> Whose hand, whose essence, what divinity
> Makes this alarum in the elements?
>
> (HYPERION, III, 103)

He falters on, gazing upon the goddess, who never answers; from her he can hardly expect an answer, so majestic she is, but the promise of power hammers on his brain. The moment comes when like Empedocles he must take on the robes of a god:

Knowledge enormous makes a God of me.
Names, deeds, grey legends, dire events, rebellions,
Majesties, sovran voices, agonies,
Creations and destroyings, all at once
Pour into the wide hollows of my brain
And deify me. . . .

(HYPERION, III, 113)

Like Empedocles the poet must suffer the forfeit. No sooner has
he announced his godhead than he finds himself struggling in con-
vulsions and the poem ends with the desperate cry of Apollo as
the goddess suddenly raises her hands, either in warning or in
blessing or in a gesture of destruction.

Of this early version of *Hyperion*, Keats himself said it was a
failure. The struggle with the Titans was too much for him.

In *The Fall of Hyperion*, he re-cast the poem, giving it a graver
music and a greater power by dismissing half the *dramatis personae*
who littered the stage. Though Saturn remains, Mnemosyne gives
place to Moneta, a goddess of more formidable aspect. The poet
approaches the throne and stands beneath her knees, seeing only
the folds of her linen garments trembling with her breath and the
light coming from the golden censers which fall from her hands.

Now no longer does he desire to be a god. What he desires is
something infinitely more difficult—to see himself. Suddenly the
veils part:

Then saw I a wan face,
Not pin'd by human sorrows, but bright-blanch'd
With an immortal sickness which kills not;
It works a constant change, which happy death
Can put no end to; deathwards progressing
To no death was that visage; it had past
The lilly and the snow; and beyond these
I must not think now, though I saw that face——
But for her eyes I should have fled away.
They held me back with a benignant light,
Soft mitigated by divinest lids
Half-closed, and visionless entire they seem'd
Of all external things;—they saw me not,

> But in blank splendor beam'd like the mild moon,
> Who comforts those she sees not, who knows not
> What eyes are upward cast.
>
> (THE FALL OF HYPERION I, 256)

It is one of the great moments in English poetry, but it is also one of the greatest nightmares. What Keats is describing is the death of the Titan, and the Titan is himself, just as Iphigenia is Goethe. Keats' imagination is so controlled, so perfectly on a level with his subject, his eye so keen and his understanding of the super-human goddess so complete that the mind recoils in a kind of horror that he should have attempted to depict himself at this moment of his grief. The figure owes something to Godwin's *St. Leon* *, published twenty years before; to odd lines of *Paradise Lost* and Chaucer's *Hous of Fame;* to *La Belle Dame sans Merci;* to the delightful lines he wrote when he was a medical student in imitation of medieval English;* to the memory of the great caves he had seen in Scotland with their basalt columns broken and lying in the sand. It is the landscape of the fallen gods. Keats is gazing

---

* On 4 January 1819 Keats carefully copied out in a letter to George and Georgiana Keats a passage from Hazlitt's lecture on *St. Leon*, a novel by Godwin. Speaking of the chief character, Caleb Williams, Hazlitt says: "He is a limb torn off society. In possession of eternal youth and beauty he can feel no love; surrounded, tantalised and tormented with riches, he can do no good. The faces of Men pass before him as in a speculum; but he is attracted to them by no common tie of sympathy or suffering. He is thrown back into himself and his own thoughts. He lives in the solitude of his own breast— without wife or child or friend or enemy in the world. *This is the solitude of the soul, not of words, or trees or mountains*—but the desert of society— the waste or oblivion of the heart. He is himself alone. His existence is purely intellectual, and is therefore intolerable to one who has felt the rapture of human affection, or the anguish of woe." Echoes of Hazlitt's lecture on Caleb Williams occur constantly in Keats' letters hereafter.

* Alexandre the Conqueroure was wayfayringe in ye londe of Inde, there mette hym a damoselle of marveillouse beautie slepynge uponne the herbys and flourys. . . . Her forhed was as whytte as ys the snowe whyche ye talle hed of a Norwegian pyne stelythe from ye northerne wynde. One of her fayre handes was yplaced thereonne, and thus whytte wyth whytte was ymingled as ye gode Arthure sayth, lyke whytest lylys yspredde on whyttest snow; and her bryght eyne whenne she them oped, sparklyd lyke Hesperus through an evenynge cloude. Theye were yclosyd yn slepe, save that two slauntynge raies shotte to her mouthe, and were theyre bathyd yn sweetnesse, as when by chaunce ye moon fyndeth a banke of violettes and droppethe thereonne ye silverie dewe.

upon himself in fear and trembling, in the certainty of death, in the pride that was not pride, but went beyond pride altogether, for it went beyond death. The heaviness of death aches in some of the lines that follow the vision of Moneta—never has any English poet seen death so nakedly:

> There is no death in all the Universe,
> No smell of death—there shall be death—Moan, moan,
> Moan, Cybele, moan; for thy pernicious Babes
> Have changed a god into an aching Palsy.
>
> (THE FALL OF HYPERION, I, 423)

The repetitions, the retractions, the icy calm which changes to desperate remonstrance, all these are the fruit of the vision, and in going deeper into himself Keats goes beyond the recognisable limits of language: he says things that cannot be said, and to our astonishment they are said exquisitely.

Keats alone of the great poets of his time saw the Titans plain, became a Titan, struggled with them, and saw his own pride crumble only at the edge of death. Though we are conscious of the agony, we are more conscious of the illumination. If Moneta is blinding white, it is no more than we expected, since she too is coated over with the "mystic gypsum" of the Titans and her whiteness is the same whiteness as Melville observed with horror in the whale, a whiteness like the breath of corruption. Only twice in literature has the vision of Moneta been equalled: once in the chapter of *Moby Dick* on "The Whiteness of the Whale", and once in the terrible chapter of *The Brothers Karamazov*, where Dostoievsky describes the death of Father Zossima.

With the conclusion of *The Fall of Hyperion* Keats was conscience-calmed at last. There is a word, *bezdarnost*, meaning the giftlessness of life, which Chekhov was fond of using with tremendous effect to signify all that was deserted in life. Keats had passed through this desert, like Blake and Hölderlin before him, and seen the same spectres of the imagination, but more boldly and perhaps with more sense of responsibility than any of them. He alone had taken them by the throat and shaken their secrets out of them. The effort of wrestling with them produced in him a kind of *acedia*—impossible to go on, impossible to go forward:

there remained only the sonnet to the Bright Star, and this already had been foretold in the first *Hyperion*, where Apollo desires to enter a star with his lyre. The last poems show no traces of the struggle with the Titans except extreme exhaustion. In October 1819 he wrote: "I should like to cast the die for Love or Death— I have no patience with anything else." He spat blood in the January of the next year, and in September he sailed for Italy.

While Keats was looking at the blood on his handkerchief, Shelley was at work on *Prometheus Unbound*. Goethe had abandoned Prometheus in his youth; Blake spent more than thirty years of his mature age wrestling with the Titans; Hölderlin came upon them when he was on the verge of madness; Keats came upon them when he was on the edge of death; and all four could only speak of the Titans fragmentarily. It was as though the wrestling was altogether too painful, too close to the bone. It was left to Shelley to write a consecutive drama of Prometheus, but there is a sense in which his vision of them is the most fragmentary of all. His Prometheus has never slept on a rock, never seen the eagles. "The heavens have gone further off," wrote Hazlitt, but for Shelley they have not gone much further off. When Prometheus speaks, he has the cultivated accents of Calderón, Goethe and Æschylus in an eighteenth-century translation, with overtones of Young's *Night Thoughts* and Blair's *The Grave:*

Prometheus   Peace is in the grave.
              The grave hides all things beautiful and good:
              I am a god and cannot find it there,
              Nor would I seek it; for through dread revenge,
              This is defeat, fierce king, not victory.
              The sights with which thou torturest gird my soul
              With new endurance, till the hour arrives
              When they shall be no types of things which are.

Panthea   Alas, what sawest thou?

Prometheus   There are two woes,
              To speak, and to behold; thou spare me one.
                         (PROMETHEUS UNBOUND, I)

The sublunary characters are not fully realised, but they possess a curious power of moving us at a distance. "A mighty darkness fills the seat of power," but it is not the darkness which shone from hooded Hyperion. We move from darkness into airy light, and back again into darkness, and the journey has the quality of one of those nightmarish caves in fun-fairs where in the darkness, as the trolley runs along the rails, you catch glimpses of blue skeletons and dripping hands caress the traveller's face, and all is nightmare until you pass into an Arabian garden where the fountains are playing and there are veiled houris with almond eyes. It is poetry, but except for a few moments of passionate indignation, it is not great poetry. The graveyards are too demonstrably inhabited by succubi, not angels, and Prometheus is Shelley himself languidly throwing his challenges at heaven, and the challenges are no more powerful than the paper boats he sailed over the Hampstead pond.

With Wordsworth the terror returns, but it is an archetypal terror, something that belongs to the time even before the appearance of the Titans. There are no names for the heroes he sees coming thickly across the moors, half-hidden in the mist; or rather, he gives them names, but we do not recognise them under their universal appellations. The soldier of the *Prelude*, the Leech-Gatherer, Margaret, the Solitary Reaper, all have the stature of Titans and for a moment one can almost believe they are the gods sent down to torment men. Seeing the London beggar, Wordsworth says his own mind "turned round as with the might of waters":

> And, on the face of that unmoving man,
> His steadfast face and sightless eyes I gazed,
> As if astonished from another world.

> (THE PRELUDE, VI)

We believe him implicitly; he has seen the vision, but there is no power behind the phantasm, no pity is communicated to us, no indication is given of his purpose. There rises out of the lonely places of his soul an endless procession of similar phantasms all pointing their accusing fingers, none saying from where they have come. "Evil, be thou my good," says Milton's Satan; then for a moment we believe him, but we do not believe, however much we try, the credentials of Wordsworth's creatures.

> The Gods approve
> The depth and not the tumult of the soul;
>
> (LAODAMIA, 75)

but the battle with the Titans is concerned precisely with the tumult of the soul, the wrestling which each man has with himself in order to discover himself.

But once at least Wordsworth saw something which, at this late date, is recognisably a Titan. It came marching after him. It had shape and form. It spoke out of the whirlwind. He had been rowing across the lake:

> But now, like one who rows,
> Proud of his skill, to reach a chosen point
> With an unswerving line, I fixed my view
> Upon the summit of a craggy ridge,
> The horizon's utmost boundary; far above,
> Was nothing but the stars and the grey sky.
> She was an elfin pinnace; lustily
> I dipped my oars into the silent lake,
> And, as I rose upon the stroke, my boat
> Went heaving through the water like a swan;
> When, from behind that craggy steep till then
> The horizon's bound, a huge peak, black and huge,
> As if with involuntary power instinct
> Upreared its head. I struck and struck again,
> And growing still in stature the grim shape
> Towered up between me and the stars, and still,
> For so it seemed, with purpose of its own
> And measured motion like a living thing
> Strode after me.
>
> (THE PRELUDE, I)

It was thus that the self, taking shape and dark disguise, strode after him, but for the rest of his life he avoided himself, took care never to meet himself and contented himself with the dim ghosts on the barren heaths of his mind. It may have been Annette's fault;

it may have been his own; it is more likely that the man who might have been the leader of the Girondins no longer struggled against the temptations of power, but surrendered all power and even surrendered himself. Though he says it at greater length, he is only saying what Rimbaud was to say later: "I could not go on. And besides, it was evil."

For Shelley and Goethe the final peace was too easily obtained; they slipped into it, without quarrelling overmuch, seeing the world and themselves, not as they were, but as they hoped they would one day be: it is significant that both of them introduced Pandora into their scheme of the Titanic struggle. "Prometheus," wrote Shelley in the preface to *Prometheus Unbound*, "is in my judgment a more poetical character than Satan, because, in addition to courage, and majesty, and firm and patient opposition to omnipotent force, he is susceptible of being described as exempt from the taints of ambition, envy, revenge, and a desire for personal aggrandisement, which, in the Hero of *Paradise Lost*, interfere with the interest. . . . Prometheus is, as it were, the type of the highest perfection of moral and intellectual nature, impelled by the purest and the truest motives to the best and noblest ends." So Queen Victoria might have spoken of Albert, but neither Hölderlin nor Keats would have recognised in this paragon of virtues the character of the Titan, if only because he lacks the two greatest qualities possessed by the Titan race—power and consciousness, the consciousness that he has fallen from grace.

These six poets saw the Titans in a different light, wearing different disguises and possessing strangely contrary impulses. Goethe's young god becomes at last the sun-scorched skeleton of Urizen; Keats, who could summon "shapes of epic greatness" whenever he desired, becoming Achilles in the trenches or Troilus shouting in exultation: "I wander like a lost soul upon the Stygian banks staying for waftage," came at last face to face with himself; Hölderlin went down into the depths of his spirit to surprise the Titans at the moment of their rebellion; Wordsworth saw the dim shapes passing in the mist and failed to recognise them, giving them no names; Blake named them to the last step-child, but failed to see them coherently, and he too came to face himself, and summoned himself to remain unannihilate; Shelley wandered about the graveyards in search of them. They all thirsted, wandered over spiritual deserts, saw chasms opening and prayed for sunlight; and having seen the Titans, they returned with their accounts of the journey— *et hic dei sunt*—only to find that they were not believed, or their spiritual adventures were accounted to be adventures of another order. Having returned, all of them behaved in the same way: they put the Titans behind them, and prayed for mercy. Goethe gazing into his microscope, Hölderlin pondering on the entrancing flow of the Neckar in his old age, Keats turning to Italy and the south, Blake endlessly dedicating himself to his art, Wordsworth recollecting in tranquillity the heat of his love for Annette, Shelley celebrating the illusory and insubstantial triumphs of life, all in their different ways were turning their backs on the world as they had seen it. For them the Tyger became the Virgin and the Rose.

It was perhaps an inevitable conclusion; the battle was unequal from the very beginning. A man does not face his naked self with impunity, and anyone who wrestles with the Titans must assume something of the stature of a Titan, and at the same time he must suffer the penalty of exhaustion. The fragmentary evidence of their contests suggests that they were all defeated. Though Blake denied mercy, he gave evidence enough that he saw no other hope:

> O noble sons, be patient yet a little.
> I have embrac'd the falling Death; he is become One with me.
> O sons, we live not by wrath, by mercy alone we live!
>
> (MILTON, 25)

In the end, perhaps, mercy was the only way.

The Green Wine-cask

WHEN the great poets at the turn of the century spoke of the Titans, they spoke with an authentic voice of things they knew well and intimately, for they had lived with them, seen them in clear daylight, stumbled after them at night, wrestled with them in great fever and despair. Gradually, as the nineteenth century advances, the mist thickens. The Titans seem to vanish completely from the world, and instead of the sculptured and only too living gods seen against the sky, and men wrestling with them, we see little periwigged demons casting shy and evil glances at themselves. Instead of Prometheus we see the dandy.

Once again there is (in the words of Coleridge) "in some sense, a Fall," some kind of catastrophe of the spirit has taken place, and the self no longer exerts itself to its full powers. There is no Prometheus; instead there is Nietzsche's "ugliest man", Ibsen's Brand sorrowing at the waterfall, Lermontov's demon, Dostoievsky's Stavrogin—a host of men filled with the lust of pride at a time when pride was no longer elemental. At the time of Homer dawn was a dancing-place; now, as the kings settled once again on their uneasy thrones at the end of the French Revolution, dawn was a damp mist floating through the streets, to become sooner than any-one could have expected a patient etherised upon a table. Pride, having become urbanised, smelt of *goulash*, stale tobacco and rubber.

It need not have been. It is perfectly possible to imagine that with the least change of the weather of the soul, with the least extra turn of the screw, an entirely different landscape might have been presented to us; the descendants of the great Prometheans need not have become demons, huge in comparison with ourselves but dwarf-like in comparison with their forebears. We can only guess at the reasons. Kant had proclaimed that exaltation was only the rebound from fear; and in this sense he was the first to detect and perhaps to invent the emerging fears which grew through the nineteenth century to flower in our time—fear of mechanisation, fear of the city-streets, fear of the irresponsible maniac who might at any moment plunge the city into darkness by pulling the levers at the power-station. Long ago Aristotle had written: "The man who needs no one else is either a god, having everything within himself, or a wild beast." But in the gallery of proud men and proud souls in the nineteenth century there are no wild beasts and no gods; only a desperate, painful and suburban striving.

In the past the proud man had thirsted after glory, desiring to take to himself the titles and powers enjoyed by the Persian Kings, to call himself Lord of the Earth, Lord of the Skies, Lord of Heaven and even Lord of Hell, but now very suddenly, and almost overnight, there appears in human history a new phenomenon: glory had become suspect. Baudelaire describes himself as the king of a rainy country, powerless and rich, young and yet very old:

> Je suis comme le roi d'un pays pluvieux,
> Riche mais impuissant, jeune et pourtant très vieux.

He sees himself as the powerless king of a country of no value, a drowned landscape where nothing lives, an abyss where nothing grows. There exists a strange fragment from Baudelaire's hand, published first by Nadar in *Charles Baudelaire Intime*, where the abyss is described:

> Symptoms of ruins. Immense buildings from Pelasgian times piled one upon the other. Apartments, rooms, temples, galleries, stairways, drains, gardens, lanterns, fountains, statues. Cracks in the walls. The humidity comes from a reservoir somewhere near heaven. How to warn people, how to warn nations? Let us warn by word of mouth those who are most intelligent. There, high up, a column cracks; the two ends are hurled

apart. And yet nothing has been destroyed. No way out. I climb down the stairways, then climb up again. Here a tower, there a labyrinth. I have never been able to make my way out. For ever I have lived in a building about to crumble into dust, a building troubled by a secret malady.

We know the name of the secret malady—it is time, but not time only. There are no cures for this disease. There are attitudes to be assumed—an attitude of the utmost nobility, patience and understanding. All this is important, but at most the attitudes are like those of the bedraggled swan in his poem who shouts from the gutters: "When will the rain fall? When will the lightning strike?"

Faced with the abyss, faced too with the gradual mechanisation of the world, the proud poet, descendant of imaginary princes, twists and turns in his agony, searching for the way out, to discover it at last in the almost mechanical dandy, who is not far removed from the famous mechanical chess-player who played at the court of Louis XVI. To become the dandy, completely concealing all evidence of hysteria, always cool and impassive, never for a moment betraying himself and utterly removed from the common infatuations of men—this is the only solution which Baudelaire can envisage; and in painting the portrait of the urban *megalopsychos*, he paints a portrait of his most extreme self.

It is not, of course, a complete portrait. There are moments when the strain of the disguise is too much, when the poet cries out in humility for the bread and the wine, when he sees himself as damned, not because he has cut himself asunder from men, but because he is suddenly made conscious that his disguise has worn thin. In the end the proud poet, who has been watching himself continually in a mirror, sees that he is no different from other men, as abject as they are, and as much in need of divine grace. It is at this point that Baudelaire touches most closely upon the territory of Pascal—divine grace: this above all; and one must wait patiently for it, praying to Edgar Allen Poe and all the saints. At this point it is no longer true that the ideal is "to become a great man and a saint for oneself". One must become a saint for God.

Yet the battle continues. Haunted by the moments of brief and dizzy rest when the trapeze has swung up to its full height, breathing the rarefied air near the tent-top and surveying the audience at a distance, Baudelaire can say at one moment: "Forgetful of the past, content with the present and resigned to the future, intoxicated with his *sang froid* and his dandyism, proud of being above those he meets, he says to himself, contemplating the smoke of his cigar: 'What becomes of these consciences is of no importance to me.'" But almost in the next breath, speaking of himself, he will say: "Lord, have pity on mad men and mad women! O Creator! Can monsters exist only as monsters in the eyes of Him who alone knows why they exist, how they have made themselves what they are, and how they could have prevented themselves from becoming monsters?" And even in the most complete and sharply etched portraits of the dandy there is implied a curious humility in the acceptance of beauty as the divine instrument by which perfection is brought about, and the revolt is not so much against God as against the anonymous tides of men, each one resembling the other, who threaten the existence of art. "Dandyism is the most rigorous of monastic rules," he wrote, exalting rigour as Valéry was to exalt the *ostinato rigor* of Leonardo. "It is the last flash of heroism in the decadence. Dandyism is the setting sun; like the declining orb it is superb, without heat and full of melancholy. But alas! the mounting tide of democracy which invades and levels all, drowns day after day these last representatives of human pride."

What is consoling in Baudelaire's portrait of the dandy is that he is not satanic, has no desire to commit an *acte gratuit* and lives in spite of himself in a state of complete responsibility—not, it is true, to God or men, but to his art. "The dandy," he wrote, "ought to aspire to be sublime without interruption. He should live and sleep in front of a mirror." But the sublimity he aspires to is a very real one, and in *Les Paradis Artificiels* he describes at length, and with amazing skill, the artist-dandy in all his complexity:

> He admires his remorse and glorifies himself, and all the while he is in process of losing his liberty. Here, then, is my imagined man, the spirit of my choice, having reached that degree of joy and serenity where he is constrained to admire

himself. At this point all contradictions cease, all philosophical problems become crystal clear, or at least appear to be so. Everything has become an affair of pure enjoyment. The fullness of this real life inspires an immeasurable pride.

(L'HOMME-DIEU, IV)

This is not the man who cultivates his hysteria with joy and terror, though it is recognisably his brother—the pure artist, remote from men, imprisoned in his own liberty, contemplating his art and his own enjoyment of his art; and his justifiable pride is no more than a spark thrown off the anvil, a sudden self-rewarding smile in the intervals of his work. Ibsen's Brand speaks derisively of the man who shrinks from immensity. He compares such a man to an owl that should be scared by that darkness to which alone his sight is adapted, to a fish who should fear the vast waters in which alone he can live and breathe, but Baudelaire consciously turns aside from the *crimen laesae majestatis*. He has no desire to be the conqueror; and his pride is entirely different from the epileptic pride of Raskolnikov, who commits a murder so that he can liken himself to Napoleon. In spite of all his rages, his oddly unconvincing attacks on women, his conviction that the sexual act is vicious and that it is performed only in "the certitude of doing evil", in spite also of his desire to shock and the strangely adolescent belief that a catalogue of horrors possesses a cumulative power greater than a single horror—a belief that was shared by Rimbaud and some of the medieval scholars—we find ourselves continually in the presence of a truly religious soul, who remains humble before his art. Like Pascal he has searched in vain for the movement of pure charity among men. He has failed to find it. In despair he summons the great artists, and among them, and only among them, he finds the certainty of his peace. And if he hates men, as he does, it is only because his pity has been sharpened to the point where their sufferings have become his own; and when he sees the blind walking through the streets of Paris, with their dark eyes turned towards the sky, or a ragged red-haired waif, or old men tottering through the mists, or the dogs at night, there is an almost Buddhist sense of compassion and a pity which is as endless as the reverberation of his poems; then at last pride completely withers away, the dandy is forgotten, there is only the terrified man communing with himself on the grandeurs and miseries of the human condition. "The dead, blind wall butts all enquiring heads at last," says Ahab, remembering a line of *Lear*, and the dead, blind walls are present to Baudelaire to the very end, though he kicks and screams against them.

The world of Baudelaire is one we know only too well; it is almost the same world through which Virgil wandered. There is the same preoccupation with the fevers of life, the smoke, the dead bodies of the young, the haunting vision of what might have been. The girl lies headless on the bed, and in some other country the lover who murdered her thinks of her continually as though she were whole. He knows that many men are murderers, and that all of us share the instincts of the massacrer. He knows the terrifying power of cities to destroy the soul and to squander men's energies in entirely useless purposes. He knows there is no power against death and nothing so menacing as evil; and if he is half in love with evil, it is only in order to discover its secrets. He knows the wolf who prowls to the north of every man's good favour and he has spoken to the *hitai*, the lame, squinting and wrinkled daughters of Zeus; and if sometimes he is tempted to employ the terrible Roman curse—*Ultimus suorum moriatur*—it is because he has too much pity for the living. Here is not the cunning and cruelty of the wild beast on the throne, but the sorrow of the caged tiger who dreams of a more natural home. So at last in madness, confused and humble, he retreats into the pavilion of his own thoughts, dreaming of foreign lands which have about them the serenity and oriental magnificence of an interior by Vermeer, warmed by the spring sun. That his vision grew artificial and confused, that he led in the spiritual world the life of an exile and an intriguer, may be forgiven him; what is important is that a fundamental humility remains, so that it is possible to say of him that no European poet ever equalled him in humility and many suffered more fearfully from spiritual pride.

There remains the dandy. It is not only in the cut of the clothes and the precision of his habits that we recognise the dedicated spirit. Baudelaire announced that the dandy must follow the most

rigorous monastic rule, not the rule of the Jesuits or of the Bene-
dictines, but of the Old Man of the Mountain, "who imposes upon
his intoxicated disciples the command of suicide". The despotic
laws to be obeyed by the dandy are the laws which men must
obey when confronted with ultimate things. "The doctrine of
elegance and singularity imposes on its ambitious and devoted
sectaries, upon men who are often full of impetuosity, passion and
courage and sustained energy, the terrible formula: *Perinde ac
cadaver!*" Translated into less recondite terms, Baudelaire is demanding devotion unto death for the sake of art, the artist's entire
indifference to his own suffering. To the outer world the artist
must show "a steadfast resolution not to be moved; the fire in him
must be a latent fire, such a fire as one may guess at, so that the
onlooker will feel that it may flare up, though it will not." So
had Baldassare Castiglione taught his pupils, and so had St. Ignatius
Loyala taught his disciples.

The dandy, then, is not a fop, but a terrible machine of
vengeance and instrument of man's pride in an age when all the
Titans have fallen. He does not suffer in any way from the German mania for destruction, because in a sense he is already dead
to the world, takes no pleasure in the world and would regard it
as the utmost nonsense to destroy something which is continually
in the process of destruction, since the world is suffering from the
creeping disease of time which honeycombs it. The dandy therefore attempts in every possible way to achieve permanence, and
like the Chinese Buddhist, he does this only by himself assuming
the elegance, the immovability, the grace and the artificiality of a
corpse. Pope said once to Swift: "I am a man of desperate fortunes,
that is a man who is dead." It is precisely his desperate, paradoxical
fortunes which send the dandy out on his mission of reforming the
world through art, through the greatest degree of artificiality. Art
alone is permanent. *Si le grain ne meurt.* . . . What was required
of the artist, as of the true Christian, was that he should die on
earth for the sake of the kingdom of heaven.

Baudelaire sometimes assumes too much. He assumes, for example, that what is required of him is required of all others; that
because the choice appears to be one between suicide and becoming
a Christian, this, and this only, is the decision to be taken; and

then he demands that the greatest art should be created in a state of god-like calm. In *Les Paradis Artificiels* he examines the means by which this calm can be brought about. In an extraordinary chapter called *L'Homme-Dieu* he analyses carefully a movement towards this god-like calm, a movement which proceeds by way of an explosion of pride induced by hashish.

It is a chapter written so deliberately and so carefully that it gives the impression of being ponderous. The examination of what Wordsworth called "unknown modes of being" proceeds gradually and with a curious air of complete certainty. It had been known for a long time that by taking drugs the intensity of self-consciousness could be increased, that an almost mystical ecstacy results from taking *canabis indica* and that fly-agaric has the effect of enlarging the pupils so that people are seen of monstrous size, and therefore in a sense more real. With hashish Baudelaire examines the "multiplication of the self", the strange state of existing on several levels at once, each one at its maximum intensity and each separate. He says deliberately—and there is no reason why we should disbelieve him—that he has no desire at all to increase the frontiers of self-consciousness: what is above all necessary is that he should enter that region of Buddhist calm where it is possible to see the world as it is *sub specie æternitatis*. The frenzied pride, the exaltation of the self that comes during a certain moment of the hashish-experience, is no more than a temporary resting-place on the journey towards the calm he desires. There comes a moment when "the worship, the adoration, the prayer, the dreams of happiness are hurled out like the explosion of fireworks with extraordinary energy", only to lose themselves in darkness. During this upward movement the hashish-eater is filled with the most gentle tenderness towards people and with a consoling sense of his own virtue; time and space seem to cease; at the final moment of the explosion he is convinced that he is the most virtuous person in the world, and at the same time his sensitivity is abundantly increased, with the result that all paintings, all sculptures—the most beautiful things he can contemplate—seem more beautiful than ever and seem to have been created for him alone. It is at that moment that he believes that he is god. Then the hurricane of pride "becomes an atmosphere of calm beatitude, silent and restful, and the universality of beings is then seen to be charged with colour, illuminated with a sulphur-yellow aura. If it should happen that a faint recollection enters the soul of the miserably blessed spirit, and he should ask himself: 'Is there another God?' then he will confront that God also and without the least terror they will debate their claims."

In *Le Chemin de Paradis* Charles Maurras spoke of the senseless desire to raise every human life to the pitch of paroxysm, but Baudelaire is not reaching out for the vertiginous heights. He identifies the god-like calm with the calm of exhaustion. He insists that the movement towards this calm follows closely the movement of æsthetic experience, so that a man contemplating a work of art, suffering with it, entering it and then withdrawing from it and observing it (though it contains within it the traces of his own forcible entry) is behaving exactly as the artist is behaving when he takes a drug in order at the same time to increase his sensitivity and to acquire the most complete calm. The paradox remains, a paradox acutely analysed by Kierkegaard in *Repetition* and *Fear and Trembling*, and stated perhaps least ambiguously by Milton in the final chorus of *Samson Agonistes*. It is the paradox that great calm may be derived from great excitement, that the soaring of pride may be merely an effort towards an almost superhuman calm, and perhaps there is no other way towards that desirable calm except through the movement of pride. It is as though the stage of an Attic tragedy lay inside oneself, and the self was audience, tragic actor and chorus, and all played and sang together, and at the culminating moment of the drama the tragic actor and the chorus were swept away, leaving the self in contemplation of the self in the enviable calm of the gods.

The significance of Baudelaire's efforts to solve the problem of himself, the continual debate in the mirror, the resourcefulness of the two combatants who continually face each other, the unerring grace and humility which lie behind these dispassionate discoveries should not blind us to the residue of spiritual pride in his own genius. It colours his work and gives some substance to those who declare that his poems in praise of Satan and Peter's denial of Jesus are deliberate acts of pride, and deliberately offensive to God. When Baudelaire says in his journals: "For my part I say the sole and supreme pleasure in love lies in the absolute knowledge of doing evil. And men and women know, from birth, that in evil is to be found all voluptuousness," it should be clear that he is stating ambiguously something that we all know to be true, and is not deliberately trying to shock, and that everything depends upon the definition of evil; yet Baudelaire's statement in his journal is only another form of the patristic insistence upon the evil of sexual intercourse, and there are many moments when Baudelaire himself seems to speak with the rage, the compassion and the intellectual authority of the early fathers.

So, too, when Anatole France said that Baudelaire "knew he was being damned, and thereby he rendered to the divine wisdom a tribute which will be counted to him for righteousness, but he was intoxicated by the idea of damnation and his appetite for women went no further than what is necessary to guarantee the definite forfeit of the soul," he was overstating his case. For Baudelaire it was not himself that was being damned; it was the whole race of men. "True civilisation," he wrote, "lies in the diminution of the traces of original sin, and has nothing to do with gas-light or steam." A race of mediocre talents was taking the place of the *conquistadors* of European civilisation, and it was necessary to shock them into an activity worthy of themselves.

He was not alone in despairing over the direction in which modern civilisation was going. Kierkegaard's insistence on the value of the individual possessed something of the same daimonic force, and there are times, reading Kierkegaard, when we seem to have strayed back again into Baudelaire's note-books, as when Kierkegaard says: "If the crowd is the evil, if chaos is what threatens us, there is salvation only in one thing, in becoming a single individual." And when Kierkegaard discusses the individual, at great length and with increasing subtlety, we find ourselves confronted with the dandy, but this time the dandy possesses a supreme consciousness of his own guilt and an infinite dependence on the heroic necessity of God. Even with Kierkegaard there is confusion between the individual and the daimonic; continually and relentlessly Kierkegaard warns against that confusion, but the more he warns against it the more likely it becomes that the confusion must remain. In *The Concept of Dread* he wrote: "The demoniacal is self-isolation and the unfreely revealed. The demoniacal does not isolate itself with something, but shuts itself up alone and therein lies the profundity of existence, that unfreedom makes itself prisoner. . . . If freedom touches self-isolation, it is seized with dread." In his journals and in a hundred portraits in his own works, and most particularly in *The Journal of a Seducer*, Kierkegaard portrays the proud man who has cut himself off from God and determines to take the leap into God's hands. He twists and turns within the prison of his pride, and even at the greatest moments of his pilgrimage towards God unconsciously he finds himself within the continuing prison. "Resignation," he wrote, "gives me the consciousness of eternity; this is the purely philosophical movement which I can accomplish whenever it is demanded of me, a movement I exact from myself by a severe intellectual discipline . . . *this movement I make of my own strength.*"

Kierkegaard was tormented by the portrait of the individual, the consciousness of his own eternity. Spinoza had spoken of that same consciousness—*sentimus experimurque nos æternos esse*, but with a ring of Platonic humility. What is this consciousness of eternity, asks Kierkegaard, but extreme liberty? "Dread," he wrote, "is the vertigo of liberty." For Kierkegaard the greatest geniuses are therefore the greatest sinners, for they put themselves up before God as individuals in the sense of being daimonic individuals; and the greatest of these sinners is Socrates, who demanded of men that they should know themselves. Reason, for Kierkegaard as for Luther, remains the enemy, and what is so remarkable in Kierkegaard is how he employs all the resources of reason to throw reason from her throne. He defines the categories of anguish as though they were categories of a Kantian critique, gravely and with a kind of resolute nonchalance, not laughing or crying or hating, but in a determined effort to understand; he explores the boundaries of his fear, and the fronters of his pride, continually setting himself up before God, but humbly in search of divine love. Never has the mystic and the trained intelligence been brought together so closely; never, except in Pascal and Corneille, were pride and humility so intimately gathered together. He turns from contemplation of the altar of God to the contemplation of the altar of himself, and lost between the two acts of worship quietly demonstrates the intensity of the darkness of the hell he is continually creating for himself, envying those who turn by custom and inheritance only to the altar of God—the peasant women, the tobacconist at the corner store, the humble folk of the world.

Quam aram parabit qui majestatem rationis laedit? At what altar, asked Spinoza, will they pray who have given offence to the majesty of the reason? Kierkegaard could not wholly deny reason, could not wholly regard his great accomplice with the pity and gentle remonstrance reserved for it by the great mystics of the past. The bewildering maze of reason, its seductions, its continual adaptability, its triumphs were only too present. He will go with reason, and then abandon it, and then return again to find reason waiting for him by the roadside, as patient as ever, and as undemonstrative. Kierkegaard realised these difficulties, his envy of those who could make the leap of complete faith was a real envy. Of his pride he spoke often, openly, and without contempt, though there is a kind of sorrow. There exists a remarkable entry in his diary relating how he went wandering in Jutland, and found himself on a summer evening on a hilltop overlooking the sea. In the stillness it was as if the dead had come to life, and he, no longer burdened with his fleshly load, walked with them in a diviner air. His whole past life rose before him, as men say it does in the instant before death, he cursed his own smallness, and his heart went out in forgiveness to all those who had done him evil:

> As I stood there alone and forsaken, and the might of the sea and the war of the elements brought my own nothingness to mind, and on the other hand the secure flight of the birds brought to mind the words of Christ, "Not a sparrow falls to the ground without the will of your Heavenly Father", I felt all at once how great and how small I was, and those two great powers, Pride and Humility, joined hands and became friends.

So had Petrarch, on another hilltop, felt the wings of Pride brushing against his cheeks; and for Petrarch too there had been elements of anguish, and both returned from their hill-top chastened. Something of this great dialogue with Pride and Humility Kierkegaard was later to place in the famous Abraham essays in *Fear and Trembling*. The serpent's bite of pride remained, and he was to remain tortured with his own individuality until he died, and speaking of his individuality Brandes was to say later, with peculiar justice: "Even in its isolation, it still has a noose around its neck, and on the other side of the narrow pass of individuality through which the flock was driven, the flock still waited."

The cry of Kierkegaard, so intense and unavailing, was repeated by Ibsen, whose most desperate cry was *"vaere sig selv"*— "to be yourself"; but when Peer Gynt is asked who he is, he replies: "What am I? I am anything you like, a Turk, a criminal, a troll in the mountains." It could hardly be otherwise. The self, when it revealed itself in this time, had assumed the tortured shape of permanent disguise; no scientist could pin it down; it baffled the efforts of the most sensitive analysts; and if Kierkegaard saw it finally as the essence of Christian faith, the burning core that prayed, he was not always to find solace in this belief—restlessly he attempted to analyse the brightness of the candle-flame. His self, under all its disguises, is supernatural: Ibsen's is only too human.

When Ibsen's Brand speaks derisively of the man who shrinks from immensity, and compares him to an owl that should be scared by the dark or a fish that fears the deeps, he was admitting defeat. This was the world as he wanted it, but humanity is not so easily outdone. Skule asks the old Skald in *The Pretender*: "What gift do I need to become a King?" The Skald answers: "My Lord, you are the King." It is at this moment that Skule utters the thought that has been eating its way into his cancerous vitals: "Have you at all times full faith that you are a Skald?" It is Peer Gynt's answer again, but with overtones which were to end with the strange convolutions of the self in Pirandello, where no single self in a man has validity, and the sum total of all his selves is zero. There are Buddhist mandalas showing the birth of the souls, each soul giving birth to others, till the portrait of the contemplating Buddha is half enclosed in the trembling cloud of souls which rise above him. The mere act of concentration upon the soul may give rise to an innumerable progeny. With Ibsen the birth of these souls is like the sudden appearance of the mysterious Boyg. "All of a sudden he ran against something, and when he put his hand out he felt it was cold and slippery and big."

Hugeness infatuated him, and with hugeness there went the desire never to compromise. To be cold, to be big, to separate himself into his constituent elements at will—these are the expressed desires of his heroes. Of his own coldness he was his own best witness, and in a long letter written to Brandes he recounted the suicide at Rome of the young Danish lawyer, Ludwig David, of whom he had seen a great deal. The youth threw himself head-foremost out of a window, in a crisis of fever. Ibsen wrote down the minutest details of the events, in the most studied and deliberate style, as if he was drawing up a report for the police. It was such a superhuman coldness as Dostoievsky possessed, yet, as he said himself "It was a human document," he was writing of a young and wasted life, while Kierkegaard wrote continually of an old and wasted soul.

There are moments when Ibsen seems to be writing on a more human plane of exactly the same problems, and offering exactly the same solutions, as Kierkegaard in the rarefied air of his imaginative theology. Kierkegaard cries continually: "Either/Or." Brand answers: "All or Nothing." "It actually seems," said Brandes, "as though Ibsen aspired to the honour of being Kierkegaard's poet." It is unlikely that Ibsen knew more about Kierkegaard that he could have read in the daily newspapers. These dreams of hugeness, of some patriarchal father who permanently refused to compromise, a winged lord of vengeance, all these may have arisen from the same causes that led Kierkegaard to invent the invulnerable Knight of the Spirit—the loneliness, the desperate misery of his own soul and the misery of the country he inhabited.

Ibsen did not invent the type. It can be found in the Icelandic sagas, or in the rustic tales of Absjornson and Moe, where too we find the Boyg, that huge monster of Norse superstition, the world-snake capable of infinite contraction and expansion and invisible, the symbol of Nordic pride. Peer Gynt dares not sin. He lacks the *daemonsk alvor*. He is "too contemptible for sinning". But when, in the famous sixth scene of the fifth act, thoughts and watchwords and songs and tears, in the manner of the medieval morality plays, take corporeal form and assail Peer Gynt, it is the very humanity of his answers which endears him to us. *Brand* is the story of a modern Lucifer; *Peer Gynt* is the morality of Everyman in modern dress.

Otto Weininger, that extraordinary young man who shot himself in Beethoven's house on October 4, 1903, leaving us indebted to him for a host of pregnant aphorisms and an essay on sex and character which Freud acknowledged as among the masterpieces of psychology, pointed out that Ibsen's philosophy is almost the same as Kant's. The peculiar aspect of the ego as the principle and ultimately the sole guide to truth was revealed anew to the young Scandinavian poet. It was at least more than a half-truth. In those essays collected together under the title *Uber die Letzte Dinge*, Weininger, in his attempt to come to grips with the problem of Ibsen, says many strange and various things, but his discussion on the Kantian influence makes it almost certain that at one time in his life Ibsen must have been saturated in *The Critique of Pure Reason*. But there were other influences, and sometimes, emerging like lightning, there is that fear which comes to light in Luther's *poenitentia*, that "absolute" fear of the terror of God.

This is nowhere more evident than in *The Wild Duck*, with its desperate symbol of the wild duck falling to the bottom of the lake, and there clutching fast to the roots of reeds in its determination never to be caught or seen by men. In this play the purest form of innocence enters in the person of the young girl who kills herself rather than shoot the imprisoned duck, an innocence which raises her to the height of Kierkegaard's Knight of Faith. In some of his last lines, too, Ibsen has described the sheer horror of not being able to leave off "falling apart from God," and in Rubek's ultimate statement of misery we are conscious of the loneliness which goes beyond all loneliness, when the soul becomes a small tattered thing, shrivelled by too much contemplation of itself:

> In front, beside a fountain, sits a man weighed down with grief, who cannot free himself from the earth-crust. He sits there and slips his fingers in the purling stream—to wash them clean—and he is gnawed and tortured by the thought that

never, never will he succeed. Never in all eternity will he attain to freedom and the new life. He will remain forever imprisoned in his hell.   (WHEN WE DEAD AWAKEN, II)

It was a scene we have seen many times before in European history, and we shall see it many times again: the relentless pursuit leads to relentless defeat, the proud man burning to a cinder, becoming no more at last than the scorched stick of a rocket which has blazed and died away in the night.

These fears, these desperate alliances and bitter feuds with heaven, were the peculiar attributes of the nineteenth century. In the previous century the subjects of poetry were universals—the Triumph of Life, the Triumph of Death, the Sight of the Sea, the Tenuity of Human Existence, the Consolations of the Marriage Bed. All these had assumed, in the practical organisation of the literary life, an importance and validity which was possessed, for example, in the time of Corneille, by words like Honour, Devotion and Duty. Those who wrote on the Triumph of Life were, in a very real sense, escaping from life, but with the great poets of the nineteenth century there is an abrupt and revolutionary change of direction arising largely as a result of the new freedoms promised by the French Revolution. To all this Ibsen was the legitimate heir, and unlike Baudelaire and Kierkegaard he tempted to portray the whole man, from the coarse homespun stockings on his feet to his noble and crowning forehead. With Nietzsche, we are once more in the realms of the Triumph of Life, the Triumph of Death and even of the Consolations of the Marriage Bed. It is as though he had brought entire into the new world the traditional universals of the eighteenth century, clothed them in Persian costumes, disguised them, and attempted in every way possible to make them equivalent to the singular and haunted men of his own generation. His Zarathustra speaks like a hero of Corneille, and it is significant that Nietzsche possessed a passion for the French tragedian. The interminable monologue goes on, the voice thickens into the low growl of a saturnine lion, and like those gossamer threads that rise from grass on a summer's day and take their light from the surrounding fields, he takes the colour of everything he reads. A sentence of Schopenhauer, a line of Corneille, another line of Plato—

all become his own. When he was young Nietzsche read a paragraph of Schopenhauer which says: "Where possible a man will hold everything and enjoy everything, but when it is impossible he will at least attempt to control everything. 'Everything for myself and nothing for others,' is his motto. Egoism is colossal. It towers over the world." It is a sentence which will reappear in nearly everything Nietzsche wrote. He will hold it to the light, examine it, watch the refraction of the light pouring through it, he will assume the guise of the man who holds everything, and the man who attempts to control everything; and the pure exhilaration, charged with genius and menace, and an incurable simplicity —he could paint only a single portrait, where Ibsen painted hundreds—streaks through his work like the brilliant blue-white of a magnesium flare. Every word is an apostrophe, every discourse a play on the word "I". Magniloquent words, overtones of ecstatic self-communion, delusions of power, a curious journeying along the edges of glaciers, everything that could conceivably shock *l'homme moyen sensuel et moyen chrétien* is brought forward as a proof of his restless desire for a world of Cæsars. His early *Unzeitgemässe Betrachtungen* contains the desolate plea: "Mankind must continually strive to produce single great men—that, and that alone, is the task." "I look downwards, because I am exalted," says Zarathustra. He approved of the phrase in Plato's *Theages:* "Each of us would like to be master, if possible, but to be God most of all." He lived among a hundred mirrors, saying of himself that he was a Cæsar with the soul of Christ, though he had no understanding of Christ, and when he rages against Christianity he gives the impression of being a new Don Quixote raging against windmills; and indeed there was something of Don Quixote about him, in his desire to reaffirm the ancient lordship of man over his fellowmen, to destroy pity, to set the gladiators fighting one another.

It is all on the border of madness and the most extraordinary penetration. In his book on Wagner, Nietzsche wrote that it was a terrible thing for a man who thought to dominate the world to discover he has no need of it. And it was precisely the discovery that the most noble man had no need of the world which terrified him. One of the characters of Dostoievsky's *The Possessed* says: "I searched for three years the attribute of my divinity—it is independence." Nietzsche never adequately defined his independence, though he sought all his life to define it; nor did he ever define the world's independence of "great men". No two philosophies could be so opposed as Nietzsche's *Will to Power* and those last humble chapters of Tolstoy's *War and Peace*, where the irrelevance of great men is made apparent.

Nietzsche writes as though the dominance of greatness was axiomatic. He wears the mitre, the chasuble and the dalmatic of a new Roman Emperor; he blesses the assembled mirrors; he groans because their answer is only an uproar of silence. "I have become one who blesses and one who says Yea. I struggled long till I attained this, and was a wrestler that I might one day get my hands free to bless. And my blessing is this: to stand over everything as its own heaven, its round roof, its azure bell and eternal security. Blessed is he who thus blesses." So Gautama Buddha might have spoken after the years of wandering in the wilderness, or Christ when he returned from the desert of the temptation; such words come oddly from a dyspeptic *privatdozent*, who derived his exaltations from epilepsy and his penetrating insights from the more cryptical passages of Schopenhauer. Yet there was value in the simplicity of his theme, in the continual reminder of a pagan affirmation of life, in his tenderness towards Greek culture and his understanding of it, in his blunt refusal to face the complicated motives of the human soul and to reinstate a superior motive —the motive of power. But when his own intellectual power led him to demand ferocity towards the weak, Nietzsche showed himself as the unforgivable ancestor of Hitler, and he who praised life most firmly became one of those most responsible for the modern abasement of human values. "Hungry, fierce, lonely and God-forsaken, so doth the lion-will wish itself," he wrote in *Thus Spake Zarathustra*. Innumerable poor old women, abandoned in lodging-houses, have had the same desire for revenge.

He wrote in *The Genealogy of Morals*:

> What then does the ascetic ideal mean in a philosopher?
> This is my answer—it will have been guessed long ago. When
> he sees this ideal the philosopher smiles, because he sees therein
> an *optimum* of the conditions of the highest and boldest in-

tellectuality; he does not thereby deny "existence", he rather affirms thereby *his* existence and *only* his existence, and this perhaps to the point of not being far off the blasphemous wish, *pereat mundus, fiat philosophus, fiat philosophus, fiam!*

(WHAT IS THE MEANING OF ASCETIC IDEALS?)

In *Ecce Homo*, he wrote:

> My destiny is that I should be the first honest man, and it demands that I should know myself in contradiction with thousands of future years. I was the first to discover the truth, and this I did because I realised that lies were indeed lies, and knew them as such. My genius is in my nostrils. I protest as no one has ever protested, and yet I am the sheer antipodes of a negative spirit. I am a happy messenger, such as has never been before, and I have known tasks so solemn and so high-reaching that even the conception of them has failed until this instant. It is only since I have come that a new hope has dawned on the earth. (WHY I AM A FATALITY)

What can one say of such things, except that they are blasphemies against men, insolent attributions of divinity by one who calmly assumes a role not intended for him? Nietzsche's great value was to question all things; he did not question himself, his genius, the role he played in the world, the lunatic strivings of his self-will. Terrible shuddering fits of epilepsy in which "countless delicate tremors and thrills ran down my body to my toes, and in this tempest I felt supremely free, no longer obedient to necessity, mighty and god-like," a great obstinacy of the will derived from much physical suffering—these are perhaps the causes of his malady—"the absolute malady, which all men should strive to attain." Like Kierkegaard he must have his "thorn in the flesh", and then when he draws it out, he will gaze at it tenderly, with reverence and worship, regarding the thorn itself as the sign of his divinity. One does not utter such blasphemies with impunity.

From the day when Schelling said: "the thought of the self and the self are absolutely one," and Fichte announced: "I am, absolutely because I am," the primacy of the human will had become a force in German philosophy. Coleridge went into a kind of summer madness as he pondered the German theorem of the will. Melville, receiving the theorem at second hand, enunciated his own theorem of the self without regard to German subtleties. "There is a certain tragic phrase of humanity," he wrote, "which in our opinion was never more tragically employed than in Hawthorne. He says No to thunder; but the Devil himself cannot make him say yes. For all men who say yes, lie; and all men who say No, why, they are all in the happy condition of judicious unencumbered travellers in Europe; they cross the frontiers into Eternity, with nothing but a carpet-bag, that is to say, the Ego."

Melville knew the rages of the sea, the unavailing thirst of a wave for the high clouds, the butting of the waves against the shore. There was in man something as wild and tempestuous as the seas, a great longing for glory, for permanence, for the sun. So he drew men exulting in their spiritual strength, free of all chains in their imaginations, though the chains clung to them, contemptible of all dangers—he, too, suffers from the European passion for infinity. But what distinguishes Melville is his extraordinary sense of responsibility towards his fellow-men, his gift of love. Towards God or himself he shows no charity, but towards his fellow-men he is abundantly charitable, and his intensity of love for them is only equalled by the intensity of his hatred of the dæmonic fate which seemed to him to be ruling the world. "The dead, blind wall butts all enquiring heads at last", says Ahab. But at least Melville will go on butting his head until the time comes when he can bear the ordeal no longer; then he will retire to the Abyssinia of the New York Customs House, defeated, puzzled, reckless of his own genius—most reckless because he refused to employ his genius until the final battle between innocence and disaster is fought in *Sailorman Budd*, and there Melville fights with one arm tied behind his back, giving the youth no weapons except his beauty.

He is closer to Baudelaire than any of the other *conquistadors* of the nineteenth century, the most genuine of Americans and the saddest of mortals, the least depraved. A singular honesty shines through all his work. Almost he is Kierkegaard's Knight of the

Spirit. He imposes no pattern. He struggles to avoid the temptations of drama, and by his very struggling against these temptations the drama becomes more menacing, more acute, more incontravertibly *honest*. There is none of Nietzsche's mechanical Superman in Ahab. who is a real man challenging a real God and demanding a real justice:

> Oh, now I feel my topmost greatness lies in my topmost grief. Ho, ho! from all your furthest bounds, pour ye now in, ye bold billows of my whole foregone life, and top this one piled comber of my death. Towards thee I roll, thou all-destroying but all unconquering whale; to the last I grapple with thee; from hell's heart I stab at thee; for hate's sake I spit my last breath at thee. Sink, all coffins and all hearses to one common pool! and since nothing can be mine, let me then be torn to pieces, while still chasing thee, though tied to thee, thou damned whale! *Thus*, I give up the spear!
>
> (MOBY DICK, CXXXV)

Thereupon Moby Dick, who can only be Leviathan, the Whale of God, sinks the *Pequod*, and the ship goes down with a fluttering bird pinned to its mast-head, drawn under with "arch-angelic shrieks", so that part of Heaven is drawn hellwards, as when the angels fell from God. There can be no doubt of Melville's intention. The drama of the *angeli deficientes* is played out in the wastes of the Pacific, with utter ruthlessness, and complete abandonment to the main theme of phenomenal pride faced with phenomenal God. Here no small vices are displayed; no small theatre is the scene; no audience, except the conscience of man, watches; all is played against a setting of incomparably more august dimensions than the Himalayas themselves—the greatest of seas. Yet to Melville and to the bewildered onlooker the dimensions of the seas are incomparably smaller than the dimensions of the will of man; and the great whale itself is smaller than a man's voice; the final greatness lies in the incontravertible act of defiance, the pursuit of the whale against all odds. "I now know thee, thou clear spirit," says Ahab, "and I now know that thy right worship is defiance."

Like Baudelaire, too, Melville is conscious of original sin, not in the sense that man has fallen, but in the sense that God has fallen. When Ahab says:

> Talk not to me of blasphemy, man: I'd strike the sun if it insulted me. For could the sun do that, then could I the other; since there is ever a sort of fair play herein, jealously presiding over all creations. But not my master, man, is even that fair play. Who's over me? Truth hath no confines.
>
> (MOBY DICK, XXXVI)

he is demanding man's quality with God, his right to demand justice, his eternal privilege to be higher than the angels. Other men go free; Melville deliberately places himself in the toils and demands that justice should be explained, demands that his voice should be heard and that God should humble himself before man, but majestically, after the due ceremonies have been performed. It is the eternal voice of Job saying: "Though he slay me, yet will I trust in him: but I will maintain my own ways before him." It is not, except in the most elementary sense, pride as it was known in his own generation: it is Prometheus in the wastes of the Pacific, and like Prometheus his pride has political purposes; and in the great passages of *White Jacket* with the vision of men congregating at the hearthstone of Adam, Melville supplies deliberately the political ends he desires to attain.

With Dostoievsky there are no political purposes, yet there is almost the same sense of awareness of his own responsibility, not only towards men and God, but to the human heart. Max Stirner, the founder of philosophical anarchism, the author of *The Ego and His Own*, which Karl Marx found of sufficient importance to refute at great length in *Die Deutsche Ideologie*, wrote: "Whether what I do or think is Christian, what do I care? Whether it is human, liberal, humane, whether it is inhuman, illiberal, unhuman, what do I care? All I ask is that I should satisfy myself." It was the inevitable consequence of Schelling's philosophy applied to the critique of pure living, but for Dostoievsky every one of these predicates was of overwhelming importance. Anarchism fascinated him, but answered none of the questions which absorbed him. "All things are nothing to me," says Stirner. Dostoievsky answers: "The whole world, everything within it, the thoughts, the loves, the deceits, the falsities, the glorious hopes of people, all these concern me, and most of all I am concerned with the discovery of God in relation to the people of the world." Stirner demanded the unlimited freedom of the individual. Dostoievsky answers, in the words of Shigalov: "Starting from unlimited freedom, I arrive at unlimited despotism." In the great battle between mystery, miracle and authority fought out in the concluding scenes of *The Grand Inquisitor*, Dostoievsky, with the utmost compassion and understanding, gives the ironic victory to the Inquisitor and sends Christ wandering helpless through Spain—a pilgrim and a beggar once more. The prodigious irony of Dostoievsky, never more cunningly expressed than in *The Grand Inquisitor*, is of a kind that defeats analysis: like Socrates he must follow the problem to the end, to reveal the absurd. He is baffled, as we are, by the endless game played between freedom and authority on all the levels of experience, but he preserves his humility, and if he describes Raskolnikov desiring to be "like some Napoleon or other", proving himself by murdering a defenceless old woman, we are aware that the main battle is *not* being fought on the level of murder and paranoia, but on the level of the hesitancies and strange manifestations of the human heart at moments of defeat.

It is the peculiar greatness of Dostoievsky that he is so absorbed by the characters he creates that he becomes them, lives their entire lives, and even gives the impression of suffering their deaths. When he discusses the characters who have stormed heaven, we must be on guard against thinking that these are the characters he most admires and most understands: there are always the fools of God, Alyosha Karamazov and Prince Myshkin, to remind us of the unalterable facts of humility and man's duty to God. But when he talks of eternity as some terrible cob-webbed lavatory in Siberia, or when in *Letters from Underground* he says:

> Do you know what I really want? That you should all go to the Devil, that is what I really want. I want *peace*. But do you know that in order not to be disturbed, I would willingly sell the whole world for a copeck? Should the whole world

perish, or should I have to do without my cup of tea? I should say, let the whole world perish so long as I can have my cup of tea!

he is talking with the utmost sincerity of certain "modes of being" which are relevant to his purpose, which is to describe the despairs and tumults of the soul faced with overwhelming defeat.

The fact of defeat is everywhere in Dostoievsky; he is never concerned to minimise it. Brutality, the rage of the defeated, is something he understands, and even pardons. "We are travelling with a corpse in the cargo," wrote Ibsen. Dostoievsky, the greatest of all those who have written with a deep sense of the tragedy of urban life, answers: "There are millions upon millions of these corpses, and I must speak about them." Through the pages of his novels there pass, one by one, the chalk-white Titans of the nineteenth-century metropolis. Under such conditions a Nechayev can arise, possessing, like this famous Russian revolutionary, a philosophy of the most complete opportunistic nihilism, raping and murdering as he pleases, plotting the fall of the monarchy even from his prison, dying bravely at last, having uttered in his brief life-time only curses on his friends. Nechayev, the ancestor of Hitler just as he is the ancestor of the Communist police-commissars, is portrayed with alarming clairvoyance in *The Possessed;* and if the new Titan is seen to be no more than the ancient streak of brutality which every man possesses as a birthright, Dostoievsky describes the infinite modulations of the proud revolutionary spirit in the twilight of imperial Russia, and he sees it as the shoddy thing that it is.

The fall of man is the theme of Dostoievsky's major work. The proud rebels, like Ivan Karamazov, encompass their own fall; having fallen, they rejoice in their humiliation, and even when they are in the depths, they swing from pride to the extremes of humility and back again. There are times when Dmitri Karamazov echoes the words of the saintly Alyosha. "I exist, and I see the sun," he says, "and if I don't see the sun I know it is there. There's a whole live world in that, knowing that the sun is there." The same drunkard and profligate will say at another time: "Dear friends, this humiliation persists, it persists to this day. Man has much to suffer on earth. What horrible suffering! I hardly think of anything but that, brother—the humiliation of man." Humbly, without the least pride, Dostoievsky watched the curious evolutions of the characters he had created.

The humility of Dostoievsky, and even the humility of his characters, is astonishing in comparison with the intolerable pride of Tolstoy, who wrote in his youthful journal: "What is wrong with me is my great heart," and who said, as he lay dying: "I see that all our plans are coming to nothing. I did what I could for the sake of others, and especially for my sake." He is Leviathan, "king over all the sons of pride," the strange genius who was so conscious of his own sin of pride that he made Pierre Bezukhov the humblest of men in appearance, though he could not conceal the haunted pride concealed within him. There were times when Tolstoy's silence seemed so forbidding that men guessed he was saying things to himself he did not dare say to others. Towards the end of his life his horror at his own pride and his intoxication of it absorbed him to the exclusion of almost everything else; and seeing himself as the symbol of a rejuvenated empire, he left his home and went wandering to his death. He is like the Bogatyr Ilya Mourom, the great Russian hero, who could shrivel into a corner of a cottage for long years on end, only to reveal himself later as the great leader of men, indestructible and possessed of a "holy soul", or like Sviatogor, the huge giant whose head touched the clouds and who possessed such extraordinary strength that he could set the whole world in motion; one day, crossing the steppe, he saw in front of him a little bag filled with earth and was about to lift it, but as he held it the bag drew him down into the abysses of the earth.

The astonishing spectacle of a great genius so eaten up with pride that he is continually overwhelmed by himself, stunned by himself, made hopelessly miserable by himself, believing himself in some way separated from divine grace, all this remains peculiarly Russian. Nothing quite like this had ever appeared on the mainland of Europe. There is a Russian word, *prostor*, which suggests the infinite flat spaces of the Russian plain and man's loneliness within it. Of this sense of intense, unrelieved loneliness Tolstoy was the unwilling victim, but at the same time he was so convinced of the greatness of his soul that he saw himself as an inevitable leader of men; and all his searchings for the truth, all his strange theories about history and morality end only in himself, in his own greatness of soul. It is as though the Italian *terribiltà* had come to life in the shape of an immense aristocratic peasant of the Russian soil. He wrote in his journal towards the end of his life: "I felt the need to be known and loved of all the world; *to name my name*, the sound of which would greatly impress everybody, so that they would troop round me and thank me for something." But even when he lay dying at Astapovo, he did not know what that "something" was.

He has told the story of his own unavailing pride with unique courage and frankness in his posthumous story *Father Sergius*. Prince Kassatkin, a brilliant army officer, commits a crime from which he can absolve himself only by entering a monastery. He lives in the monastery quietly, doing good works, taking his vows and behaving like every other monk until suddenly and almost unexpectedly he finds that he has become a saint and a miracle-worker. "Yes, Prince Kassatkin had become a worker of miracles; impossible to doubt it. He could not fail to believe in the miracles which he himself performed, from the little cripple boy to the old woman who recovered her sight in answer to his prayer. Strange though it seemed to be, it was a fact. Victory, perfect happiness seemed to have been obtained. It was time to rest in the proud consciousness of the heavenly reward justly won after so much effort; everyone proclaimed Stepan Kassatkin a great saint, a worker of miracles. Was not this unanimity satisfying? Is not the voice of the people the voice of God?" Prince Kassatkin broods over this sanctity which he has won without any effort and even in spite of himself. It seems to him monstrous, and at the same time delightful. He says: "People come from a great distance to see me, they write about me in the newspapers, the Emperor knows me, Europe —unbelieving Europe—knows me." He knew himself to be a flaming torch who inspired other men, who gave them the grace denied to himself; and all the time, with an outward show of humility, he knew himself to be proud, proud beyond reason, beyond the least hope of divine grace. He prays: "Lord, King of Heaven, Consoler, Spirit of Truth, come down upon us, purify us of all stain, and save our souls, Most Blessed One. Deliver me from the stain of human glory which oppresses me." But when he had said these words, he remembered how many times he had prayed in exactly the same way before, and how unavailing it had been. He did not know whether he loved, but he knew he was loved, and at the same time he knew he had no humility, nor any purity. At last the old holy man commits an abominable crime on an unfortunate feeble-minded girl, escapes from the monastery and goes to live with a rich peasant, "where he works to this day, labouring for the peasants, tending the sick and teaching the children."

Tolstoy does not ask us to believe the ironical ending of the story; it belonged to the classic tradition of Russian literature, and Dostoievsky will sometimes end his stories in the same way. The inference that he is describing himself is clear. Plato had said that the man who lives alone would partake of the character of the beast or the god (οὔτε Θεῖον οὔτε Θηρίον), and the whole emphasis of Tolstoy's story is that a man may be both, must indeed be both if he lives alone. He is like the portrait of dæmonic man painted by Gregory the Great who "walks with himself along the broad spaces of his thought and silently utters his own praises".

In one of those revealing fragments which light up, as with a blinding flare, the works of Nietzsche, there comes a dissertation on the mask which explains, if it does not excuse, many of the more baffling phenomena of pride in the nineteenth century:

> I could imagine that a man with something costly and fragile to conceal would roll through life clumsily and rotundly, like an old green heavily-cooped cask of wine: the refinement of his shame requiring it to be so. A man who has depths in his shame meets his destiny and its delicate decisions upon paths which few ever reach, and with regard to the existence of which his nearest and most intimate friends may be entirely ignorant. . . . Such a hidden nature desires and insists that a mask of himself shall occupy his place in the hearts and heads of his friends.   (BEYOND GOOD AND EVIL, 40)

The "old green heavily-cooped cask of wine" was the sign of the times; it rolled and trundled, leaking a little, no longer fresh, continually and explosively effervescent, and always in danger of spontaneous combustion. Neither Pan nor Hubris nor the Titans could recognise themselves in it, yet it was indisputably their child, born from their flesh. The great statues of the fallen Titans, which had come to life at the touch of Goethe and Keats, were at last falling into ruin and crumbling to powder; the intoxication had gone out of life; power was being taken from men's hands and given over to the machines. *Pereat mundum*, shouted the old Emperors, as long as my divinity or my kingship remains. Let the world perish, say these strange interlopers of the nineteenth century, as long as I have my cup of tea, my glass of wine, my grey skies, my guilt, my sense of sin. It is a strange transformation, and of all these minor giants only Melville, in his endless Pacific seas, seems to have found an adversary worthy of him, for like Job, when he demanded answers from God, Melville was given the vision of the Leviathan; and for him it was enough, and indeed too much, for in the White Kingdom of Leviathan he was never at peace. He could not be; the vision was too blinding; the rest of his life was a waiting by the edge of the sea, at that strange Customs House in New York, where he searched in vain among the contraband for the white whale of his dreams.

The Nymph and the Lake

IT IS related that when the poet Arthur Rimbaud was born, his eyes were wide open, and as soon as the nurse placed him on a pillow on the floor, he began to crawl laughing towards the stairway. It is hardly more than one would expect. His brief and prodigious life had about it the aura of a legend; he fits into no pattern and everything about him is instinct with a kind of heroism. At the age of sixteen he wrote one of the great masterpieces of French poetry; at the age of nineteen he had abandoned poetry forever.

The single masterpiece—for it is by far the greatest of his poems—is a delirious account of man's powers over the elements, his imaginary conquests, his triumphs and his remorse. A drunken boat becomes conscious of itself, steers away from the imaginary Americas of the mind and goes in search of the visionary monsters of the world. These is a sense in which the voyage of the drunken boat is an answer to the shattering visions of Leviathan and Behemoth which God demonstrates to Job as the most exalted creations of His own powers. *Hast thou entered into the springs of the sea? or hast thou walked in the search of the depth? . . . Hast thou entered into the treasures of the snow? or hast thou seen the treasures of the hail?* Yes, says Rimbaud, I have seen them all; and when we have read the poem we are convinced that he has entered by some magical process into the creation of things, but when all is over, when the poet has been scorched by "the blue fires of delirium", and driven over "silvery suns, pearly waves, brazen skies", and seen the Floridas "mingling flowers with the eyes of panthers", and men's skins all rainbow-coloured—when he has explored every imaginable vista of the glory and splendour of the world, he comes back at last, with infinite sadness and regret, to the voyage as it really was:

> Si je désire une eau d'Europe, c'est la flache
> Noire et froide où vers le crépuscule embaumé
> Un enfant accroupi plein de tristesses, lâche
> Un bateau frêle comme un papillon de mai,
>
> (LE BATEAU IVRE)

and with the spectacle of the child at dusk watching his frail paper boat sailing across a puddle, the final act of humility is accomplished.

But in a sense there was almost no humility in Rimbaud. Miss Enid Starkie has shown how, by means of cabbalistic spells, he deliberately desired to make himself the equal of the gods; like the ancients he believed the poet could create a whole universe. In the famous letter of 15th May 1871, written shortly before or after the composition of La Bateau Ivre, he claims the powers of Prometheus:

> The first study of the man who wishes to be a Poet is knowledge of himself, wholly. . . . I say that one must be a visionary, make oneself a VISIONARY. The poet must make himself a *visionary* by a long, immense and reasoned *derangement* of all the *senses*. He seeks in himself every kind of love, of suffering, of madness, he exhausts all the poisons in himself in order to keep only their quintessence. Unspeakable torment in which he has need of all faith, all superhuman power, in which he becomes among all the Great Invalid, the Great Criminal, the Great Damned—the Supreme Scholar!—for he comes to the *unknown*. For the Poet is truly the thief of fire, charged with the government of humanity, the animals even; and he must make his discoveries felt, touched, heard. If the things he has dredged from down there have form, he gives them form; if they are formless, he gives them formlessness.
>
> (LETTRE DU VOYANT)

Rimbaud speaks here with extraordinary assurance. He is young, athletic, full of certainties, and he knows precisely where he is going—he will create a new world. He is not Rimbaud, but some-one else: a god or a magus. He says several times "*Je est un autre.*" Or else he says: "It is wrong to say *Je pense*, one should say *on me pense.*" In his farewell to *Une Saison en Enfer*, he exclaims: "I, who called myself angel or magus, having forsaken all morality, now return to the earth." It is Prospero's cry, but it is not con-vincing: that complex pride did not entirely die. The primacy of the self, its powers of creation, its peculiar ambivalences, all these keep echoing long after we have closed the book. We hear the organ-note of Rimbaud again when Bergson, in a terrifying phrase, declared: *Le moi, infaillible dans ces constatations immédiates, se sent libre et déclare.* . . . "The self, infallible in its immediate state-ments, feels itself free and declaims. . . ."

In the famous essay *L'Homme-Dieu* in *Les Paradis Artificiels* Baudelaire spoke of the voice rising from the hashish-dream which said: "Now you have the right to regard yourself as superior to all men; none can understand or ever know all that you feel; they would be incapable of understanding the benevolence they inspire in you. You are a King whom the passers-by fail to recognise." Rimbaud acquires the same sense of omnipotence without hashish. By a concentrated splitting of the senses—*un long, immense et raisonné dérèglement de tous les sens*—he will discover what lies behind the senses; the curtain of the senses will be torn aside; behind this curtain he will seek out the perfection he desires. Per-fection he must have; all the treasure of the world is to be found there; he asked for nothing more, and desired nothing less.

But Rimbaud, unlike Baudelaire, is possessed by a fierce humility. *Le Bateau Ivre* ends with a confession of humility, in the child sailing his frail boat across a puddle. *Mémoire*, one of the most miraculously perfect evocations of childhood, ends with the same lustreless puddle, "*l'eau couleur de cendre,*" and within the un-moving boat there is a child whose arms are too short to pluck the blue and yellow flowers. That is all; and it is enough. It is all our human misery, and since the misery completely encompasses us, "*la science est trop lente, que la prière galope!*" "Science is too slow, may the prayer hurry on." The fierce, vertiginous prayer must take the place of the human art, and it is in these prayers and magic spells, which fill *Les Illuminations* and *Une Saison en Enfer*, that Rimbaud gives the impression of complete mastery. Here he is at his simplest and his best, and his most humble:

> O saisons, O châteaux,
> Quelle âme est sans défauts?
>
> Oisive jeunesse,
> A tout asservie,
> Par délicatesse
> J'ai perdu ma vie.
>
> (CHANSON DE LA PLUS HAUTE TOUR)

It might be Eve speaking after a temptation by Lucifer in a play by Arnoul Greban. If it is humility, it is also the enjoyment of humility; not a strident enjoyment, but one which knows the delicacies of its place. Yet there are moments when pride breaks through, and Rimbaud clamours loudly not for a single Hell in which he could be punished, but a separate Hell for each separate sin: *Je devrais avoir mon enfer pour la colère, mon enfer pour l'orgueil, et l'enfer de la paresse; une concert d'enfers.* "I should have my Hell for anger, my Hell for pride, and a Hell for laziness —a whole concert of Hells!" Or else he will scream out in his agony a prayer more pitiable than any composed by Baudelaire, and just as Baudelaire in his prayer will call upon his nurse and his mother, so Rimbaud, independent of all living things, living in a world of enchanted landscapes only, will summon up the remembrance of things past, and once again we see the pool with the paper boat: "*Pitié! Seigneur, j'ai peur. J'ai soif, si soif! Ah! l'enfance, l'herbe, la pluie, le lac sur les pierres.*" The small pool is the symbol of his love, just as the vision of the golden birds in their millions flashing in the heavens is the symbol of his pride—*Million d'oiseaux d'or, O future Vigueur!*

"Not by curse of their will is man so lost, but love eternal can return, so long as hope abideth green in leaf." The words of Dante in the *Purgatorio* are like echoes of Rimbaud, who looks always into the unimaginable future, while Baudelaire looks always to the unimaginable past. The visions of glory abound in Rimbaud, but it is a recognisably earthly glory, though bathed in a heavenly light, paintings by Poussin coming to life as the poet breathes on them. He is never tenuous. Baudelaire is half in the shadows, half-illuminated by a red glare; Rimbaud is the poet of the clear light of dawn. Everything has the sharpness of dawn, and it is this love for the dawn-light which gives him the strength and the power to suggest an unfolding universe, as fresh as a flower. On the last page of *Une Saison en Enfer* he utters his final prayer: "For we are engaged in the discovery of divine charity. . . . Dawn will come at last; and then, armed with an ardent patience, we shall enter the splendid cities; then it will be lawful to possess the truth in a body and a soul." But when autumn came, he had already written: "Autumn already!—But why should we regret the eternal sun if we are engaged upon the discovery of divine clarity—far from the men who die upon the seasons."

It has been necessary to insist upon Rimbaud's humility if only to insist more emphatically upon his pride. Never was a man so incorrigibly filled with the most extreme of virtues and the most extreme of vices. The vertigo of pride, the desire to make himself truly "the thief of fire, charged with the government of humanity, the animals even," were for him almost commonplaces; he was the first to invent a language which perfectly expressed this desire: "The insane and infinite leap into invisible splendours, inconceivable delights—the fearful secrets for every vice—the terrifying gaiety before the crowd." Gregory's great phrase is held up to the light, and instead of the solitary continually singing his own praises in the broad spaces of the solitary mind, there is the spectacle of the young poet creating a vertiginous heaven for himself alone.

In *Crimen Amoris,* one of the most sustained of Verlaine's poems, Rimbaud is described as a young god, the most beautiful of the evil angels, crowned with flowers, standing among the silk hangings of a palace in Ecbatana, a youth like a portrait by Giorgione, lost in a dream. Around him the other evil angels, his brothers and sisters, dance wildly, while the pages serve wine, and the music surges like the waves of the sea. Then very abruptly the young god takes leave of the dancers, kisses them and ascends the high tower with a torch in his hand; as dawn comes, he is heard saying: "I am he who will become God!"

"O angels and men," he cries. "We have suffered too long from the battle between good and evil. Let us humiliate ourselves, sinners that we are, and let us humiliate all our desires—let them become but the most simple of vows. At last the seven sins must marry the three saintly virtues. And let there be a sacrifice to universal love."

At this moment he throws down his torch, the sound of the raging fire comes to his ears, and "the enormous quarrel of red eagles drowned in the dark waves of smoke and wind" takes the place of the Persian palaces. Once more we are in the presence of Capaneus; pride is a kind of raging fire. The dancers die singing, but Rimbaud remains on his high pinnacle with folded arms, contemplating the deluge of fire, praying quietly, prepared to die "in the joy of the song". Then night comes down with its thousandfold stars on a celestial countryside *"sévère et douce"*, where the branches of the trees wave like wings and cold streams murmur over stones; sometimes there is a flash of light from a leaping wave, and sometimes a mist rises towards the heights of the ravines, "as though to some determined end." After the evocation of a night so saintly that the angels seem about to descend, Verlaine ends with an evocation of Rimbaud, the adorer, the one who is lost and found, the infernal bride:

> *Et tout cela comme un coeur et comme une âme,*
> *Et comme un verbe, et d'un amour virginal*
> *Adore et s'ouvre en une extase et réclame*
> *Le Dieu clément qui nous gardera de mal.*

(JADIS ET NAGUÈRE)

It is then at last, but only by a peculiar grace, that the heaven-reaching boy is transformed into an apostle of blessedness. Like Rimbaud's own *Chanson de la plus haut Tour*, Verlaine's *Crimen Amoris* ends with the vision of peace and exhaustion.

"At first," said Rimbaud in one of his extraordinary fragments, "I expressed darkness and silence; I noted the inexpressible." He was not alone in desiring to say the things that had never been spoken. Stephane Mallarmé also possessed this desire. He possessed none of Rimbaud's furious courage. He was content with lesser things—the exploration of the virgin whiteness of paper, and somewhere in this virgin whiteness he hoped to imprison the self, conquer it, examine it, strip it to its essentials. The quest, for him, was urgent and continual. This nervous scholar, who contemplated the universe from the classroom and the editorial chair of a woman's fashion paper, possessed one weapon forbidden to Rimbaud. Rimbaud assaults the fortress. Mallarmé digs underneath, or creates around the fortress the image of its own absence. He wrote once: *Je dis: une fleur, et, musicalement, se lève l'absente de tous les bouquets.* It is permissible to enquire how Mallarmé invokes himself. *Je dis: moi-même, et, musicalement, se lève l'absente de tous les moi.* The self is a fleeting nymph, never wholly possessed; he can barely describe her, and when she appears first in *L'Après-midi d'un Faune*, she is no more than a perfect whiteness caught momentarily on the surface of the river; then she is gone, to return again only in the heated imagination of the faun. This "animal whiteness", this "prelude of pipes craving the flight of swans" is white like the page, like the virgin's body, like the pattern of stars. What is required is that the faun (or the poet) should thrust upon it the shape of his own imprint. The airs are Sicilian, the graces belong to a former period of Theocritean happiness, and somewhere at the heart of them Mallarmé is in search of himself, a self which has become translated to another age and almost to another planet.

Rimbaud sings; Mallarmé composes with endless difficulty, sounding each phrase multitudinously against his ear. Mallarmé will not throw himself at the Kingdom of Heaven; he will build it slowly, brick by brick, with more "ardent patience" than Rimbaud ever thought possible. Like Rimbaud he must gaze at the pool, knowing, as Melville said, that "meditation and water are for ever wedded." But he does not see a boat—he sees only, on the sunlit waters, the pure white of a virgin thigh. And there the difficulties begin, for out of this whiteness he must construct a whole world.

L'Après-midi d'un Faune describes a purity absent from the far greater poem, *Hérodiade*, which describes the awakening into consciousness of a young girl. She speaks quietly to her nurse as she watches herself rising from the depths of a mirror:

> *O miroir!*
> *Eau froide par l'ennui dans ton cadre gelée*
> *Que de fois et pendant les heures, désolée*

> *Des songes et cherchant mes souvenirs qui sont*
> *Comme des feuilles sous ta glace au trou profond,*
> *Je m'apparus en toi comme une ombre lointaine,*
> *Mais, horreur! des soirs, dans ta sévère fontaine,*
> *J'ai de mon rêve épars connu la nudité!*
> *Nourrice, suis-je belle?*

The nurse answers that she is indeed beautiful, but her very beauty is such that she must walk alone, proud and disdainful, for the rest of her days:

> *Temps bizarre, en effet, de quoi le ciel vous garde!*
> *Vous errez, ombre seule et nouvelle fureur,*
> *Et regardant en vous précoce avec terreur:*
> *Mais toujours adorable autant qu'une immortelle,*
> *O mon enfant, et belle affreusement et telle*
> *Que. . . .*

But the unknown name (is it Hubris?) is never mentioned, and the nymph once more disappears within her own beauty, until the nurse asks: "For whom is the unknown splendour of your beauty?" Then the nymph answers, echoing down the ages the cry of Seneca's Medea and the heroines of Corneille: "For myself." It is only then that we realise that the nurse is a projection of the nymph's mind, as she continues her dialogue of self-love.

It is all so quiet that we hardly know what is happening. The lapidary style, the extraordinary beauty of the rhythms, the sense that we are present at the birth of a ferocious tyranny, the apparent absence of all drama almost prevent us from realising that we are witnessing one of the most terrifying and murderous dramas of all —the gradual disappearance of beauty into its own mirror. Desperately the nurse calls back to the retreating image: "How naïve you are, my child! One day this triumphant disdain must grow less." But we know that it will never grow less, the tragic disease can never be cured, and Herodias is heard chanting her magic spells, living already in a world of her own, drowned in her mirror:

> *Mais qui me toucherait, des lions respectée?*
> *Du reste, je ne veux rien d'humain et, sculptée,*

Si tu me vois les yeux perdus au paradis,
C'est quand je me souviens de ton lait bu jadis.

Drinking the milk of paradise, Herodias drowns, desiring nothing human and incapable any longer of recognising humanity. Like an ancient Greek chorus the nurse reminds her of her inevitable fate, but Herodias only delights in her fate, in her separation from the world, in the infinite cunning abysses of herself where she hides herself. She speaks to herself, admiring herself, "a deserted flower in gardens of amethysts"—for a moment the preoccupations of lesser poets of the *fin-de-siècle* return; we do not believe in the amethystine garden, but we are compelled to believe in "the sombre sleep under the first earth" where she finds herself, the landscape of unending ice which is reserved for the proud:

> *J'aime l'horreur d'être vierge et je veux*
> *Vivre parmi l'effroi que me font mes cheveux*
> *Pour, le soir, retirée en ma couche, reptile*
> *Inviolé sentir en la chair inutile*
> *Le froid scintillement de ta pâle clarté,*
> *Toi qui te meurs, toi qui brûles de chasteté,*
> *Nuit blanche de glaçons et de neige cruelle!*

In this astonishing portrait, so beloved by Des Esseintes, in a landscape of "white nights of ice-clots and cruellest snow", we see the self talking to herself, dying to herself, achieving at last the final apotheosis of death, which is not to die only, but to die completely; and then at last, as the drama moves on to its inevitable conclusion, the self sees herself in childhood again, but unlike Rimbaud seeing the child crouching by the puddle and sailing a paper boat, she sees herself aimlessly sorting pebbles by the sea-shore—nothing will ever be built—the sorting will go on forever—there are no dreams possible, for the self-regarding beauty is tragically cold and meaningless. Her last words to herself are: "You lie, O naked flower of my lips," and at once we enter the world of the *mensonge*, upon which Valéry was to seize later with quite extraordinary effect, making tower upon tower of *mensonges*, till each in the progress cancelled the other, and only the last tower, suspended above the universe, remained. Hopelessly, having come to the end of all journeys, the nymph Hubris-Herodias pronounces her *coda*:

> *J'attends une chose inconnue*
> *Ou peut-être, ignorant le mystère et vos cris,*
> *Jetez-vous les sanglots suprêmes et meurtis*
> *D'une enfance sentant parmi les rêveries*
> *Se séparer enfin des froides pierreries.*

Mallarmé is not always so cold. Once, at least, he conveyed a sense of purely human glory when, in an almost Chinese catalogue, he spoke of

> *Tison de gloire, sang par écume, or, tempête!*

But generally a coldness clings to him; he is in love with absence, the vase without flowers, the hollow in a bed where a woman once slept, the suicide's emptiness. But there were times when he could speak clearly and almost effortlessly concerning consciousness. In *Hérodiade* he had drawn the portrait of pride from the moment of its awakening to the moment of its death. In *Un Cygne* he drew a portrait of pride in mid-flight. Once again there is the background of unblemished whiteness, "the hard forgotten lake which haunts beneath the frost the transparent glaciers of flights unflown." All is cold and illimitably chaste; above this cold winter landscape flies the Swan:

> *Un cygne d'autrefois se souvient que c'est lui*
> *Magnifique mais qui sans espoir se délivre*
> *Pour n'avoir pas chanté la région où vivre*
> *Quand du stérile hiver a resplendi l'ennui.*
>
> *Tout son col secouera cette blanche agonie*
> *Par l'espace infligée à l'oiseau qui le nie,*
> *Mais non l'horreur du sol où le plumage est pris.*
>
> *Fantôme qu'a ce lieu son pur éclat assigne,*
> *Il s'immobilise au songe froid de mépris*
> *Que vêt parmi l'exil inutile le Cygne.*

This portrait of the Swan is not very far removed from a similar portrait painted by Baudelaire, who showed the proud Swan wandering through the muddy roads of Paris, croaking: "When will the rain fall? When will the lightning strike?" Mallarmé has shown the Swan in the same attitude of supreme disdain; for all eternity it remains in mid-flight, its reflection permanently mirrored and imprisoned in the lake.

Mallarmé's extraordinary challenge to poetry did not end with him: others were to explore the same landscape more fully. Among them was his son-in-law Paul Valéry, whose imagination was lit by an Italian sun and who wrote French as though it was a language strange to him, yet he wrote the language with more precision than anyone since Pascal. In him the themes of *Hérodiade* and *Un Cygne* assume even greater conviction; and they are the spring-boards from which he leaps into the unknown territories of the self-mirroring mind. There is something almost grotesque in his passion for pursuing the strange creatures of pride. His detachment from his own work is almost superhuman; he sees himself seeing himself seeing; there are even moments when we derive the impression that by an act of will he can, like a man seeing an infinity of reflected images in parallel mirrors, see himself see himself to the *n*th power, till at last, among all those disappearing and diminishing images, he finds the self he sought.

The complexities in the mind of Paul Valéry were endless. He was hardly twenty-three when he wrote the first draft of *The Introduction to the Method of Leonardo da Vinci*, from which his invocation to pride has already been quoted. He returned to the examination of the self-seeing mind continually, but it is in the later portraits of M. Teste that he is most convincing. Valéry describes the *megalopsychos* of his own generation. It is oddly disturbing to discover that he is not far removed from the similar figure invented by Aristotle. He is described as a man who speaks in a dull muffled voice, he talks without gestures, walks at a brisk military pace, greets no one, and enters a room as though he did not see it. He has a large brooding head, the massiveness of a man confronting all problems with the effrontery of genius. "When M. Teste spoke he never lifted an arm or a finger: he had killed the marionette." He spoke, if he spoke at all, in sudden startling apothegms; he had thrown his books away and burned his papers; he lived in the region of pure thought. The first interview with M. Teste takes place in a bare room. Rudely, without any warning, M. Teste dismisses his interlocutor and falls asleep, and Valéry, who watches him, is convinced that he is following once more the motions of his own mind as it sinks into unconsciousness, conscious even of his own unconsciousness. It is in this sense that M. Teste assumes the shape of a mechanical chess-player endowed with a brain which solves all metaphysical problems by a studied coherence; he is more closely akin to Baudelaire's dandy than to Rimbaud's *voyant*, that visionary who split his mind into fragments to see what lay behind. M. Teste deliberately holds his mind together; he refuses to employ sensation as a weapon; he will cut clear through the mind and track his own soul to the source by logic, and by logic alone. But sometimes we find ourselves reminded of Amiel's famous saying that *le néant qui s'aperçoit, c'est la pensée pur*. "The nothingness aware of itself is the pure thought." In a very real sense M. Teste is *néant*, the perambulating zero, the logical mirror of the whole universe.

The attempt to describe the monster is not wholly successful. It is significant that the two most successful fragments of the continuing interview occur in a bare bedroom and at the theatre—the two places seem to have been chosen as deliberate extremes. Valéry is continually pointing towards the contrast between the intelligence of M. Teste and the non-intelligence of the rest: the visible sense of superiority is a little too marked; the pride of M. Teste is only too evident. But while M. Teste disdains the world and people, and takes refuge in his pride, he is sometimes aware that the pride he shares with his creator offers barriers to the discovery of his own soul. It is not perhaps enough—it may never be enough—to kill the marionette, for other marionettes arise to take the place of the marionette who has been killed, and sometimes, when he effaces himself, he only insists upon himself the more; and when Paul Valéry accompanies M. Teste to the theatre and listens in the darkness to the amazing dialogue which M. Teste has with himself, we are conscious of M. Teste as a blinding patch of darkness among the dark shadows of the stalls, a sibylline oracle speaking from the black mouth of a cave which is himself. Very often M. Teste is heard muttering to himself: *Maturare*. But in fact he does not mature; he is always the same; the problems he attempts to solve are always the same problems, and his methods of solving them are just as unchanging.

The relevance of M. Teste, however, remains. Sometimes we ask where we have seen him before. Then it occurs to us, painfully and a little unexpectedly, that in his determined fury to unveil the secrets of the human soul is he not a little like the Adolf Hitler who wrote in his Landsberg prison a document which has explained at length nearly all the traps into which the human soul can be made to fall.

M. Teste derived from the marriage of Stéphane Mallarmé and Leonardo da Vinci, but the Nymph in *La Jeune Parque* is the daughter of Herodias alone. Herodias is dead; out of her pure and virgin body there has been born a nymph as cold as Hubris, a stalactite regarding itself in a mirror of surrounding stalactites, and she too performs the ritual of gazing into these mirrors with deadly insolence, a slave to herself, a demon in love with her daimonic powers. Once, many years before, while listening to the waves breaking on the Ligurian coast off Genoa, while the thunder pealed and the forked lightning writhed, Valéry had dedicated himself to "the penetration of himself". *La Jeune Parque*, completed in 1917 when the war was at its height, was the first-fruit of that peculiar oath. Originally it was to have been a short poem of perhaps twenty-five lines; in its present form it is more than five times the length of *Le Bateau Ivre*. The poem, composed so assiduously over four years, so scrupulously put together that nearly every word was checked against an etymological dictionary, is one of the masterpieces of our time; and almost incomprehensible.

Like Mallarmé, Valéry has been accused of being a difficult poet. The charge is hardly accurate, for he is relatively comprehensible in nearly everything he wrote: only *La Jeune Parque*, in default of a commentary, must always remain obscure. The nymph gazes at herself in the mirror of the lake, she is bitten by a serpent (but the serpent is only perhaps the awakening of consciousness, or the fear of death), her tears fall, and this is all; but as we follow the drama intermittently, by the flicker of lightning, coming out of darknesses into brightness again, we are aware that something of enormous proportions is being achieved: the poet is writing the drama of consciousness, passing through all the veils of the self till at last, as at the end of a tragic play, we are aware of some nameless crime. It is a drama where there is no movement except the movement within the soul, a mystery play without God, and in a sense it is the complete obverse of Ernst Toller's *Massen-Mensch* which projects a comparable drama of anonymous tragic heroes against a stage which embraces the whole continent of Europe. Valéry remains content with the circular stage of the brain.

Valéry had long ago suspected that his obsessions with the self would lead him to pride. He had discussed pride at length in *The Introduction to the Method of Leonardo da Vinci*, coming to some conclusions which might have been disquieting to him if he had realised he was unconsciously borrowing from a funeral speech by Bossuet. Years later, in a letter written by Mme. Teste, we learn that she had discussed the strange behaviour of her husband with the Abbé:

> M. l'Abbé, who possesses a grave and charitable curiosity concerning my husband, and a kind of pathetic sympathy for a man so separated, told me quite openly that M. Teste inspires in him sentiments which are extremely difficult to separate. He told me the other day that the faces of my husband are innumerable!
>
> M. l'Abbé believes him to be "a monster of solitude and singular self-knowledge", and he went on to explain, though regretfully, that my husband suffered from a pride which would have been altogether abominable and satanic almost, if it were not that his soul was so tense and so bitterly turned upon itself, and if it were not that he knew himself so exactly that the disease, perhaps, was enervated in its very beginnings (*que le mal, peut-être, en était comme énervé dans son principe*).   (LETTRE DE MADAME TESTE)

Nevertheless, the game of pride in *La Jeune Parque* is played, as in *Hérodiade*, to its final conclusion, but the conclusion itself is no longer the same. Mallarmé had chosen the death that comes from pride; Valéry chooses the death that comes from the sun, with all its possibilities of rebirth; for him the death of the soul is not final, since always an awakening is possible, and in the last lines of *La Jeune Parque* there is a canticle in praise of the Sun almost as perfect as those which had been written by Leonardo da Vinci and by St. Francis before him.

But pride remains: it is the constant theme of Valéry, never to be exorcised except by the magic conjuration of the sun, or by death itself. The self talking to the self, at all the levels of the self's experience, has never been so precisely stated; the rounding of consciousness on itself, its seeing itself at odd angles in the mirror-glass, its cries of greeting, its wantonness and unexpected diversions, all these are contained in those poems which seem sometimes as evanescent as wind or sea-foam, and at other times to have been graven on rock. Taine had said that "there was nothing real in the self except the thread of its events." Valéry accepts its unreality, but only as one would accept the unreality of a ballet: the dance continues whether we believe in its tangible existence or not. Our beliefs, indeed, have little to do with the divine shadow-play of the soul speaking to itself. It was Taine again who said one could follow by an interior light this spirit of truth which shines amid the darkness of the soul and itself leads the meditative man on his journey through these subterranean galleries. Valéry is prepared to believe, or pretend to believe, that the "spirit of truth" indeed lies there, and by a process of rigorous awareness the artist can reveal the plan of these galleries, and the nymphs who walk singing among them. In this world, so tenuous that we follow lamely and with the greatest difficulty, Valéry seems at times not only to be capable of resurrecting the very sound of the voices he heard there, but he can even re-create the timbre of the echoes heard in the long galleries of the soul; and we are not in the least surprised to discover that there exists among these galleries a world coloured like Poussin's paintings and inhabited by the half-archaic forms of Greek gods; for the Mediterranean light shines on them, and everything is bathed in that unearthly and glittering sunlight.

There are, however, difficulties at the very beginning. Valéry, like many French psychologists, believed that consciousness was itself an error, an accident by which two incompatible nerves or tissues had produced, perhaps by rubbing together, a kind of sore-ness, an intense sensitivity; the self grew within the mind as a pearl grows within an oyster. But the pearl is sterile; it cannot give birth, it is easily wearied, it is restricted in its movements and suffers a fatality by which in the end, after too long a contemplation of itself, it must die; and the greatest enemy of all is *ennui*, the *acedia* of the theologians, "that pure *ennui*, which derives from no misfortunes or infirmities, and has its source in life itself and the clairvoyance of the living being; and this absolute *ennui* is nothing more than life when it is completely divested of everything that conceals it, when it gazes upon itself." One of the major themes of *La Jeune Parque* is precisely the awareness of *ennui*, the sigh of the nymph drowning in the lake as she remembers that it has all happened so many millions of times before, and is purposeless; for in the regions of the soul no values have any importance, and all that remains is the pure act of vision endlessly repeated. This is not the *ennui* of Baudelaire, nor even of Mallarmé; it is infinitely more frigid. *L'idéal est une manière de bouder; Bouddha boude*, wrote Valéry; the execrable pun should not blind us to the truth which lies behind it. "*D'où vient cette froideur?*" Polyeucte complains, and the answers is not entirely unexpected: "*Dieu même a craint de la mort.*" The *ennui* which lies at the heart of the self-regarding mind, like the dark night of the mystics, is like a continual presentiment of death. It is in this sense that the explorations among the mirrors are among the most frightening of all experiences; and Valéry was perfectly aware of their dangers.

In this world of categories and shining lights, of revolving mirrors and nymphs in a Greek sunlight, Valéry is at home. He can see the whole trembling universe balanced upon the stem of the self, death coming out of the darkness to cut the stem down. The stem of the amazing flower desires glory, but it is of that kind which was expressed in the strange sentence of Mme. de Guion, which delighted Schopenhauer: *Midi de la gloire; jour où il n'y a plus de nuit; vie qui ne craint plus la mort, dans la mort même; parce que la mort a vaincu la mort, et que celui qui a souffert la première mort ne goûtera plus la seconde mort.* "Noon of glory; day when there is no more night; life which no longer fears death, within death itself; for death has conquered death, and he who has suffered the first death shall not taste the second." It is a phrase which should be placed as an epigraph to the famous *Cimitière Marin*, where Valéry's obsession with the self meets his obsession with death on the shores of the Mediterranean, the tideless sea. Immortality confronts death, and in the poem Valéry describes at length the slow dance of the thoughts of the dead:

> *Maigre immortalité noire et dorée,*
> *Consolatrice affreusement laurée*
> *Qui de la mort fais un sein maternel,*
> *Le beau mensonge et la pieuse ruse——*
> *Que ne connaît et qui ne les refuse,*
> *Ce crâne vide et ce rire éternel?*

So he goes on, after the strange reminiscence of Machiavelli in the fourth line, to describe the passions of the dead, and their perplexities, their living absence, dreamlike and continual in the enchantment of the graveyard near the sea, where the doves have almost the immobility of the tomb-stones and the grave enquiries of the pre-Socratic philosophers are still overheard in the bright glittering air; till at last, with a prayer like the invocation to the sun at the conclusion of *La Jeune Parque*, Valéry calls upon the wind to open his book and scatter the pages abroad, almost as Prometheus summoned the naiads to his presence.

Where Valéry achieves his greatest success is in the marriage of the purest lyrical poetry with a quite peculiarly modern precision: *his words have definitions*: it is not in vain that the etymological dictionary was always by his side. When he speaks, for example, of the temple, he is nearly always using the word in its ancient Roman sense of "the dedicated heavens". "The greatest liberty," he wrote, "comes from the greatest rigour," and he was obedient to this axiom which derives directly from the *ostinato rigor* of Leonardo. But pride and the endless research of the self led him to continual evocations of the self in all its forms:

> *J'y trouve un tel trésor d'impuissance et d'orgueil*
> *Que nulle vierge enfant échappée au satyre,*
> *Nulle! aux fuites habile, aux chutes sans émoi,*
> *Nulle des nymphes, nulle amie, ne m'attire*
> *Comme tu fais sur l'onde, inépuisable Moi! . . .*
>
> (FRAGMENTS DU NARCISSE, I)

So it is, following Mallarmé, that he refuses even in his pursuit of the soul's secret places to consider the vague, the undefined, the imperfectly observed. He will throw into the darkest recesses a golden light of the Mediterranean sun:

Je me voyais me voir, sinueuse, et dorais
De regards en regards, mes profondes forêts. . . .

(LA JEUNE PARQUE)

Mallarmé concluded the great *Hérodiade* with a vision of the child by the seashore playing with pebbles—perhaps the pebbles were only the words which, with great difficulty, he had elaborated into a poem; Valéry ends his two greatest poems, *La Jeune Parque* et *Le Cimitière Marin* with the evocation of Mediterranean landscapes and a hymn to the sun. Mallarmé's arctic nights are absent. The same fears are there, but they are felt in a warmer air: the sun shines on the soul's torments. For him all emptiness is fullness; the sunlight is always singing. He delights in the moment of birth, the buds springing on the tree, the sunrise appearing over the Mediterranean islands, the moment when the palm becomes conscious of itself, the moment of awakening from sleep and that other and still more delightful moment when sleep is about to come; for him these moments are those when the self is most fully realised, and he is content to lay a trap for them and wait patiently till they appear—not the single self, but the innumerable selves at their perpetual dance. Against the universe every single living thing utters its note of proud defiance, and all the selves are at this game of defying the monster:

Non, dit l'arbre. Il dit: Non! par l'étincellement
De sa tête superbe,
Que la tempête traite universellement
Comme elle fait une herbe!

(AU PLATANE)

For Valéry there are no locked gates: the mind passes at ease from the inner room to the outer air, *entre le vide et l'événement pur*, and night is no more than the knife which peels the skin of a fruit—the great abstractions which rule over our lives cut, but hardly separate; in the morning the fruit will be whole again. He delights in the heights, *l'incorruptible altitude*, only because the air is fresher, one breathes more easily, the soul sparkles more strongly in the rarefied air; and if, as he says in the rare preface to the English edition of *La Soirée avec M. Teste*, he "suffers from the sharp disease of precision," it is only because "I tend towards an extreme form of the strange desire to understand." Therefore there are no gestures except the incontrovertible gesture, no effort to please except the effort which springs from a direct sensuality, no struggles with the demon, for the demon is as compliant as a woman, and only too anxious to reveal his secrets. *O pour moi seul, à moi seul, en moi-même*, sings the Nymph beside the Mediterranean lake, but we should be mistaken if we detected in the proud voice the note of Hubris alone. When Hubris leaves the Arcadian mountains and descends to the shores of the Mediterranean, she sheds her violence and is wholly tamed. She no longer strikes down men, but allows them to live and sleep with her, finding their consolation in the treasure she reveals.

The self, the *inépuisable moi*, pursued Valéry to the end of his life. In the last of his poems, *Sémiramis*, the note of urgency disappears, the final surrender is made, Sémiramis ascends like the Rimbaud of *Crimen Amoris* into her high power and prepares for death. At this moment she utters her proudest boast:

My heart is vaster than the whole Kingdom; there is no tower so high that from its summit I cannot see the frontiers of my soul.

I desired to be so great that men of later times would never be able to believe that I have existed. So beautiful and so powerful that they would only be able to think of me as pure spirit. And is not the greatest glory that of the gods who think themselves inconceivable?

"Impossible, unbelievable," they will say of Sémiramis. "Impossible—and therefore divine. . . ."

Now I shall rest beside this altar and pray to the sun, soon in its full strength, and demand that it shall make me into smoke and ashes. And then, at this very moment, there will come from me the Dove, which I have nourished with so much glory and so great a pride.

(SÉMIRAMIS, II)

Thereupon Sémiramis dies, the Dove ascends into the blue heavens and nothing is left except the altar smoking in the sun.

It was a fitting end to his poetry. He had gathered together all the strands of French pride: and when it was over, there was only the flight of a bird and an altar in the sun. We had been led to expect as much. French pride does not dress itself in armour; it is dressed in the colours of the seasonable earth, it greets men with kindness and enquires about the nature of the soul with gentleness. There are moments when even Lear behaves like Beelzebub, when the Spanish mystics seem to be playing a desperate game of dice over the soul, when the Germans with their annihilating visions appear merely contemptible and when the Italian *terribiltà* only unnerves us. Then we remind ourselves of the dying words of Sémiramis, or of the quiet boast of young Arthur Rimbaud:

Ce n'est rien; j'y suis; j'y suis toujours.

So Pindar might have spoken as he gazed at his athletes, or Michelangelo as he gazed at the altar-wall of the Sistine Chapel; so might a French peasant speak in the evening of his life, knowing that he would appear again among his grandchildren. In such words, without harm to anyone, European pride achieves its greatest glory.

Vertigo

THE nymph still looks at herself and admires herself in the water, as she has done since the beginning of time. Long before Hubris entered Arcadia, the terrible intoxication was known. The gravest crimes, the most senseless adventures have sprung from the self-regarding gaze, and though we make poetry of pride in the West, and pretend to ourselves that there are some forms of pride which are legitimate and others which are not so, the most deathly instrument placed in the hands of man remains the mirror.

We live in an age of machines; our pride as men is taken from us; nationalism remains as a sign of the deadly mirror. It was not always so. There was a time, as we have seen, when pride was a human thing, to be feared, but never to be feared so much as today. The pride of the Athenian tragedies is not the same as the pride which enters the penitential psalms of the Middle Ages, though Superbia is evidently descended from Hubris. The kind of pride which graces the French is rare; all over the world a grotesque image of pride stalks like a wild thing. What is strange is that although we can trace pride through many branches of history, there is no final law, no final consciousness contemplating itself; only a continual development. Just as love changes, and the habits of love change, so the pride of man changes, and the habits of self-consciousness change. Œdipus and Satan would hardly recognise themselves in the admiring glances of Valéry's *Narcisse*, but it is demonstrable that *Narcisse* springs from the same general causes. The "I" changes, and the "I" that it contemplates changes: in the history of the aware *persona* there are infinite transformation scenes.

But though the "I" changes, we are made oddly conscious of national similarities, even of a kind of national progress. The forms of Spanish pride can be recognised, even though there are moments when we are compelled to wonder at the survival of a deep-seated primitive core which has nothing whatsoever to do with the influences which came demonstrably from the Visigoths or the Romans. French pride is gay and sensual until Corneille stumbles over the *matamore* in *L'Illusion*, and Pascal, with greater daring, stumbles over the abyss. German pride destroys, and Italian pride is a great vaunting of man's powers, and the English continually drag in their adored Beelzebub with his perennial cry: "Don't you think I'm a funny old man?" and at the distance of hundreds of centuries we recognise the white-faced Titans in the portrait of Charlie Chaplin, chalk-white with horror at the world around him. So the actors pass across the stage, now disguised as nymphs, now as Titans, now as heroes forsaken of the gods, now as Lucifer, son of the morning, and then again as Lucifer, prince of darkness; then Beelzebub and Mephistopheles emerge from the trap-doors, and in their place there is suddenly Queen Superbia surrounded by lion-cubs, a mirror in her hand, adoring servitors all round her, till suddenly she vanishes and there is only the naked woman of the German engravings contemplating herself in her glass. At this point in the transformation scene an extraordinary change occurs, for the naked woman turns incomprehensibly into the naked man, the Renaissance hero, the *conquistador* and the *condottiere* rolled into one, till age and contemplation weaken him, and he becomes the Faustian magus, who gives place to the dandy, the epileptic visionaries of Dostoievsky and the cerebral M. Teste living alone in a bare room so that he may admire the grandeur of his comprehension untrammelled by the presence of objects for contemplation, a *sunyassi* of the intellect enjoying his home-made Himalayas.

What is strangely absorbing is the process by which pride is continually changing sex, as the goddess Kuan Yin is born by parthenogenesis from the god Gautama Buddha, and the peculiar sense that we are witnessing a continuing development, and at the same time there is no development—only a single actor strutting across the stage, occasionally disappearing into the wings to change his costume; then he comes bowing towards us, who are his mirror; he smiles and gazes at himself, not admiring himself but admiring the impenetrability of his disguise. One suspects that he will have his place on the stage to the end of time.

It is too early in the history of European consciousness to discover the real causes which have led to this aberration. Nothing comparable to this tradition of awareness exists in the East. Self-awareness, of the peculiar intensity it has reached in the West, has no place in the philosophies of China, and only the most scattered hints can be found of similar states of mind in India. "To become a god, to break through all frontiers and to reach the heights——" This is the eternal cry of western man. The Indian replies softly: "We are already gods, the frontiers are there to amuse us, the heights beckon us and we have only to walk for a little while and we will possess them entirely." Thereupon he points to the real, the irrefutable Himalayas.

Yet there is evidence that something approximating this sense of pride may be found in India, and it is not only in the West that men take vertiginous delight in watching themselves in mirrors. We find all over the world, even among the most primitive tribes, the studied glance, the desire for supremacy, the mirror worn as an ornament of the gods. But once we have left the rarefied air of European pride, how different is the atmosphere and how delightful the rebuke of Krishna to Radha as it is related in the *Prema Sâgara*. Radha believes she has her lover in her power. In her conceit she tells the god: "Beloved, now I may go no further, but do you set me upon your shoulder and bear me along." The god answers: "Let it be as you desire." The story continues:

> Then the god, Sri Krishna Chand, seated himself on the ground and allowed her to climb on his shoulder, and he smiled to himself, for he was the destroyer of pride and the knower of secrets. Then when she had set forth her hand and was about to ascend on his shoulder, he vanished. So she remained standing there, with outstretched hands. So it is that the moonlight, taking offence at the moon, may linger behind a cloud, and the radiance of her fair form, emerging and spreading over the earth, gave out such beauty that she seemed to stand upon

the earth on sheeted gold. Then a stream of tears came flowing from her eyes, and she could not drive them away even when the bees, attracted by the sweet savour, came near her face. Heaving great sighs because she was separated from him, she stood alone in the forest, so that all beasts and birds and trees and climbing plants, hearing the sound of her sobs, were crying too. (PREMA SÂGARA, XXXI)

Here there is no fall of the Titan goddess, no desperate resolve to grapple with the god, there is not even a Narcissus peering into the shadowy lake; it is as though the story of Narcissus was being told, but it ends with the voice of Echo resounding mournfully through the forest and the mirror perilous is forever forgotten. Yet there are moments, as in the famous paean of self-praise by Krishna in the *Bhagavad Gita*, when the authentic accents of leaping pride are heard; then "the gambling of the cheat and the splendour of splendid things" take wing like the unknown bird which wings its way through the great speech of Herod at York. "I am all things," says Krishna. "I am the offering and the sacrifice, I am the fire-giving herb, the butter and the fire. I am the treasure, the lover, the source, the ending and the eternal seed. I am being and not-being, I am eternal life and sudden death." And so he goes through the catalogue of power, intimidating by his majesty, saying one moment that men have only to bring him a leaf, a flower, a fruit, water, and they will be cherished in his saving arms, and the next moment he demands the whole gift of all men, and one begins to wonder whether he is indeed a god, or only one of the heroes of the *Mahabharatta* in disguise, for they too possessed the same passionate love for gambling and conquest.

What is certain is that there is a vast difference in the self-awareness of the East and the West. One even suspects that in the East the dangers of the western form of awareness were known and deliberately guarded against; that the *sunyassi* deliberately places himself beyond the reach of the "gnawing self" by taking up a solitary resting place far from the haunts of men, renouncing all the blessings of the world, and even hope itself, holding his mind in check until thought ceases, his eyes turned towards the Himalayas, which are demonstrably so much greater than anything he could desire or possess. One begins to suspect that St. Anthony would not have been tempted with *superbia* if there were Himalayas in the regions of the Nile.

Some clue to the difference appears perhaps in the *sutras* of Patanjali where complete detachment of spirit from the phenomenal world is demanded of the acolyte, "for unless there is this pure detachment, then the direction of our thoughts is coloured by the appearances of this world; and the contemplator becomes caged, like one who enters a burning building when the stairs have collapsed behind him." The absolute detachment demanded by the Indians is so foreign to the West that we are almost bewildered when we contemplate it; their calm is not ours; like Othello, we are too apt to say, "If after every tempest come such calms, may the winds blow until they have awakened death." Though the calms come, we do not desire them; our natural habitat has been for too long among the vertiginous reaches of the spirit. "The eye of the sea is one thing," said Patanjali, "and the foam another; leave the foam and look with the eye of the sea." But try as we will, we see only the foam glancing in the sunlight, delighted when it dashes among rocks, happiest when it spins highest, and we seem to feel there is some purpose in the mad backwards and forwards rush of the brilliant waves against the rocks, and we forget the calm immensity of the surrounding sea.

From the earliest times European man has striven against the current and thrown his challenge at God. Unlike the Chinese, he does not attempt to conform to the laws of nature, but attempts to seek them out, reveal their hidden strength and use this strength against nature herself; and if he loses himself in the attempt, he is only too apt to regard defeat as a sign of his own authority. The medicine of immortality (φάρμακον ἀθανασίας) tempts him continually. Through the whole of Western history there rings the continual implacable cry: *Non serviam*.

This cry and this history have made him what he is. The initials of tragedy were on his forehead from the beginning. Dark guilt, repentance, the insane stare, the belief in his own majesty and power, the knowledge that the gods were against him and are ready to strike the first treacherous blow, all these were the marks of his spirit; and there is no reason why we should catechize him for being what he is. He has found his deepest source of satisfaction in pitting his wits against God, and there is no evidence, in this age of skyscrapers and atomic bombs, that he has completely failed. The same impulse which led the Babylonians, the earliest Europeans, to build the heaven-storming *ziggurats* led to the building of skyscrapers; the impulse that led Etana to fly on eagles' wings into the sun led to the airplane; the measurements of the Egyptian river-watchers led to the atomic bomb. It was a game which Western man has played well while it lasted, but he seems from the beginning to have been conscious of an ineluctable fate. Sometimes, during the game, he would pause for a while, see the mirror break, watch the nerve-ends twist in upon themselves, and he found himself confronted with his original loneliness, his emptiness and a shattering silence. Then, gathering his strength about him, he would throw himself forward in vertiginous flight in that strange progress which was away from himself, and yet deliberately deeper into himself, hiding his fears by inventing greater and greater images of himself. Then again there would come those terrible pauses, while he bent down and started sobbing like a child.

Confucius said once there were four things he preferred never to speak about—uncanny happenings, feats of strength, rebellions and ghosts. The wanton nymph speaks of nothing else. All that the Chinese mind deliberately refused to absorb, she accepts eagerly to herself, until she (or the Western mind in its pride) came to live in a world which was almost entirely inhabited by these four things. The danger is that we may continue to live in this world, 'for there is little likelihood that we can turn aside; at best we can swerve a little way towards the East. Even then there are dangers, for by the marriage of Eastern and Western philosophies we create bastards, or employ the East as a mirror in which we see ourselves amazingly magnified. Something of this kind happened in the thirteenth century when the *chansons de geste* introduced the luxuriance of the East, and the hero, the image which men constructed of themselves, was tinted with oriental colours. Something very similar has happened in our own time. When T. E. Lawrence came to describe his own most intimate construction of beliefs, setting himself against the deserts of Arabia, he saw himself magnified in the desert mirage:

Life in the mass was sensual only; there could be no rest-houses for revolt; its spirit was accretive, to endure as far as the senses would endure and to use each such advance as basis for further adventure, deeper privation, sharper pain. Failure seems God's freedom to mankind. Omnipotence and the Infinite were our two worthiest foemen, indeed the only ones for a full man to meet, they being monsters of his own spirit's making. In fighting Omnipotence, honour was proudly to throw away the poor resources we have, and dare him empty-handed.

(SEVEN PILLARS OF WISDOM, LXXIV)

It is the landscape of vertigo, the Caucasian rocks with Prometheus assailing the heavens, the mirrors descending and the ghosts coming out of the dark like bats. We believe him, but the next moment our belief is held in suspense, and we ask ourselves: What is Omnipotence? What is the Infinite? What purpose is served by throwing away all available weapons? Rimbaud had also penetrated that Phoenix-land, only to find *extase, cauchemar, sommeil dans un nid de flammes*. There was sleep once among the the nest of flames, when Adam lay stretched out upon the grasses at night, guarded by the angels with the flaming swords. So it is, throughout the history of Western pride, the proud man is filled with regrets and desires nothing so much as to leap into innocence and childhood again, for only children live in the happy delusions of innocence, believing they can perform all things with magic gestures and words; the toad becomes a house, the leaf becomes as broad as the whole heavens and the children themselves become whatever they desire. In this sense the nymph Hubris, the Titans, the Queen Superbia regarding herself in the mirror, even the dandy are mythologies introduced to enable men to return to their childhood; the figures are themselves magic spells, and the gestures are part of an ageless ritual. We might have guessed as much when, after reading *Le Bateau Ivre*, all the great voyages of the conquerors, all the visions, the triumphs and the explosions of naked pride are seen to resolve themselves at last in the portrait of the child crouching in the evening beside a puddle with his paper boat.

This is not, of course, the whole story. There is a moment when the childhood visions of omnipotence cease abruptly, and there comes the realisation that the world is as it is; then sometimes there arises in the child a sense of envy against the world, the bitter knowledge that he is chained to the rock and can no longer perform miracles, but still he must struggle against the world and attempt hopelessly and spasmodically to re-create it in his own image, blaming God because God assumes the powers which are given to men in their childhood. The tragedy of the human condition is that when we were children we thought all things were possible to us, and when we grow older we look back to childhood as a time when everything was possible. But the development of self-consciousness and the extremes of self-consciousness do not spring entirely from the visions men have when they look back to their vanished childhood; many other forces have been at work. Over the centuries there has been a development of the cerebral cortex: somewhere in that maze of nerves, by some chance crossing of fibres, there has grown a sense of awareness of oneself. Some roughness somewhere, an open wound, a clot, produced by magic or design a third eye which watches and gives commands; and in this mirror of the mind's eye men see themselves with pitiless lucidity, wishing sometimes that it were impossible. At some time in the course of human history the nerve of consciousness and the nerves responsible for man's power over surrounding objects met: from that moment man's destiny was determined. He knew then that he would never be satisfied; he would continually demand more and more power, and these demands increased until they encompassed the whole world. Now that we have conquered the world, we have only the stars to go to.

It would seem that the endless dangers of the game of pride are an infatuation to the West; the young Aryan princes of the *Mahabharatta* who gambled their lives or their kingdoms away are our ancestors, and the fatality upon us cannot be wished away. We are all caught up in the game; we cannot, like one of Euripides' soldiers, go and make a private peace of our own. And even if it should happen that we reach the sun or encompass the whole universe, we may gamble it away for the sake of our pride. Somewhere, in some lesion of the European soul, there may be a place where we can drop the requisite medicine; but at this late date it seems unlikely. The cure may be as fatal as the disease.

Our modern world is faced with the intolerable consequences of our pride. Our rulers, and most especially the Communist rulers, suffer from the sin of pride; they believe so firmly in themselves and their infantile theories that they are disposed to wreck even their own people, slaughter them, starve them to extinction, ruin whole provinces, so that some idiot phrase—Capitalism, Socialism, the dictatorship of the proletariat—shall have meaning by virtue of the sacrifices offered in its name. These rulers are not afraid to desire that the whole world shall be possessed by them, yet all histories show that victories are hollow:

> O Silence is filled
> With the triumphal song of the victors,

wrote a Chinese poet. After the last victory, after the last conflagration of the ego, only silence remains.

It may be that the virtue of humility no longer has any meaning, and perhaps it is no longer true that "Prowde folk God wyth-standyth, to folk in lownes he spryngeth his grace." The world, as Rilke said, may have passed out of the hands of God. The day of the Titan gods may have come again, and the men who will come to power in our generation may be entirely fearless of God. Power for the proud man means having it both ways, having it every way, any way. That vision has its severity and its ritual and the most exquisite humility rarely dawns on him. Rough-shod he rides over men and over the face of God. And so it may be to the end of this world, now that Hitler has stamped on the world the mark of his own inhumanity, and thereby made us all more in-human to one another. In the world of Maidanek and Auschwitz the divine image in man and the deadliness of sin have no place.

There is a curious disease suffered sometimes by Malays which leads them into a frenzy of murder, a revenge and self-liberation through revolt. They cry out wildly, their eyes roll, they slash with their naked knives, and as soon as they have seen blood flow they spare no one, neither friends, nor children, nor kinsfolk. The disease is known by the name *amok*, the ancient war-cry of the Malay pirates. "This disease passes for the devil," wrote Henry

Fauconnier in *The Soul of Malaya*, "but perhaps it is only despair, and the desire of death, brooding at the bottom of his heart. But stronger even than this desire is the ecstasy of mortal combat, a defiance flung at humanity."

For too long the West has flung its defiance at humanity, hardly knowing what it was doing, and hardly caring. The spiritual wantons go in search of their own; and it would not be so bad if they corrupted only the young, yet they corrupt all men. Nearly all our leaders have been proud, vain, boastful and hyterical. Trotsky defended revolution because "it leads humanity from out of the dark night of the circumscribing I," but in fact neither he nor Lenin were devoid of that coarsest kind of spiritual pride which led them to send millions to their deaths as long as their idiotic theories were put into operation; and what is said of the Communist revolutionaries may be said equally of the Fascists. Trotsky, who "looked often at himself", in the words of Lunacharsky, was only the type of the revolutionary *matamore*, boasting of triumphs which belonged to others. Sometimes, but not always, there comes a nemesis to pride. Trotsky bludgeoned with an axe; Mussolini hanged on a meat-hook; Hitler reeling towards his death in the catacombs of the Berlin Chancellery, are the evidences of the punished pride of our time.

Meanwhile, not all Europeans are spiritual wantons. There are some who see with pitiless lucidity that the splendours are mostly on the surface, in the texture and beauty of the skin, and the real splendour lies in love and youth, and an adoration of life so great that it puts to flight the terrors of pride. In the paintings of Grünewald, of Giorgione and Vermeer there is a glorious humility; so there is also in Van Gogh, who once wrote to his brother Theo: "It is better to be conquered than to conquer, better to be Prometheus than Jove." It may be that we must learn from the artists if we want to survive. It is the painters rather than the poets who teach us to be humble, exchanging our own beauty and singularity for the beauty and singularity of the earth we live on. Goethe's *Faust* is a perennial warning: the Gretchen tragedy, the Helena scenes, the reclamation of the sea-shore, the desperate return to the womb of the Mothers—all these are but tragic episodes which

set forth the bankruptcy of *"unendliches Streben"*. The humble
man strives patiently, and with love, to establish a relationship with
the We; if he strives endlessly, and without love, to exalt himself
at the expense of the We, his acute and anguished sense of solitude
can only grow deeper. Pride rules us, and pride must be abased.
It was Dante, the proudest of men, who wrote: "Brother, the
quality of love stilleth our will, and maketh us long only for what
we have, and giveth us no other thirst."

But in our own age the quality of love too often goes by default.
For the first time it is possible to imagine a world in which no love
exists, a luckless world ruled by machines, the sovereignty of man
given over to the machine state. Pico della Mirandola proposed to
define man as the being who is obliged to choose, touched by a
divine restlessness, always recreating his ends in the light of new
inspirations. But if his field of choice is reduced, if divine restlessness is exchanged for obedience to machines, if inspiration has no
place in the new emerging State, then man will have succumbed
to the powers he has invented, and though his pride remains—
pride over all the soaring achievements of our age—man himself
is reduced almost to extinction, no more than a small filament obeying the larger and undiscovered purposes of science. Once he believed himself the center of the universe, the possessor of divine
gifts, a being on whom God breathed the breath of eternal life.
Now the vision fades, and we see that love was a very tender thing,
and pride implacable. In the age of machines "the holy and glorious
flesh"—*la carne gloriosa e santa*—becomes no more than a play-
thing. It would seem that an inexorable destiny moves towards the
annihilation of man.

As man moves further and further towards the circumference
of things, a numb and frozen nullity, having lost the vision of God
and his own dignity, aware only of his powers to dominate the
material universe, and how those powers turn ultimately against
him, we watch the curtain rise on the last sad act of the tragedy,
helpless as children on the seashore watching a naval battle far out
to sea. At most they can shout and fling their pebbles, but only a
miracle will enable them to decide the issue. Meanwhile the battle
goes on, and no one hears the cries of the despairing children who

throw their pebbles on the sea—those pebbles which are as precious as bread on the waters. We do not know yet whether their cries are in vain.

So we watch and pray, hoping against hope for the day when love returns to the earth. It has happened before that the world has been saved from pride. A Jesus, a Buddha, a St. Francis arises to demonstrate the vanity of things, pointing to worlds of incomparable splendor remote from our own, where the virtues of humility and tenderness are exalted and pride is abased. They are the creators who fashioned new universes when our own was dying. They walked in humility and grace, in the holy light of their dreams, setting their faces against the *tenebrosi*, the dark ones, the painters of shadow. The old world died on their hands, as they announced the new way. We see now, more vividly than ever before, that either a new Redeemer will arise or Prometheus will be consumed in his own flame.

We have come to the end of the ways; the red cock crows on the roofs; no one listens to the note of warning, which has been uttered repeatedly through the centuries. Millions of men have died in agony because some among them have been obsessed with their own pride, and they will continue to die unless the regimen of humility takes hold of us. We are witless against pride, and it is time that our wits should be gathered together, before it is too late. We cannot apportion the blame. We have seen pride ride like a winter wind through all the adventures of Europe, bringing in its train the evil Nemesis; and though the theologians thundered against it, and the tragic poets saw the vision of the darkness ahead, no one could ever banish it entirely from men's hearts. We painted the Son of the Morning in the most glowing colours; and as he walks through Isaiah, Ezekiel and Revelations he is always the most entrancing of the angels, the colour of flame, like Prometheus. Now we live in a world where the flame may consume us all. Pride, the furious leaping and falling flame, haunts us and may haunt us forever, though we are beginning to learn the nature of the penalty which must be paid—the evidence lies all around us in a world in ruins; in the concentration camps; in the laboratories of the scientists; in the vast graves. Now that we have captured the power of the sun and can put it to our own uses, it may be that the world will be destroyed for a while, to emerge again, as the world of Cronus gave place to the world of Zeus; certainly we were never so close in spirit to the world of the Titans.

Once there were sanctuaries and holy places where men walked in delight of God, and the world was filled with a glory; all things were shining; the women came down to the wells in the evening, and there were flowers and food for the asking. Before pride came, there was no ruthless self-seeking, the humble were exalted, men loved one another and adored the earth and everything upon the earth, because life was almost too short for anything except adoration. Either those times are passed or they have never been. Occasionally in some villages of Asia it is still possible to come upon these patriarchs of another age, who behave with a simple dignity and friendliness which suggest that pride has never entered them; they live for the world alone. For them the earth is eternally being reborn and eternally perishing; the sun glows in their faces, and the white moon is a mysterious stone shedding a blessing. They do not fear themselves, and everything made by their hands is ennobled by the making; and though they have no desire to compete with the gods, they talk to the gods as familiars. The corn and the vine reach their fullness and are then destroyed; men also grow great and then weaken and die. They neither fear the lightning nor attempt to shine like flames, and are pleased with everything that is laid before them; these are the salt of the earth, adoring the earth, and they have turned away from pride, if pride ever entered them, because they know that "every good gift and every perfect gift is from above, and cometh down from the Father of lights, with whom is no variableness, neither shadow of turning."

London 1937
New York 1960

Although pride is the most significant of human sentiments, always present and constantly luring men to destruction, surprisingly few efforts have been made to
portray her features. Artists seem to have recoiled before
the task of reproducing her image. Occasionally they have
attempted to solve the problem by fusing together the
elements of earthly glory—kings, eagles, lions, finely
caparisoned horses, beautiful women regarding themselves
in mirrors, but only a handful of them have succeeded
in suggesting the menace behind the splendour. One of
the most successful is a miniature showing her on horseback, wearing a turban, armed with a spear, sitting im-
periously on a saddle made from a lion's skin. She is
perfectly calm, and not yet riding for a fall.

Orgoille, from a thirteenth century manuscript in the Bibliothéque Nationale.

Hochfart, from a fifteenth century German woodcut. The accompanying text describes her as riding a dromedary with a gold harness.

Superbia, from a colored German miniature contemporary with the Codex of Rüdeger Manesse, c. 1280, which shows similar portraits of knights in armour.

Orgeuil, from a rose window in Nôtre Dame, Paris.

Orgeuil falling before Humilité, from the Album of Villard de Honnecourt, c. middle of thirteenth century. The inscription reads: Orgeuil, si cume il trebuche—*This is how pride trips.*

DIE HOFART

Hans Burgkmair (1473-1530) portrays pride as the incarnation of imperious vanity.

Prima nefandarum vitiofa Supbia rerum
·Mater et omnigeni fons fcaturigo mali

*Heinrich Aldegrever (1502-1555) portrays pride triumphant, in
full command of her mount.*

SVPERBIA·OMNES·DESPICIO

Georg Pencz (1500?-1550) gives pride the wings of an immense peacock and a white horse. "I despise all things," she says into her mirror.

Pieter Bruegel the Younger (1564-1637) seems to have been alone in depicting the pure horror of pride. There is the inevitable woman contemplating herself calmly in a mirror, but she is surrounded by fantastic siege engines and leering griffins determined on her destruction.

Marten de Vos (1532-1603) painted Superbia as a modern Queen set against an antique setting. Her dwarf has serpents in his hair.

Superbia.

Jacques Callot (1592-1635) was a contemporary of Breughel the Younger, but his description of pride is chaste and decorous. The devil seems to have been added as an afterthought.

A Few Notes

The Nymph Hubris

THE description of the statue of Nemesis on page 6 comes from A. B. Cook's monumental study, *Zeus, A Study in Ancient Religion* (Cambridge University Press, 1914), I, 269, from where I have also taken the inscription on the pedestal. The two subsequent quotations will be found in Pausanias, I, xxxiii, and Ammianus Marcellinus, xiv, ii, 26. The description of the altar to Nemesis derives from *Zeus*, I, 267. The mystery of the origin of Hubris and Nemesis may never be solved, and the difficulty becomes all the greater when we discover that the Greeks themselves are quite extraordinarily confused. Theognis 105 states that Hubris is the father of Koros, and Solon, Fr. 8 just as categorically says that Koros is the father of Hubris; Nemesis is sometimes confused with Leda, and the origins of Pan are innumerable: perhaps after all Herodotus is right, when he sees Pan as originally one of the gods of the Egyptians, meaning that his origins are wholly lost in antiquity. What is certain is that he was originally a god of the pasture, and at various times he assumed various powers, and there is a clear distinction between the Pan of Arcadia and the god Pan who was worshipped in a cave at the source of the Jordan river near Caesarea-Philippi. Once at Troizen he was styled λυτήριος, the deliverer, and of all the attributes he possessed, this seems to be the most constant, but the deliverance was achieved by the utmost sensuality. By the time Pan reached Sicily, he had become an altogether more delicate god: the son of Zeus and Thymbris, a Sicilian river nymph. It is possible that Thymbris is only another name for the nymph Hubris.

The explanation of the origin of the Titans I owe chiefly to Ellen Harrison, while a full account of the Roman ceremony of the puppets is given in Warde Fowler, *The Roman Festivals*. Fowler completely fails to understand the purpose of the ceremony and can only surmise that it has something to do with ancient river-rites. Ellen Harrison has, I think, proved her case, and the ritual of immersing the Titans in the Tiber may very well derive from similar ancient rituals in Greece; it would be strange indeed if the Titans were not continually feared in Greece: hence the ceremony of drowning them. The classic text from Nonnus' *Dionysiaca*, introduces innumerable problems. Gypsum is the first mineral to appear in the evaporation of sea-water, it absorbs water, is unaffected by acids and was commonly employed to preserve wine— Petronius in the *Satyricon* mentions huge flagons of the great Falernian vintage hanging suspended from the ceiling and coated with gypsum. It would seem very likely that gypsum was at one time used to preserve the dead. The full text of the dream of the dead occurs in Hippocrates, *Regimen* IV, xci-xciii:

> If anyone sees the dead in a dream dressed in white and clean, it is a good omen; and to receive something clean from them indicates both health of body and the healthiness of things that enter into it, for from the dead come food and increase and seed, and for those to enter the body clean indicates health.

The Rage of the Lions

THE discussion on the various forms of Ate and the powers of Hubris at the beginning of this chapter owes much to Frederick Althorp Paley's *The Tragedies of Æschylus* (1870), which even now gives the most complete picture of the interactions of these vast and nebulous forces. It is not, of course, complete, nor could it be: very many books would be needed to show the delicacy and the ever-changing attitude of the Greeks towards Hubris. I have also omitted any discussion of the peculiar identity which occasionally occurs between Athene and Hubris. Athene's wider powers are amply illustrated by Evelyn Abbott in his *Hellenica*, p. 44: "Athene is the divine power which keeps watch over the impulses of men, and punishes them when they would pass beyond the appointed limit. . . . In her we see the intellectual conception of life which makes men responsible for their mistakes as well as their crimes, and punishes with equal severity the presumption and the baseness of man." A detailed exploration of Hubris in Æschylus is also given by F. M. Cornford, *Thucydides Mythistoricus* (1907), from which I take the following fine sentence describing the ghosts who haunt the *Agamemnon*:

"On this invisible scene walk the figures of Hubris and Peitho, Nemesis and Ate, not the bloodless abstractions of later categories, but still clothed in the glowing lineaments of supernatural reality".

But when on the same page he goes on to describe Hubris as "simply Agamemnon dressed in the robes of a legendary person," it would seem that an unnecessary simplification has taken place: Agamemnon is more than Hubris, just as Hubris herself is more than Agamemnon.

I have deliberately omitted from this discussion any reference to the famous speech of Diodotus (Thucydides, III, 45), because the division of the categories of pride seems here to be too mechanical. Diodotus explains that daring springs from poverty, while covetousness, insolence and Hubris spring from wealth; but this was not the belief of Æschylus, who saw a kind of poverty even in a king's triumph. Diodotus is more convincing when he says: "When, in the hour of triumph, fortune presents herself to a man's side, then is the conqueror in deadly peril." The hard division between the categories of the sins was one of the traps into which the medieval scholars fell with grave unction; having solidified the categories of sin, they solidified the *sinfulness* of sin: so St. Thomas Aquinas when discussing sin sometimes gives the appearance of discussing stock-market reports from Hell, and thereupon with delightful gusto he makes mathematical enquiries into futures, and suggests increasing investments in hard, mechanical categories of "the good". This is a danger which the Greeks, continually changing their categories, sometimes in the most arbitrary manner, nearly always avoided.

The Roman Triumph

No COMPLETE enquiry into the Roman Triumph, and the strange changes which occurred during its development, has yet been produced. The greatest changes seem to have come around the year 150 B.C., with the exhaustion following the Punic wars and the ruthless five-fold destruction of Carthage. Very little has been said here concerning the Etruscan cultural influences on the procession, though these were considerable—the *bulla aurea* wound round the *triumphator's* neck, the triumphal chariot itself, the heavy gold crown and the red-robed lictors with their bundles of twelve rods are all clearly Etruscan. Greek influences through Egypt were also considerable. See, for example, the astonishingly, vivid account of the triumphal procession of Ptolemy II Philadelphus through Alexandria on the day of his accession, given by Athenaeus, *The Deipnosophists*, V, 195-203, which is quoted *verbatim* from a lost History of Alexandria by Callixeinus of Rhodes. In this procession, which occurred in 285 B.C., no prisoners are sacrificed, and the *bacchanalia* is married to a quite extraordinary exaltation of divine kingship.

The whole *ethos* of Roman history is contained in the Triumph. The naked pride of the Romans appears here in all its forms, subtly changing with the years; and nothing quite like this triumphal procession occurs in any other culture, though the Triumph continues in Europe, and Mantegna's paintings at Hampton Court witness to the hold which it had on the renaissance mind. The last stages of the survival of the Roman Triumph can be seen in the German concentration camps, in the long march towards the gas-chamber and the incinerator.

The chapter concludes with an illustration from Seneca's *Jason*, but all of Seneca's plays and many of his letters might be quoted to show how he wrestled with the demon. At odd intervals, and very frighteningly, Seneca will suddenly discourse on pride, as of a thing which wholly involved him. He wrote to his friend Lucilius, suggesting that he should avoid "all such things in his gestures and outward attire as are most noticeable in themselves: as a rugged attire, a rude head, horrid beard, contempt of money, coarse lodging, and whatsoever leads to fame *that opposite way.*" This "opposite way to fame" was to provide one of the major terrors of the Desert Fathers.

Perhaps the most revealing of all Seneca's statements on pride occurs in the famous letter on death, where pride is never explicitly mentioned:

> What is freedom? you ask. It means not being a slave to any circumstance, to any constraint, to any chance; it means compelling fortune to enter the lists on equal terms. And on the day when I know I have the upper hand, her power will be nought. When I have death in my own control, shall I take orders from her? *Ep*, LI.

Of this attitude, Lecky in his *History of European Morals*, I, 222, has perhaps said the final word: "In the later Stoicism self-reliance reached its climax in the deification of human virtue, the total absence of all sense of sin, the proud stubborn will that deemed humiliation the worst of sins."

The Medieval Monument

I OWE many of the stories about the desert fathers to Miss Helen Wadell's admirable work. The briefest and best description of the sufferings of St. Anthony occurs in Palladius, *The Book of Paradise*, edited by Sir E. A. Wallis Budge, London, 1914, I, 13:

> And the Evil One was working upon him every shameful deed according to his wont, and at length he even appeared unto St. Anthony in the form of a woman, and the rest of the things which pertain unto pride he was performing readily.

The Terribiltà

THE translations from Pico della Mirandola on page 98 are based on excellent versions which appeared in the American literary magazine *View* during the autumn of 1944. Pico della Mirandola's debt to the beautiful chapter XV of the *Divine Hierarchies* of

Dionysius the Areopagite is indisputable. I tried to find some excuse for quoting part of this chapter in the text, but failed. Afterwards, it seemed to me that it should have been quoted only because it provides a commentary to Capaneus, for the puzzle has been why Capaneous should have played with the fire, and what there was in the nature of fire which should have been so tempting to the proud. Dionysius perhaps supplies the clue when, speaking of the earthly flame, he says:

> It is that which is spread everywhere, intermingling with all things, shining by its very nature and yet hidden, and manifesting its presence only when it can find material on which to work, violent and invisible, victorious by main strength, violently assimilating to itself everything it triumphantly seizes, and so renewing all things with its life-giving heat and blazing with inextinguishable light: never defeated, unchangeable, darting upon its prey, changeless always, as it lifts that which it gathers to the skies.

Beelzebub

THE fragment of the Herod play has been included in the original, because no translation does justice to the superb poetry. The text of the York plays is corrupt, and it is too late ever to know the name of the great poet who wrote this play. I append a rough translation of the fragment, which begins without any clear indication of perspective: the clouds, the sky, the planets are wholly fused together in a general invocation:

The clouds set in clear skies enclose these regions
Where in the midst are Jupiter and Jove, Mercury and Mars:
Droves of them hurl themselves over my kingdom.
I rejoice to stir up their thunder: they blow when I bid.
Saturn is my subject, whom subtly I hide,
And at my leisure I lay the god low.
Speedily I ride the rack of the red sky.
I throw thousands of thunderbolts whenever it pleases me.
Venus owes her voice to me,
She whose delight is to play with princes.

The Sun, Prince of Planets, set proudly on high
Shall send forth his beams to gladden our dwellings;
The Moon at my will shows his power,
And Emperors in castles bestow great mercies on me.
And lords and ladies are obedient to my desires.
I am fairer of face and more beautiful to behold
Sixty-seven times more than anything on earth,
Than glorious gulls that are gayer than gold.

(L. TOULMIN SMITH'S YORK MYSTERY PLAYS, P. 123)

I would like here to thank Miss Eva Golson for her help in translating several of these lines. It is odd that the proud tyrants should demand a mathematical form for their pride; but Herod's 67 does not nearly approach Plato's Tyrannical Kings 729.

I am aware that the verdict on Pope on page 142 is not entirely fair. There are other references to pride in the *Essay on Man:*

Pride then was not, nor arts that pride to aid;
Man walked with beast, joint-tenant of the shade. . . . (II, 151-2)
Pride still is aiming at the blest abodes,
Men would be angels, angels would be gods. . . . (I, 189-190).

Arthur O. Lovejoy, in an essay called "Pride in Eighteenth Century Thought" which occurs in his *Essays in the History of Ideas*, Baltimore, 1948, makes a spirited defence of Pope's treatment of pride; but Pope's cleverness continually obtrudes, he is not dealing with pride but with "an idea of an idea of an idea" of pride. Nor does he ever approach the power of Byron's wit. All that Pope ever said about pride, and much more, is contained in two lines from Byron's *Vision of Judgment:*

His Darkness and his Brightness
Exchanged a greeting of extreme politeness.

I have omitted references to Dunbar's *Dance of the Sevin Deidly Sins*, for the incongruous figure of Pride "with hair wyld back and bonet on syd" seems to be no more convincing a portrait of pride than anyone performing a Scottish reel; and the conclusion of the portrait is even less convincing, as he watches Pride skipping through the fire and giving forth "hiddous granis". Somehow these groans fail to be terrifying, as for example Chaucer's "mirour perilous" is terrifying. Cowley describes the proud man in his essay *On Liberty* as one who "struts and looks big upon the stage; he thinketh himself a real prince in his masking habit, and deceives too all the foolish part of his spectators; he's a slave *in Saturnalibus*." But Dunbar's little devil deceives no one.

For the same reason I have omitted D. H. Lawrence's perennial cry against the proud man. It is not convincing, and the author of the cry was as proud as anyone in his own generation. When D. H. Lawrence wrote in his essay on Cézanne: "The man of flesh has been slowly destroyed through the centuries, to give place to the man of the spirit, the mental man, the ego, the self-conscious I," he was whipping himself.

The hatred of Italian pride is continual in Elizabethan England, and perhaps the simplest and most heart-felt cry against the Italianate form of pride is William Cecil's: "Suffer not thy sons to pass the Alps, for they shall learn nothing but pride, blasphemy and atheism." (*Memoirs of the Life and Administration of William Cecil, Lord Burghley*, London, 1828-31). But there are many other references, and Greene in particular raged against "the pride of Italy". Mostly, it seems to have been envy.

The German Agony

IN GENERAL German pride is the least rewarding, the most fleshly and the cruellest. From Beowulf to Hitler it thunders grotesquely and dangerously, always in the same tone, brandishing cudgels and opening its mouth wide to swallow the world. That the theme should be so continually repeated, with such little change, suggests that the danger is a permanent one, and the evil has not yet been eradicated.

The Pride of France

FRENCH verse does not go well into English prose, and still less well into English verse. This is especially true of some of the finely wrought crystalline passages quoted here from the works of Mallarmé and Valéry, in which the French genius for gazing in mirrors acquires its clearest accent and decoration. But it is also true of the earlier periods. In France the light comes clear down from the heavens: there is no smoke, no diffusion of the image. Though the wanton nymph is stripped to the skin, she appears to be clothed, and though she whispers she appears to be accompanied by a full orchestra. Rendered into English, her words lose their lucid majesty, but it seems best to give an approximate translation, if only to demonstrate once more that a good deal of the finest French verse becomes the purest nonsense when adapted into English.

p. 169   I have won all, I have won all, I have achieved a masterpiece, a great deed.

p. 170   Lucifer, king of enemies, you howl like a famished wolf, when you would sing or laugh.

p. 170   My nobility and my great beauty have been changed into deformity, and my song into lamentation, my laughter into desolation, my light into melancholy shadow, my glory into dolorous rage, my joy into incurable grief. Only my pride remains, unaltered and unchanged, since the day when it was forged long ago in a vanished paradise; and now it grows worse, never in any way growing smaller.

p. 170   Harsh and eternal death is the portion of the damned; and we are all held on the chain of harsh and eternal death. We have deserved our fate, and we submit to it. Harsh and eternal death is the portion of the damned.

p. 171   *The Vain One:* I raise my head and show my well-formed body to all: and all are happy to greet me.

The Superstitious: You prize too much your body of flesh, which is no more than carrion. You must die, and those who speak of death tremble.

The Vain One: My beautiful green eyes shall not become food for worms.

The Superstitious: You must make this leap. You cannot escape. It is the only certainty.

The Vain One: Rebellious death will not dare to take me so young and so beautiful.

p. 181   Pierced to the very depths of the heart, in sudden and mortal assault, miserable avenger of a righteous quarrel, and unhappy victim of an unjust rigor, I remain motionless and my downcast soul surrenders to a fatal blow.

p. 182   In so great a misfortune what remains? I, I, I say, and that is enough!

I am the master of myself and of the universe! I am, and I want to be!

Without giving a reason or any account of my desires, I want what I want, because I want it.

p. 183   I satisfy both the people and the countries, and everywhere my verses are my only supporters. My pen is honored by their singular beauty, and I owe only to myself my fame.

p. 184 (top)   I remain motionless in this mortal terror, and everywhere at my feet I see a precipice. I see the nature of my crime and your justice, and I know that Heaven is not pure before you.

p. 184   Master of the universe without being master of myself, I am the only rebel on this height of power. I am enchanted by the flames I fight, and only with reluctance do I love what I want to love. In vain does Rome urge stately ceremonies for my marriage. I desire to dawdle and delight in interruptions, and I dare not resist the dangerous desire of preparing always and achieving nothing.

p. 185   The pitiless thirst for glory, whose blind and noble ecstasies hasten my death so that my memory shall live, halts for a few moments my impetuous feelings of inexorable envy, and permits me to give a sigh of love on this melancholy and propitious day, before surrendering to thee my life.

Fear not that so beautiful a longing should dare to contest a heart with thee—that heart which is the most faithful slave of your famed rigor. This troubled and lingering gaze lures an unexpected benefit, and does not hinder surrender. True, it complains; and the surrender is begrudged; but there is no need to blush for shame. I shall blush only in secret.

. . . . .

I glory in it, but conceal in myself a terrible load of griefs, I have silenced all my desires and torn out my heart. Beloved Prince, if thou canst see in this confession where my genius lies, observe its rages. I die content; honor gives me her due. But I would have been more content if I could have lived for thee.

Pascal's Abyss

THE reference to Pascal's confession on page 194 is given in Sainte-Beuve, *Port Royal*, I, 465. These astonishing words are taken from a collection of letters on Port-Royal published in 1734 and purport to have been contained in a letter from Mère Angelique de Saint-Jean to Arnauld. There seems to be no reason to doubt their authenticity.

The Nymph and the Lake

p. 282   If there is a water in all Europe that I crave, it is the cold black pond where in the scented evening a crouching child, overwhelmed with sadness, launches a boat as frail as a May butterfly.

p. 284   O seasons, O castles, what soul is without fault?
Lazy youth, enslaved by all things, I have lost my life through delicacy.

p. 286   And all this like a heart and a soul, and like a verb, adores and opens into the ecstasy of virginal love, and implores the merciful God who will keep us from harm.

p. 287   O mirror! Cold water congealed by boredom, how often and through how many hours in your frame, grief-stricken with dreams and in search of my memories, like leaves buried in a deep trough beneath your ice, I appear within you like a distant shadow. But, O horror, in your austere fountains, those evenings when I have known nakedness in my spare dreams. Nurse, am I beautiful?

Strange times, and may Heaven guard you from them! You wander, a lonely shadow and a new fury, gazing deep in yourself precocious with terror, but always as adorable as an immortal. O my child, and fearfully beautiful, and such as . . .

p. 288   But who would touch me, reverenced by lions? But I desire nothing human, and if you see me, my eyes abandoned in Paradise, a sculptured thing, it is when I remember your milk which I drank long ago.

I love the horror of being virgin and desire to live in the terror my hair brings me. So in the evening, as I lie in bed, a reptile unviolated, I feel in my vain flesh the cold glitter of your pale light. You who die, you who burn with chastity, white night of ice-clots and cruellest snow!

p. 290   I await an unknown thing; or perhaps, not knowing the mystery and your cries, do you hurl your supreme sighs, bruised by childhood, conscious among reveries of being separated at last from the cold stones.

Brand of glory, blood of foam, gold, tempest!

A swan of long ago remembers that it is he, magnificent but freeing himself without hopes for not having sung the country to live in, the boredom of the sterile winter gleamed. His whole neck will shake off the white agony inflicted by space on the bird that denies space, but not the horror of the earth where his wings are imprisoned. A phantom condemned to this place by perfect brilliance, he remains motionless within the cold dream of scorn worn in his ineffectual exile by the Swan.

p. 296   The ideal is a manner of sulking; Buddha sulks.
          Whence comes this coldness? God himself fears death.

p. 297   Meager immortality, black and golden, the fiercely
          laurelled comforter, who makes of death a mother's breast,
          the beautiful lie and the pious ruse! Who knows them not
          and never refuses them, the empty skull and the eternal
          laughter?
          I find there such a treasure of impotence and pride that
          no virgin child escaped from a satyr—none, whether
          cunning in flight or brave in failure, none of the nymphs,
          no companion, none are enticed to me as you, my inex-
          haustible self, as you appear on the wave.

p. 298   I saw myself seeing myself, and gilded from one glance
          to another, my own deep forests.
          No, said the tree. It said: *No* by the gleam of its superb
          head, which the storm treats universally as though it were
          a blade of grass.

p. 300   It is nothing; I am here; I am always here!

INDEX